The Book of the Earth

JEFF GROSS

ISBN-13: 978-0-9888262-5-0

DEDICATION

To my family, and to Helene Massieu, whose astonishing care, wisdom and dedication inspired this book.

ACKNOWLEDGMENTS

A great debt of gratitude is owed to the late Masahilo Nakazono, O Sensei, whose studies and theories are the basis for this fiction. Fiction which I fully expect will become truer and truer the more the veils fall away.

1

It was on the lightly snowing morning of January 1, year 2000, that a 35 year-old Japanese healer in a white robe, fresh off the plane from Tokyo, stepped out of a New York City Yellow Cab in front of the United Nations, an 18-inch-long metal cylinder tucked tightly under his arm. No flags flying on the tall flagpoles, the iron gate leading to the plaza locked and the plaza itself swept clean all the way to the East River, not a soul in sight either there or coming out of the General Assembly building fifty yards beyond the gate on the right, this was not quite the picture he had been led to expect. But so convinced was he of his destiny, so infused was he with the glory of his mission that the slender healer did not pause for a second to reflect upon what such signs might mean. Instead, without further ado, he quickly vaulted over the head-high gate and, oblivious to the cold piercing the thin cloth of his ceremonial robe, oblivious to the barking security guard who burst out of the guard shack scrambling to meet him, glided up the ten granite steps to the plaza on cotton feet and headed for the building entrance, looking neither right nor left, certain that nothing could stop him now.

For the gift, the priceless treasure he bore in the airtight metal cylinder was nothing more nor less than *Chi No Maki*, the Book of the Earth, an ancient Shinto scroll buried 3000 years ago. Not a copy but the original of a text written in a slanting script, a long-forgotten hieroglyph called *jindai moji*, divine writing. A document which, legend had it, (for the healer himself had never been permitted to see the scroll owing to his specialization in healing, rather than actual priestly status), related the true history of the different regions of the world, the story of the continents and the five races, and the rise and fall of Atlantis and Mu. A document containing information about the whereabouts of shrines and buried objects holding the code for world salvation. Such absolutely vital knowledge that the ancestors had left specific instructions: the Book of the Earth must only be unveiled once human ears were at last ready to listen, when things couldn't get much worse, when the future of the planet lay clearly in the balance, when the

3

human race, disgusted with itself, would choose either finally to wake up, or extinguish itself for good.

Unfortunately for the poor healer, whose name was Yuichi, at virtually the exact same time on that ill-chosen day, that same lightly snowing Saturday morning, in that very same woeful place with the 185 flagless flagpoles standing like dripping white sentinels, no less than 799 other zealots with world-saving truths of their own suddenly materialized out of nowhere, sending the UN guard fleeing to his shack to call for reinforcement. Normally, if 800 people massed in front of the gate, the New York police, (who viewed the UN as a priority, crucial to the image of the city), would be on them in a flash and the mess would be cleaned up in no time flat, before anyone came within arm's-length of the gate. But this situation, this demonstration, was unprecedented, one minute the zealots weren't there, the next minute they were: Rajasthani *sadhus*, Dominican ascetics, Tibetan *tulkus*, stage magicians, computer gurus, telepaths, weekend mystics, Forteans, advocates of every possible branch of pie-in-the-sky holiness and convenience-store enlightenment, pouring from the gutter like sewer rats, flowing over the fence, and pulling in behind the Japanese man.

Straight as an arrow, undeterred, Yuichi strode up to the building anyway, fully expecting the front doors to open as he arrived. And in fact, a greeting committee was indeed in place: a phalanx of security guards on the other side of the thick glass doors, thick-necked soldiers in flak jackets and blue uniforms pointing their machine guns right at the Japanese man as if to emphasize what the flagless flagpoles and the closed gate should have told him from the beginning: that the UN wasn't open on New Year's Day, and January 1st, 2000, was no exception.

"Ho?" said Yuichi, an untranscribable sound midway between Huh and Hoo, which sometimes meant "Is that so?" and other times meant "Very strange..."

Resolute, Yuichi pulled the metal cylinder from his belt anyway, holding it out to the soldiers at arm's length, like a gift, an offering, as he sank to his knees, head bowed. And there on his knees he would have possibly stayed forever, snowflakes melting on his bald head, snow piling up on his back, had the crowd not turned on itself.

It started when a magician from Sedona, Arizona, ripped a talisman off the neck of a druid from Bird in Hand, Pennsylvania, who mistakenly slugged a fruitarian Stalinist in reprisal. Timber, like a tree, the Stalinist fell straight over into a flock of nuns busily excoriating a flock of Scientologists, leaving habits in tatters as he clawed at them to break his fall, a last conscious act before cracking his head on the slick pavement. Spurred on by the smell of blood and the sight of half-naked nuns, the rest of the horde abandoned all remaining pretense of civility, and, with a deep-throated feral explosion, began to get to work, determined all of a sudden to settle questions of schism and doctrinal inconsistency right there, right then, as if the dominance of the next millennium depended on it.

The wind howled and swirled, the skies opened up and let loose a blizzard which turned the UN into a spectral ghost ship. On the street side, by the sculpture of the revolver with the knot in its barrel, a feminist Aikido master was set upon by four Korean Tae Kwan Do missionaries and beaten to a pulp. On the other side, her back to the cracked globe of the world, an anti-vivisectionist in a gingham skirt pelted any conspicuously carnivorous looking types wandering into her perimeter with pork chops, chicken livers, blood sausages, etc... extracted from a bottomless knapsack. The expectation being, apparently, that at some point, some moment of flash illumination, the animal bits flying through the air would cause them to see the error of their meat-eating ways. A dubious hypothesis made even more so by a lucky (beef) kidney toss which left a blood-stain so massive on the thigh of a jowly Mormon's standard-issue polyester trousers that the poor fellow quite simply snapped and came after her. Further along, a gang of redneck Vegans surrounding a half dozen Muslim dervishes until a massive black man, Minister of the Church of Apocalypse, Profanity-Allowed, mowed them down one by one, fists flashing, and deep baritone voice bellowing righteous scripture from the Book of Revelation: "For the great day of his wrath is come and who shall be able to stand?"

Discreet by design, eager as possible to avoid any violent incidents that might tarnish the image of the United Nations, an organization at least theoretically dedicated to peace, the security forces in place around the plaza, Navy Seals, Army Rangers, and SWAT teams hunkered down at the US Mission across the street watched the feed from the security cameras, but stayed where they were, out of sight, waiting for the situation to evolve. The near-military precision of the mass arrival was certainly suspicious, and the level of violence was unusual, but they looked like the usual scruffy bunch of wingnuts and New Age whiners, so the security forces stayed put, on alert, but confident that security measures already in place were adequate, that whatever the reason for the fire, it would soon burn itself out.

It was then that the heavy artillery rolled in from Times Square, three water cannons, a handful of Plexiglas-helmeted horses, and ten riot trucks full of New York's finest in brand new armor who hit the ground running, jackboots crunching. Technically, the United Nations was international territory, beyond the jurisdiction of the New York City police, but after four depressingly-uneventful days on the all-leaves-canceled pressure-cooker of Operation Millennium, and no action to speak of on New Year's Eve either, technicalities and protocol were less high on the list of priorities than using this new repressive toy before some new budget crunch made the Mayor decide the Special Events Riot Squad wasn't really necessary after all.

The first of them, a good two dozen, hollering like Apaches, headed straight for the massive black man and the Muslims, leaving the Quakers and Amish for later. A second truckload took the left side where it quickly subdued a good score of rival diet freaks, tearing them from each others' throats, tossing them to the ground and zapping them with stun guns so they would stay put. While the horses kept the onlookers back on 1st Avenue, and the water cannons bombarded anyone already inside the plaza foolish enough to try to climb back over the gate to freedom, four other truckloads, another 96 men in all, unloaded and circled around the flanks to the back of the plaza like scythers cutting wheat, indiscriminately flattening two great human swaths, eight whistling Christians, a swarm of screaming Hindus and dagger-waving Sikhs with unraveled turbans and torn beards, any number of animists, exercise gurus, channelers, alien worshippers, and fifteen suicidal Buddhists doused in lighter fluid, but not a one of them with a lighter that worked in the blizzard.

Such was Yuichi's calm presence, so soothing his charisma, so unthreatening his demeanor, that alone of the 800 trespassers he might have made it to safety unscathed if not for the anti-vivisectionist. If not for the fact that right by the statue of the gun with a knot in its barrel, she caught up to him, putting him between her and the enraged Mormon. Innocuous enough as to seem invisible at times, the Japanese man might have slipped by, if the Mormon had not lunged, and if Yuichi, imbalanced by the pull of the woman's hands on his shoulders, unrooted by the mixture of snow and blood dripping from the woman's knapsack, had not had his feet shoot out from under him. Out and up in an accidental, but picture-perfect, side kick, a brick-filled slipper straight to the Mormon's teeth.

A kick moreover quickly succeeded, in the windmilling, arm-waving attempt to regain balance, by an accidental roundhouse punch connecting one metal cylinder with one Mormon solar plexus, a blow so straight and true that it emptied the Mormon's lungs and bent him double -- straight into the path of a wicked, and equally accidental, Japanese elbow to the chin which knocked the Mormon cold. Within seconds Yuichi was stretched out next to him, smothered by the police.

9:15. The snow had let up. Face down, cheek smashed into the wet plaza ground, a truncheon in the middle of his back, pinning him like an insect, and a boot on the back of his head for good measure, Yuichi watched a last few legs run by, saw a glimmer of gingham skirt, watched, heart-sinking, white-knuckled fingers welded to the scroll, until everything vertical on the plaza except the sculptures and the law had turned horizontal, and the view to the Pepsi sign and the power plant across the East River was clear once again.

Sirens wailing, ambulances pulled in to collect the injured and spirit them away to any hospital that could take them. The remainder, those still healthy enough to move under their own steam, were scooped up, tossed into mobile processing units and armored buses and, driven, dreadlock, stock and barrel to the highest security prison available on such short notice: the brand new, but already overcrowded East City Jail, a massive floating facility anchored on the East River just up from the Brooklyn Bridge.

A good five hundred saviors, those with organizations behind them or socks full of money, were released inside the hour, bailed out at $10,000 a head. But $10,000 was exactly $8728 more than Yuichi still possessed for the one day he had expected to spend in New York. Some three-dozen more, mostly sadhus and Yogis competing unattached, managed to escape on their own by dematerializing in time to catch the end of the Sugar Bowl, which for the first time in years had managed to land the matchup for the national championship, but Yuichi was not among these either. Behind bars was apparently where he was destined to remain on his first night in this new country, behind bars with all the other loser saviors, the Roman Catholics, the Essenes, the Baha'i, the Tupi Guaranì, and the Southern Baptists whose money was locked up in Swiss bank accounts which they couldn't access on Saturdays or holidays.

Did Yuichi join those howling their various dogmas and unique visions, did he join those tossing their excrement at the guards, did he add to the cacophony of mantras and promises of ever-more-imminent divine wrath which no amount of fire-hose water from the orderlies seemed to calm? No. Perplexed though he might be by the turn of events, Yuichi sat cross-legged on the newly-painted pink concrete floor of his cell, chanting quietly, serenely, no louder than a hum.

In the interest of the late-risers apparently, the TV ran all day long with the strange story of the hair-pulling free-for-all, the saviors-run-amok. They showed the photogenic clutter of bleeding, dazed, moaning weirdoes stretched out in the black slush, and a finale... not of Reverend Y, the massive black man, being hauled off kicking and screaming by eight cops, not of Wella Balsam, the famous movie actress, not of the flesh-tossing anti-vivisectionist, but the footage of a white linen-robed "monk" (who wasn't *exactly* a monk, but who cared?) attacking a short-haired ox in a mercilessly-cut, Mister Mack's Mormon-blue suit. It came off like a joke for bar hoppers and card players to nod at while patting themselves on the back, a nice light diversion from the rest of the minor hangover grimness, the not-entirely-unexpected waves of suicides in all the most affluent countries of the world...

2

Chrissie Luna no longer had enough energy and conviction to start anything on her own any more, and turning 40 on Christmas Day certainly had not changed that. At the party in her honor, she had tried her best to put on a show, to convince everyone she wasn't lonely, that 40 didn't mean anything, that it wasn't so bad that none of the stray dogs she made her habit of collecting as lovers had turned into men who could actually care for someone else. She served drinks, she served food, she put on the happy mask she thought no one could see through, and when she got loose enough, she cracked a few jokes, making sure to laugh right afterward in that manly laugh she used to signal that a comment was risqué. "I'm the only one on the planet who would have to host a party in her own honor..." she said, keeping the laugh short, a comment of such breath-taking self-denigration that no one knew what to say and the party fell silent. All except her mother, who just snorted, a harsh, cynical I-told-you-so laugh which she kept up the rest of the evening, until it gradually seduced everyone else into almost loathing Chrissie as well.

Ten days after the New Year's Day riot, on a Monday night, Chrissie half-watched a report on "Imperial League," something about scouts for the Mets baseball team scouring the occupied territories for likely Palestinian pitching prospects, and a second expose of a scam by the United States Olympic committee, which had sent school buses to the Kenyan highlands in a poorly-camouflaged effort to sabotage Kenyan domination in the long distance track events. Chrissie couldn't see what was so bad about giving children the choice to ride on a bright yellow school bus, instead of making them run to school where you never knew if you might turn into someone's meal, but TV always made her drowsy and she was too tired to pursue it.

Waking up from time to time during the night, she caught a report about the terrible cold striking the eastern seaboard, then an interview with a psychologist about fear letdown, which they were observing in the aftermath of the New Year, when none of the promised calamities (Y2K, planes falling out of the sky, newborns suffocating in incubators, terrorists) had actually come true. Afterwards she caught a docu-tragedy on the handing over of the Panama Canal which she switched off after ten minutes, then, (an hour later?) something about the building of the Space Station followed by a documercial about how they had gotten the Buddhists from the riot to do a spot for Zippo lighters.

At four or so, Chrissie made herself a banana split and watched a documentary about the renewal of the ivory trade which was immediately followed by a story about the latest fad among New Yorkers with too-much-money: bailing out saviors. There were limousines, costumes, dolphin ice-sculptures on thematic buffet tables, there was champagne foaming up out of magnum bottles and people in perfectly-cut clothing getting together in circles, arms around shoulders, making weird sounds and laughing. "A new millennium demands new trends," the androgynous so-called "Clinical Aesthetician" they had hired to play the role of the expert was so taken with himself that it made Chrissie's stomach turn. "Bailing!" he said, with a dirty little wiggle of his nose, as if selling some hot brand-name erotic thrill. "Try it!"

Even though Chrissie, as a phone/outcall cosmetics salesperson wasn't anywhere close to what you might call "too-much-money," the TV had started her to thinking. The way she saw it, a prophet was at least a shot at something. Perhaps it would be a big gamble, a long shot that your particular prophet's madness would be any less insane than all the rest you heard. But logic alone said one of the 800 "saviors" at least would have to be telling the truth, and what if his prophecies came to pass? If you helped him in some way, then on the day you died you could tell yourself that you had contributed to something worthwhile, that your life at least hadn't turned out as meaningless as everyone else's... That's what she thought, her heart as close to gold as she knew how to get it.

Which is why it hardly mattered that three days later, when Chrissie Luna had finally made up her mind to actually do the good deed, Yuichi, lamb to the slaughter, televised dispatcher of Mormon, was absolutely, positively, the only holy man still behind bars. That also was Chrissie for you: always the last one on to a fad.

The certified check at the bank, the bail formalities, even the wait at the prison while they fetched the prisoner, dressed him, gave him back the white cotton shoulder pouch with his personal belongings, and brought him back to the light: Chrissie barely noticed the time fly by, lost as she was in armpit-sweating romantic-fantasy-run-wild about this dangerous man she was about to deliver from bondage. This chance to start over, to be someone completely new. Was it safe? Who cared? What if it were love at first sight for him? What if he, of all people, turned out to be the father of her children? The Japanese madman outside the UN? Why not? Stranger things had happened. Anyway, a little paternally-engendered mean streak wasn't the worst thing for a child. Made a kid stand up for himself, nothing wrong with that.

And then he appeared, and despite promising herself to remain cool, aloof and in control, she had almost shredded the butcher-paper wrapping of the heavy winter coat she had picked up for him at the Salvation Army store on Spring St., just in case. With his shaved head like that and white linen robe and guerilla shoulder bag, even from a distance, when she could see him, and he couldn't yet see her, she found him handsome, (the cranial stubble maybe?), more handsome in real life than on TV. And this even though he looked a trifle cross at being released, and actually seemed to be fighting the guards to slip back inside. Not that the new Chrissie took it personally. How could it be related to her? Look at the sight-lines, it was impossible, he hadn't even seen her yet. Or had he? Shit, here we go again, she thought to herself but tried to maintain her smile anyway. She hoped he wouldn't notice the sweat in her armpits, and began to wish that she hadn't worn her "Love: Stop the Violence," T-shirt, in case whatever the T-shirt actually meant should give him the wrong idea.

"Miss Chrissie Luna?" the orderly confirmed her identity for no real purpose, saying the "Luna" part with an unnecessary emphasis which made Chrissie want to melt into the linoleum floor. "He's worried about some scroll or other," the orderly continued slowly as if Chrissie were some kind of total moron. "Will you explain to him that he's just going to have to go on and forget his scroll for now, that it is being held as evidence in a battery case? Assault with a deadly weapon, they told him. He's gotta understand, he'll get it when he gets it."

If the "monk" didn't speak English, Chrissie thought, that was no reason to treat *her* like a total idiot, but she took a deep breath and tried to put it all behind her. "Umm, hi, I'm C..." She tried to be helpful. And what did it get her from the monk? What did it get her? A look! An out-of-my-way, shut-up-bitch look which she wouldn't take from people far more important than this pathetic last-man-out so-called monk would ever be. She all but turned around right there and asked for a refund on the bail pronto. Just imagine having children who look at you like that!

"You don't understand," Yuichi told the guard through gritted teeth. During the last thirteen days he had been as passive and obedient as they could wish, and when they had informed him that he was to be released, he had thanked them, all very polite. But they had neglected to mention that he would have to leave the scroll behind. Unfortunately, no matter how Yuichi presented his case, how earnestly he pleaded, or groaned, or told them the thing was just impossible, that he could not leave without the scroll, that the future of the planet depended on it, the prison flunkies simply refused to bend.

"No *you* no unnastan' pal," the guard said slowly, clearly, even more slowly than for Chrissie, (she was pleased to note). "Now I'm only going to say this once. This... the lady... who put up your bail... OK? Now... you... gots to go now... *capisce?* You're out of here, OK? Case closed..."

"Hi, I'm Chrissie?" Chrissie said more firmly this time, taking over. Shaking her head, she tossed him the half-shredded package, with a cavalier, confident, worldly flip.

"Yuichi. Pleased to meet you." He spoke soberly, crisply, (nothing like a simpleton actually), bowing politely, but keeping one hopeful eye on the orderly, in case this was all a big joke, American sense of humor, in case the large black man suddenly spun around and produced the scroll after all.

"Preased to meet you," she answered, grimacing ever-so-slightly, hoping that he hadn't noticed her "l" turn to "r" when his hadn't, (why had she done that?) then belatedly adding a clumsy bow of her own. She took a deep breath, determined to start over, start afresh no matter what they said about how you never get a second chance at a first impression. She pointed at the package. "It's a coat...I thought...I mean I didn't know if...I thought maybe you might not have one..."

"Thank you very much," Yuichi nodded and smiled briefly to put her at ease. What else was there to do about the scroll?

"Thankyouvellymush," Chrissie said. "I hope it's the right size," she said, laughing nervously, pointing at the coat so that he would know she was not referring to the size of his sex-organ, except that the way she did it, and the way he was holding the coat in front of his crotch, he probably still didn't know, so she let loose with her risqué laugh just in case, here we go again. "I thought you'd be bigger. (Omigod, what must he be thinking now?) It's Austrian, supposed to be very warm. Does it fit OK? Cause I can take it back, actually probably not, but it doesn't matter, I didn't pay that much for it." (How long was she going to keep groveling?) "The date for your preliminary hearing is Monday the 24th at 10, New York Supreme Court," Chrissie said, setting her jaw and putting on her business voice. Maybe expressing gratitude was beyond him, that was often the case with these New Age types, all concern and love for the universe, but nothing for basic human beings. "If you're not there I'll lose the bail money. So I hope you're there..." she sighed, putting an awkward period on another big mistake, and turning on her heel, ready to part company.

"I hope I'm there too," Yuichi said, with a little sympathetic laugh of his own.

"I don't know if you have a place to stay," Chrissie blurted out, she didn't know why. "But you're welcome to stay with me for a night or two. Or until the hearing..."

"Very gracious, thank you..." Yuichi bowed humbly.

"It's nothing, really, there's plenty of room..."

Chrissie's apartment was a fifth floor loft that you reached by a big, old, open, clangy warehouse elevator. To the left of the entryway were two bedrooms, and straight ahead was a beautiful, vast, room with oak floors, a space which included, on the left, where the windows gave onto Spring St., a wet-bar, on the right, an open kitchen with a double-door refrigerator large enough to live in, a dining table for twelve, and straight ahead, at the back of the room by the windows which gave onto Lafayette, a couch and sitting chairs set up around a steamer trunk and lovely Isfahan rug. Everything was neat and ordered, carefully placed, the wall full of CDs, the pictures from vacations and parties, the three televisions in three parts of the same room, kitchen, wet-bar and sitting area, the "Joy" brand dishwashing soap, the posters of Rome, Paris, Egypt, the places she only dreamed of going to, and the healthy, lush plants, so many bricks in the wall Chrissie had raised around herself in the losing battle to remain of good cheer.

"Make yourself at home," Chrissie said, throwing her pocketbook onto a chair in the entrance, her armpits gushing anew, feeling like twin Niagara Falls. Yuichi took off his shoes, virtually obliging her, even though shoe-removal was not house-policy, to follow suit. "Care for something to drink?" She recovered quickly. "Beer, wine, coffee, tea, Diet Coke?"

"Tea?"

"Tea it is," she said, automatically checking her message machine as she passed the bar, a message machine which, once again, registered zero. "Oh..." she opened her agenda and made a little note to herself to remember, first thing tomorrow morning, to cancel the week's appointments, and change the answering machine message, telling everyone she was going to take a couple of weeks vacation. "You like sugar?" she asked, opening the refrigerator door and extracting a pitcher full of ice tea to which she quickly added a dozen ice cubes from the freezer door, before transferring the suspiciously-colored brew into a tall crystal glass. The kitchen seemed to energize her. She moved smoothly, a model of efficiency, she felt confident again, and vowed that this time she would stay confident.

"No sugar, thank-you very much."

"Here you go," she said, holding out the drink with a big smile. She could teach him English, he could teach her...

"Tea?" Yuichi took the glass, polite as ever. It didn't exactly look or smell like tea. And ice in the middle of winter?

"It's my special mixture, Darjeeling and Red Zinger, tell me what you think? You make yourself at home, OK?" she added without waiting for an answer about the tea. "I'm going to freshen up."

A quick shower, a few phone calls, a Diet Coke and a flurry of activity in the kitchen (more like a hurricane, nobody but nobody was faster on Formica than Chrissie Luna), by the time the evening news came on the small kitchen TV, Chrissie had all the makings of a party going. Not that she wanted to be like one of those socialites with the plastic earlobes: this wouldn't be an ice-dolphin, limousines and chanting affair. Just a nice little party. An intimate get-together to give her a chance to introduce her savior to her friends, (and yes, admit it, to show off a bit).

She had invited everyone from her birthday party, except for rude Jim O'Brien, an Irishman straight from Dublin who thought he was much more charming with a jar or two in him than he actually was. O'Brien had just about succeeded in sticking his finger up her in the bathroom that night, but instead had crashed to the tile floor in an eggnog stupor, tearing her very-expensive Anti-Flirt French panties on the way down, and throwing up on her even-more-expensive French white satin shoes, the drunk.

"My friends are really friendly, you'll see, I'm sure you'll like them," Chrissie sang over her shoulder, just assuming Yuichi would be there. She chopped up some shrimp, tossed them into the sour cream dip, ripped open a large bag of chive-barbecue-beef-flavored ruffled potato chips, put everything in special bowls and thought that maybe she should have invited Jim O'Brien after all, just to see the look on his face when he figured out who had moved in.

"Getting-to-know-you..." Chrissie's special custom-made doorbell trilled its special cheery chime at eight on the dot, turning her instantly from just-average-nervous to psychotic-with-a-smile. "Here we go-oh!" TV off, wipe hands on apron, apron off and onto hook behind door, double-check smile in hallway and open door with a big cheery hello to... none other than Jim O'Brien himself, ohmyegod, chest out for hug, big bouquet of flowers in one hand, fifth of Black Bushmill's lubricant in the other, the brain-dead podado-head smiling fit to swallow a pint jar whole, glass and all.

"Heard there was a pordy," O'Brien said, stepping into the apartment before really being invited, and blowing into his hands to warm them, as if after that there could be no legal basis for throwing him out. "What's the occasion?"

"Jim! How nice, what a surprise, come in," Chrissie said. The noisy freight elevator had already left, groaning, wheezing, clanging on its way down, no doubt for the next bunch of friends. What was she supposed to do, throw him out by the scruff of his sweat-red neck? "Jim, I want you to meet Yuichi. He's a monk from Japan who will be staying here for a while. The party is in his honor..."

"Not a monk, a healer," Yuichi bowed.

"Same difference. Jim O'Brien, from Oierland," O'Brien introduced himself holding out first the Black Bush then the flowers to Yuichi in lieu of a handshake before drawing each back and laughing heartily at his own joke. "Yamaguchi is it?" he said, tossing the flowers to Chrissie without even looking.

"Name is Yuichi," he said, bowing. "Pleased to meet you," he added, noting the thick coarse hairs sprouting from the bridge of the Irish man's blackhead-covered nose: heart problems, probably linked to the alcohol. The unpleasantly loud voice, the lack of awareness: liver problems too, certainly much anger.

Chrissie pulled a vase out for the flowers, shooting Yuichi a smile topped off with a confident wink. This great party idea of hers was rapidly turning into a total fucking nightmare. One shot, two shots, three, the elevator kept going back down, but kept coming back up filled with people for a party at Melissa's, Chrissie's fashion-model neighbor on the sixth floor right above. A party where they were doubtless already having such a good time that Chrissie could almost hear the laughter and clicking of stiletto heels through the ceiling, almost hear the fine silk designer undergarments floating through the air like feathers and hitting the ground as the no-fluids orgy began. Had she given everyone the wrong day for the party? Chrissie wondered, before deciding that was unlikely, impossible even. "Can I get you anything?" she said, looking for an opening, any excuse whatsoever, to get away from the kitchen and hit the phones without the men noticing. To figure out what the hell was happening, where the hell everyone was. Not even her fucking mother had shown. "Some food? Anything?" They would have to scrape five layers of smiles off her face to know what she was thinking really.

"Nah, we're fine," O'Brien waved her off.

"Something to drink then..." The loft apartment should be buzzing with people, people at the bar, slightly envious people placed casually around the dinner table, people stepping out on the balcony for a quick breath of fresh air, and stepping back in, red-cheeked, commenting about the cold.

"No, it's really great, you sure can cook. Enough food here for an ormy."

"Napkins?" She was almost beginning to hate the Japanese monk, hate him so much, the way he kept nodding and bowing, encouraging the Irish lout. What kind of monk was this? It crossed her mind that maybe it wasn't Jim O'Brien who tried to finger-fuck her after all, she couldn't remember, no it had to be him, Mr. Irish Hurler had been such a champion hurler she had to toss those Barney's white satin shoes, for which she had paid quite a lot of money, thank you very much.

"Nah, just use me sleeve."

"I have to use the restroom," she finally blurted out, almost sobbing, certain that this time they would see right through her, but not really caring anymore.

"Be right in," Jim said, winking, still gentleman enough to stand when she did, (which she appreciated) holding the bottle out to her and taking a big swig. "To the hostess!"

"Getting-to-know-you..." the doorbell finally rang, and Chrissie reappeared, party-face intact. Deliverance, huge sigh of relief, only now did she remember that she had told everybody 9:30.

"Hello-o. Hi! I'm so glad you could come!" It seemed like everybody had arrived at once, and on time to boot, goddammit. "You don't know how glad..."

To Yuichi, the rest of Chrissie's "friends" looked every bit as out-of-balance and fractured as the first one. No one he could look at and say this is a man, or this is a woman, no one there who gave the least sense of self-knowledge, of seeking, or serenity, humility or awe. In the shape and color of the face, in the intonation of their voices and the energy given off, you could see the state of their livers, their lungs, their kidneys, their gallbladders, their spleens, their stomachs, their large and small intestines, their hearts. Sometimes people were sick because they chose to be, but mostly they were sick because of ignorance.

In this, Chrissie's friends were probably not much different from the patients Yuichi had treated in Japan. They didn't know when they were out of balance, so they didn't know when they had to correct themselves. They thought their moods and angers and sudden preference for certain colors and foods were a sign of "personality," they had sex whenever they itched and ate whatever they wanted as if they were immune to the changes in energy when summer turned to fall or winter turned to spring or war raged on in a faraway land. Their sickness ruled their lives, their paranoia, their phobias, their I'm-not-a-morning-person common-sense, and they held onto their sickness because it was the only thing that made them different from the rest, made them feel unique.

But in their loneliness, their drifting they could not help but respond when in the presence of someone like Yuichi. The serenity, the unlined face, the way he listened and looked them straight in the eye, seeing but not judging... It made them feel good, gave them a sense deep inside that perhaps all was not bad music and indifference, doomed planets and ecstasy in pill-form. And it caused them to want to confide in him, to reveal innermost secrets all at once.

"Chrissie's really a great girl, if you could only get her to shut up every so often..." said the daughter of a famous model agency owner, on anti-depressants because of the men coming after her to get to the models in her father's stable.

"Yeah and you hear the way she serves the food?" said an art director with cancer of the uterus, drinking scotch. "Here are some shrimps, here are some salmons. She adds an "s" to everything, like that makes it cute. It's a new millennium for Chrissakes, would somebody please fucking tell her? The world is not cute."

"And look at the wine she serves! So *parvenu!*" added an oily-haired French painter named Hippolyte, sticking his hand out to shake. "My friends call me Hip," he said, which he thought was very clever marketing for a painter, except that because of his congenital inability to aspirate it sounded more like "My friends call me Eep," which no quantity of perfect blue-gray Gauloises smoke rings could make sound cool.

Even Chrissie's dotty mother, who only fifteen minutes after arrival already sported twin white stripes of onion dip on her yellow Spandex shirt, twin stripes bisected neatly by a third stripe of parvenu Bordeaux, was not immune to Yuichi's spell. "Young man, do you have any idea what it's like to make a child? The hope of it? And then forty years later see the result? And they wonder why parents turn to drink..."

Unaware of her guests' true feelings, the object of their "confessions," Chrissie Luna watched them crowd around Yuichi and felt so happy that she had to stifle a sob. She forgave Yuichi for encouraging O'Brien earlier, and began to like him all over again. Let Yuichi have his moment in the sun, sure, she was happy to keep herself occupied with party business. She popped some new Japanese salsa music on the music system over by the couch, ever-so-slightly too loud, poured Chateau Lafitte for some, got out the ice pick and cracked ice for *caipirinhas* for others, (the ice crushed directly by the freezer just wasn't the same, too coarse), then waltzed here and there with platters of food, making double-sure everyone was fine. Wrapped up in a rare cocoon of happiness, surrounded by friends, she danced off again over to the kitchen, armpits dry as the Sahara: this was the best party she'd given in years. Was it so much, every so often, to ask for proof that you were worth something? To get an evening when everybody looked at you clean, because they respected you, because they saw the quality of your heart? Looked at you clean, respectful, like they looked at Yuichi...

When everyone had finally left, and Yuichi (gold star number three) had helped her clean up, when the last ashtrays had been emptied, the last wine bottles tossed in the recycle bin, and the garbage bags compacted, tied-up and set neatly in the hall outside the front door, Chrissie finally worked up the courage to pop the question. "So where would you like to sleep?" she asked idly, fitting a last few glasses into the dishwasher, adding the dishwasher powder, setting the machine in motion, then picking up the ice pick and idly cracking a few more ice cubes, a delay which she thought helped reinforce the impression of how anxious she wasn't. "You can sleep in my bed, or there's always the couch but it's kind of old and not very comfortable. Up to you," she added quickly, but the harsh way she had said "couch," compared to soft tone used to day "my bed," and the way she had not even given him the option of staying in the guest bedroom, left little doubt as to her preference.

"Chrissie, I have to tell you something," Yuichi said almost apologetically, taking her hand. The time had come to do more than listen. "I understand about biorogical crock ticking," (biorogical crock, he said deliberately, so that when she made the usual transliteration, she would hear "biological clock," and not be offended). "But I have to tell you something: I'm not a man. Not really."

"Not reary? Of course you're not, (the nerve!)," she said, laughing lightly, her heart sticking in her throat, taking his phrase to mean he thought he was some kind of god and therefore sex was out, when all he was trying to say, in all humility, was that he was not a man in the sense of men she had clearly known all her life, with their excessive appetites and fundamental cowardice. And... that sex was out.

Chrissie Luna stormed to the couch and opened it, then stormed to the window to air out the apartment, quickly, then stormed over to the kitchen to sponge off the already spotless counter again before returning to the couch and angrily making the bed with sheets and blankets she extracted from the steamer trunk that served as her reserve coffee table. A whirlwind of activity which used the last of her day's supply of nervous energy, and helped her decide that "I'm not a man" didn't actually mean rejection, it just meant please be patient and, probably, sweet dreams. "Sweet dreams to you, Yuichi, make yourself at home, OK?" she said. "You know where the bathroom is, I'll put out a towel for you. Anything you want, you just help yourself."

3

Chrissie Luna slept dreadfully that night, fighting her pillow to a draw, dying of thirst, dreaming of Satan in hell, then of the madman who stabbed George Harrison just before New Year's, and nearly strangling herself twice in her sweat-soaked sheets. In the morning, she woke up feeling stiff, Achilles tendons so sore she was barely able to bend her ankles, mouth coated with such a terrible sour taste that two brushings and three different brands of mouthwash later she still didn't feel fit for human company. Not to mention her puffy eyes and the pores on her cheeks and nose which seemed unusually large this morning, an ungodly mess which no combination of ice, astringent, mask or makeup in her considerable cosmetology arsenal would likely conceal, not even Preparation H. Only her sense of obligation to her guest helped her overcome her desire to go back to bed immediately and die. At the very least, she thought, she should check to see if he was still sleeping. If he was, she had just the excuse she needed.

Unfortunately for her, not only was Yuichi awake, but by the look of him, bare-chested, rippling stomach glistening with perspiration as he moved placidly back and forth over her Isfahan rug, east, west, north, south, he had already been up a good while. Even his bedding was neatly folded at one end of the couch! She didn't know what to say. The very notion was a slap in the face, an open condemnation of her party and of her, her weak, dissolute nature. A condemnation which made her so angry her knees locked and her legs froze. "By what right..." she started, but standing still made her so unsteady that she almost fell over and had to grip the kitchen counter to remain upright.

Still miles from the espresso machine, she smiled apologetically even though, seemingly, he had still not noticed her presence. If he thought she was that worthless, why didn't he just say it, rather than moving back and forth like that giving her the cold treatment? Why didn't he just say it? 'Chrissie, I saw your mother, and I know what you will be like in less time than you think, and I don't want to have anything further to do with you. Therefore if you would kindly just retire so I don't have to look at your frightful face, then I will take a shower and be out of your hair for eternity or longer.'

He had just walked in and taken over. Just walked in, settled into the living room, not the guest bedroom but the living room. He had made everyone else take off their shoes and adapt their schedule to *his*. In her own apartment she couldn't even put on some music and/or the Breakfast Show to smooth out the rough edges, because Mr. Holy Man mustn't be disturbed. Not to mention that some asshole had moved the fucking remote control during the party and she felt far too weak to track it down, since it had never occurred to the nitwits at remote-control-central to include some sort of tracking/beeping mechanism in the damn things in the first place. "Who's that?" she snapped, pointing at the photo on the coffee table, a round-faced, smiling man with a long, flowing white beard, yet another intrusion on the proper order of things.

"Good morning Chrissie!" Yuichi said cheerily.

But Chrissie did not lower her trembling, accusing finger. If he wanted to start something just to give himself an excuse to leave with a good conscience, then they would have it out right now, she was in no mood to be appeased. How easy it was to say one thing one moment, then retract it once the damage was done. "Who is it? I said."

"This? My Sensei," Yuichi said, smiling.

"Your sin-say, of course..." Chrissie said, picking up a pencil and applying it to the phone pad so hard that the lead broke, great, what else Lord, what else?

"Lie down, please," Yuichi said, designating the rug, "Yuichi fix, maybe feel better..."

"Coffee," she said, not offering but gasping, the way, when people drowned in the movies, they said "air."

"Coffee later. For right now, you lie down..." He spread his bedding out on the rug and pointed firmly to the floor.

"Excuse me?" Lie down? Fat chance. What was she, his poodle?

Without a word, he just stared at her, until finally she had no choice but to lower herself with difficulty to the floor. Yuichi was a different man now, suddenly less soft, less meandering. He did not chatter, he did not smile, he did not try and put her at ease, but simply kneeled on his haunches next to her, in *seiza,* put his hands over her, on her shoulder and hip, closed his eyes and took a deep breath, pressing down.

"Ow," Chrissie said, but still he did not react other than to switch his hands to the other shoulder and the other hip, which hurt almost as much. After that he took her right hand in his and placed his fingertips on her radial artery to check her pulses. Then he took a deep breath and exhaled, then another, in and out, punctuated by a soft "Now you..." when she failed to follow his lead. Then he switched arms, listening to the beat under his fingers, "hearing" through them her entire history, imbalances present and congenital, and the conditions one could do nothing about, those things handed down from the ancestors, the heavy heritage that made each race play the role it was supposed to play in this dance of death. Chrissie Luna's pulses were primarily flat, *kyo* condition, except for the heart meridian which was definitely *jitsu,* not that he was surprised.

Already at the prison, on first sight, he had made an initial diagnosis. The feeble, squeezed, nearly transparent energy envelope, sign of a condition she had probably lived with for quite some time now, ebb and flow defective since puberty. The constant chatter, her nervous laughter, the nose split in the middle with a slightly bulbous tip: sign of a too-full heart meridian. The roots of gray hair showing through the dye, the bags under her eyes, the floating, reedy energy: sign of depleted kidneys. The unhealthy pallor in the cheeks: sign of blockage in the lung meridian. The obvious lack of confidence, the hint of weak constitution: sign of depleted stomach meridian. Weak, exhausted, starved for love...

Now, with his hands on her, the story was filling in, becoming more complete. The solar plexus energy had clearly been blocked for years in the attempt to produce a convincing two-dimensional façade. In the neck and crown the chimney needed to be opened up, the energy allowed to circulate and not block her throat. The pain in her tendons, and the watery, low voice were only confirmation of his earlier diagnosis of depleted kidneys, a condition called "cold poisoning" resulting from excessive ingestion of cold drinks and raw foods. And since water rules over fire: it was this that was no-doubt partly responsible for the heart as well. "Sickness come because energy imbarance," he laid the Japanese pidgin on doubly thick because he sensed she would find it more authoritative. "Western medicine say doctor must to fix everything, Japanese medicine say sick person fix self. In west,

19

doctor big expert, doctor work on you, in East, doctor work with you, guide you. Difference. You responsible for health, nobody else. You responsible for listen body and eat right food. This call medicine of future, patient become very aware, aware always more and more. Unnastan?"

For forty-five minutes, kneeling on one side of her, then the other, Yuichi ran his hands over nearly every inch of Chrissie's body, the arms, the back, the thighs, the feet, sometimes soft and so sexy, sometimes hard, especially in her abdomen and shoulders, where she felt she was almost going to black out from the pain, and sex was about the last thing she wanted to think about. Sometimes, he didn't touch her at all, but stood over her supine form and held out his hands in such a way that the heat penetrated to her very core and she felt like she was almost floating. And then he massaged her feet, working his way from heel to toe, heel to toe, time after blissful time, and she thought she had died and gone to heaven.

"How do you feel?" he asked an hour later, when he was finally done, hovering over her like some beautiful statue of grace, smiling as if he knew already how she felt. Her breathing had turned deep and even, the color had returned to her cheeks, the tension wrinkles across her forehead had all but vanished.

"Wow!" Chrissie exhaled, opening her eyes ever-so-briefly, then closing them again, and shaking her head at a loss for words. The early morning anger was now a silly, distant memory. She felt unutterably drowsy, and it was all she could do not to slip away to dreamland right here on the living room floor.

"Good," he smiled back, bowed, touched his forehead lightly to the floor, said "Thank you," rose to his feet and disappeared into the bathroom to wash his hands.

With considerable act of will, Chrissie finally managed to pry open her heavy eyelids and unglue herself from the floor five minutes later. She padded back to her bed, collapsed into the cocoon of her down comforter and buried her grateful head in her pillow, regretting her morning mood, and praying Yuichi wouldn't hold it against her. It was a rare man who would massage your feet without even being asked, a rare man indeed. "I'm not a man..." Wasn't that what he had said last night? Well if that's what not being a man was about, then sign her up. If he had torn off her sopping panties, and maybe tried that little Japanese heat trick on her clitoris for a few seconds before mounting her and thrusting himself deep inside her, Chrissie thought, she wouldn't have pushed him away. But for the moment, in a strange way, she was happy he had not tried to take advantage of her after all.

4

Chrissie slept the sleep of the dead and awakened a full two blessed hours later, feeling surprisingly alert and alive. Not to mention hungry as hell, and nothing in the fridge she really felt like eating. "I'm going to go buy some food. You want to come? It's not far," she said, putting on her coat to give the impression, once again, that it didn't make a whit of difference either way if he joined her or not.

"Sure, good," he said, collecting the photo of his Sensei, putting it back into the thin cotton shoulder bag that held his money, passport and toothbrush, and slipping on his coat.

"We're just going to the store..." Chrissie said as if to imply how pathetic it was to collect all your worldly goods for an absence of 20 minutes max.

"New York City," he said, laughing.

"Yeah, I s'pose." (New York City? What the hell was that supposed to mean?) She put a finger in the air, and checked her agenda, then walked to the phone, canceled the week's appointments and changed the message. "Hi this is Chrissie, I'm off in Miami Beach for the week, leave me a message."

"So how did you like my friends last night?" As they stepped out of the elevator downstairs, Chrissie could take the suspense no longer. Except that outside, change the subject, the night had apparently been so cold that fire hydrants had frozen and exploded, turning sidewalks into gleaming, treacherous skating rinks and leaving a line of jagged ice crown-of-thorn sculptures up and down Lafayette as far as the eye could see.

"Cold..." Yuichi said, as vaguely as possible.

"Cord? Ah cold!" she said. "Cold, sure is..." If the monk didn't want to talk about her friends quite yet, that was certainly his right. Hey, with hands like that? He didn't have to say anything ever again. She brushed her hand against his once, accidentally-on-purpose, hoping he would take the hint, which he didn't, then again a little more obviously, a few buildings later, in front of the travel agency advertising, among others, flights to Tokyo for $1250.

A harmless little game which served no other purpose than to get her heart racing again for nothing, to get him to apologize for knocking into her and to cause both of them to be so distracted as to neglect to notice that they were not, in fact, alone. Witnesses to their little dances including: one weaselly-looking G-man, one wired-jaw Mormon, unaccompanied, but wearing a sandwich board on which he had written in magic marker, "There are eternal laws which have existed forever whose bounds cannot be passed," and six small gangs: black, white, poor, rich, young, old – representatives of all the little sneakered, jacketed and capped tribes that had sprouted as the millennium approached and life, in spite of auspicious financial reports from the White House, got progressively, inexorably worse. Not an underclass, but the "What the fuck" class, the First World poor, with enough money to eat, enough money to clothe themselves a dozen different ways, enough to protect themselves against the cold, just not enough money to buy enough entertainment to heal the deep-down despair, to help them find meaning in anything other than destruction. A rainbow coalition of hope-deprived, Hollywood-reference, miserable *sanpaku*-eyed people eager to fuck up this Jackie Chan motherfucker once and for all.

"It's high noon motherfucker!" said one whose eyes showed a dangerous amount of white above the iris.

"It's showdown at OK Corral, Bruce Lee," said another, with eyes showing white under the iris, yin *sanpaku*, too much alcohol and drugs, a death-wish for sure.

"It's Rambo Eight, and Terminator Five-time rolled into one..."

"Care for a cigarette before you die?"

"Any last wishes, mo'fucker?"

A bit of continuous attention which refused to go away no matter how Chrissie tried to explain it, "Mercury must be in retrograde..." no matter how many accessories they used to try and disguise Yuichi, a scarf, sunglasses, lipstick, base makeup, rouge.

Long before they had turned off West Houston and onto LaGuardia in sight of the Grand Union grocery which was their original goal, poor Yuichi, still his old confident self, but skating wildly from curb to door-stoop looking like the late Jackie O herself, had managed accidentally to incapacitate a good two-score action Jacksons, Puerto Ricans, Cubans, Blacks and Whites, to convince a G-man that whoever had told him to tail Yuichi and watch for signs of sedition must be off his rocker, and to re-fracture a stupidly pugnacious Mormon jaw.

"Yuichi! Please!" Chrissie finally latched on to him and helped him get his footing. Having your own private vigilante force was not without its pluses, but she couldn't help but wonder if in some crazy, strange way, his habit of getting in fights was not a subtle attempt to leave her by going straight back to jail. It would certainly explain the packing of the worldly goods. Not exactly what you call a confidence-builder, when a man all but says that being behind bars is less painful than spending twenty minutes with a gal shopping for groceries, but this was clearly neither the time or place to have it out. The sooner she got him back inside, the better it would be for both of them. "No offense?" she said, praying he wouldn't take this wrong. "But maybe it would be better if you went back to the apartment?"

"Maybe..."

"OK, I'll tell you what," Chrissie said. "You go back to the apartment and wait for me. I'll pick up the groceries and get a key made so you can have your freedom. You remember how to get back? Right at the corner to

Spring, Spring to Lafayette, then right to number 226. Shouldn't take me more than fifteen minutes. Twenty max, OK?"

"OK."

Shouldn't, but did. Thirty minutes, an hour, an hour and a half, two, still in full makeup, sitting cross-legged, head-down, Yuichi waited patiently on the stoop outside the door, trying his best to be invisible, wondering whether Very-Strange-Angel had not encountered some misfortune, debating whether to dive back out into the violence to search for her, but deciding against it.

Back in Isohara, Yuichi had spent a month with a cultural facilitator to prepare him for the mission, to initiate him in the ways of this other world. He had warned him of a strange angry people, warned him of the vulgarity, the impulsiveness, the inability to consider consequences, the capacity to profane the most sacred things, so Yuichi wasn't really surprised. What else should one expect in the temple of the five senses, the temple of the star-god, Susano-wo, who vomited in palaces and took pleasure in breaking down dikes or doing any old thing he pleased? What Yuichi hadn't been prepared for was the intensity of it, for how, the longer he stayed here, the worse it seemed to get. But then, in a way, this too was beginning to make sense. A sickness could not heal itself, a sickness always fought to stay alive, why shouldn't the dying star-god try to beat him down? Moses, Jesus, Mohammed: in the history of the world, what missionary of a new current had not been met by hostility? Kanagi, the scientific-material current which had gradually grown to dominate the world over the course of the last 3000 years, could hardly be expected to give up without a fight.

About his mission, Yuichi still had not the slightest doubt. Was it not his Sensei, the incarnation of the ancestors, who had interpreted the prophecies and signs? Who had entrusted him with this mission? And the ancestors did not make decisions based on impulse, imagination or dream: they acted out of knowledge. Which meant that somehow, somewhere, deep down, O Sensei could not have been unaware that the delivery of the scroll on New Year's Day would turn into a riot, that both Yuichi and the scroll would end up in jail, and that there would be other trials and tests to face before it was all over. All was certainly as it must be, no cause for complaint.

5

So what was Chrissie's excuse when she finally appeared over three hours late, a bag of groceries in her hand? She had forgotten.

"I'm so embarrassed," she couldn't stop saying as they rode the elevator up to the fifth floor. The idea of chastising him for trying to get into fights so as to leave her had slipped her mind altogether. And not that Yuichi was really bursting with eagerness to go out sight-seeing, but the key she had promised him? Forgotten too.

"How can I ever make it up to you?" she said, armpits gushing (shouldn't she be over that by now?), nerves so shot that she fumbled with her key ring for an eternity before finding the right key and letting them in. "You must be dying of thirst, I am," she said with a weak smile, putting down her purse in the usual place, glancing hopefully at the answering machine which, once again, showed a big fat red zero, and continuing straight over to the kitchen without a hitch. (He probably hated her.) "How 'bout a nice cold drink?" she dropped the groceries on the kitchen counter, and opened the refrigerator, already bored with what she had just bought. "Tea?" she said grabbing a bag of pre-washed mini-carrots almost instinctively and munching one then another while scouring the refrigerator to try and decide what she might want. To be honest, she was a little surprised nobody had called to thank her for the party, not even Jim O'Brien who always came up with something vulgar to say to her machine the day after. There was nothing in the refrigerator, so she shut it and opened the freezer door. "I hope you're not too angry..." she said, a little too loudly. She shifted the frozen broccoli to a lower shelf, and rearranged the orange juice concentrate in the door. A dish of ice cream was what she really wanted. Eeny meeny miney mo, she chose chocolate cream cookies then rejected that in favor of Sven Golly quadruple cream light peach ice cream, because of the special fruit chunks.

"Not angry, just glad you're OK. I thought maybe something bad had happened to you."

"No, nothing bad happen me," Chrissie answered. She tossed the ice cream bucket on the counter, quickly materialized scooper, spoon and bowl and helped herself to a comfortably large portion.

"New York City is very dangerous I think," Yuichi said. Ice cream in the dead of winter! He couldn't believe such a lack of basic animal common sense.

"Ah, you just have to get used to it."

"Ho?" He wondered if, in addition to forgetting to return to the apartment when she had promised and forgetting the key, she could possibly already have forgotten the gauntlet outside. Get used to it?

"Did you tell me what you want?"

"What I want..." By this point, Yuichi had only one, very precise desire: to recover the scroll, deliver it as soon as the American justice system saw fit to release him and it, then settle into a seat on JAL and leave this place behind. Sprung from jail by this strange forgetful angel, he now found himself locked up in her prison, in her apartment, at the mercy of her whims and moods. If that was the way it was, then that was the way it was, no choice but to accept it. But you didn't have to be O Sensei to understand that the condition of her health, and her incredible forgetfulness could well have catastrophic consequences long before the court date, after which the two of them could once again, mercifully, go their separate ways.

This morning, all in stride, he had given her a treatment with no specific ulterior motive, no intention other than to repay her kindness by giving her back, however briefly, a sense of her own balance. Now, whatever treatments he would give would not be so much out of altruism as out of concern for the mission, for the scroll. It was not a question of healing, because healing cannot occur in the absence of accord and collaboration. Not to mention: her condition was so entrenched, an imbalance so deep that it would require much longer than ten days for it to be reversed anyway.

"I don't remember if you take sugar," she said, having decided that it was indeed tea that he had asked for, handing him a glass of fresh crushed ice colored with the same vile *gaijin* blend as yesterday. "Help yourself, I'm going to hop into the shower, OK? No hard feelings, right?"

"No hard feelings, thank-you very much," Yuichi said, popping out a cocktail laugh of his own to put her at ease and mask his intention. He waited until she had disappeared into her bedroom, until he heard the shower go on and the shower door open and shut before springing into action, sliding over to the kitchen on sock-covered cotton feet and quickly putting her very-best-friend the refrigerator out of action... by pulling the plug.

"Oh my God," she cried when she discovered the wounded appliance three hours later, discovered an ice crusher that refused to spit out crushed ice, discovered four gallons of ice cream beginning to grow soft in the massive industrial freezer, discovered mini-carrots and celery stalks locked in moist darkness, betrayed, beginning to marinate as the refrigerator vegetable trays filled with condensation runoff, bearing the brunt of the breakdown of the never-failed-before FrostawayTM design.

It took the man from AAAAAAppliance twenty minutes after Chrissie's phone call to get into costume and character, to put an extra dab of grease on an already greasy CAT baseball cap, to grind some iron filings into the fabric of the blue overalls with the name Wade stitched on the breast, to dip his fingers in used 40W motor oil so that the fingernails were packed and the fingers had that grime-ground-in-too-far-for-soap look. Twenty minutes to slip back into a shotguns-in-the-pickup-back-window, tobacco-spit-on-the-side Alabama accent which gave him that don't-argue-with-him-he's-not-too-bright edge that most of the other appliance repair con-men in New York City also used to such good effect. Twenty minutes costume and ten minutes driving time, that would be just about right. Especially for a refrigerator, on account of the emotional tie, you had to get there within the half-hour, while the wound was still fresh.

Thirty minutes, thirty endless, painful minutes, time enough for Chrissie to empty the entire "ruined" contents of the behemoth into garbage bags, except for the Diet Coke, the batteries and a number of vegetables which Yuichi assured her could be resuscitated by cooking. (As if he were smarter than a late-night documentary she had watched on botulism, salmonella and Legionnaire's Disease!) Thirty minutes, time enough for Yuichi to start some rice cooking on the stove and to begin sharpening the knives preparatory to chopping the vegetables for a different kind of dinner, something he had planned to do anyway, even if the refrigerator had not "broken down."

In fact, "Wade," aka Shmuel Goldman, whose family owned half of Connecticut, and who had graduated from Yale with a double Masters degree in psychology and theater arts, had found no way to make a more lucrative living than preying on the Big Apple's too-comfortable fractured citizens. Taking advantage of their curious dependence on the devices that made their lives easier. Taking advantage of the endemic fear and fragility that resulted when computer circuits made machines too intelligent, and the everything-provided-urban-living made people too helpless. A six month correspondence course in consumer electronics, a three-month course in Yokel at the Defense Language Institute in Monterey, California, regular visits to the gym to keep the muscles pumped and believable, (especially the biceps coming out from under the short sleeve, with the vein showing down the middle), and enough horse-sense to know how to replace electronic circuit boards and write out a bill, that's all it had taken for "Wade" from Rowayton, Connecticut. The rest was acting.

"Nice place you got here," Wade said when he stepped inside the apartment, taking off his coat in such a way as to leave a deliberate grease stain on the wall and laying the accent on so thick it sounded like "nass ple-uz."

"Thank you. It's right over here." Chrissie almost instantly developed a hint of a drawl herself, the age-old chameleon reflex kicking in.

"Somewhere ah can drop mah coat?" He followed her to the kitchen, deliberately dragging the heels of his Timberlands across the wood floor. When the refrigerator came into sight, he slowed down a notch, blew his nose loudly into a bandanna, and mopped up the excess three, four, five times before stuffing the rag back in his pocket. "I call them guys runaways..." he said with a laugh which only deepened the horror lines on her face. So far, so good. By the look of her, she was the perfect mark: recent appliances, trembling hands, and a Japanese cook who probably cost her a pretty penny. "So heu-wut we got he-ah?" He put his toolkit down in front of the refrigerator, rubbed his hands together, cracked his knuckles and noticed the pulled plug right away. "Ah, the Frostaway..." he said, shaking his head.

"What?" Chrissie asked, but this time he didn't answer other than to wave his hand in a way that said it was time for women and children to step back and let a man get to work.

In the appliance repair grift, the accidentally-unplugged-refrigerator scenario was as routine as you got. You opened the doors, put on the stethoscope and listened to the sides, then shook your head, put on a pained expression and pursed your mouth as if the news was grim, gave the side a little wipe with your snotrag, told them you were probably going to have to take it down to the shop and then offered to try to take care of it on the spot, but no guarantees. "Suit yourself..." In this particular case, the only variable was the Japanese cook, who was giving him a slightly-too-piercing I-know-what-you're-up-to sidelong look, and who would have to be sounded out pronto before proceeding. "Can I help you?" Wade gave it his deepest drawl, ken-ah-hay-ulp-uuu, turning slowly and tilting his head as if to say, where I'm from, we mind our eyes or else.

"Sorry?"

Solly? Ha! With an accent like that, he certainly wasn't a fraud cop. "You got a problem?" Wade laid the hush puppies and Pepsi on even thicker. There were two possibilities, either the cook was some sort of wise guy and had pulled the plug accidentally-on-purpose for some fucked-up reason or another, or he was just as unaware as the rest, and thought that by watching carefully he would help keep the bill down, and thus somehow wash away the sin of having the appliance go down on his watch. Or third possibility, now that he thought about it: hadn't the Jap said Solly? The name Solomon wasn't even close to Shmuel, but what if the Jap had Jew-sniffed him and was just letting him know he was onto the "Wade" disguise?

"Tell your boy to keep his eyes to hisself, or I'm outta here," the repairman tossed out at Chrissie, as if only the presence of a woman was keeping him from kicking the cook's ass right then and there, regardless of the knife in his hand, or the generalized repair guild guidelines advising against picking fights with customers.

"Yuichi! Please..." It was too much. Unsettled by the refrigerator, now all Chrissie could see was that apparently the violence on the street wasn't enough. Now Yuichi had to bring the conflict inside her apartment as well. Whatever gold stars she had once given him, she now took away. Bring a wolf into an apartment and what do you expect? She could already hear her mother's I-told-you-so remarks. Like Chrissie needed a broken refrigerator and *that* as well. "Enough!" she snarled at Yuichi, her face a grim mask, her eyes shooting lightning bolts, her mouth pinched, her teeth clenched. "Leave... him... alone."

"That's better," said the repairman when Yuichi finally averted his gaze and got back to his cooking. "Now perhaps we can get some work done..."

Rolling up his sleeves, and putting on a terrific show of chin-scratching and head-shaking for Chrissie's benefit, Wade proceeded to remove about a zillion screws with a power drill and to make six separate trips down to his truck for various parts, before gluing it all back together, pocketing the leftover screws and finally plugging it in. In spite of Yuichi's raised eyebrows, the bill, including a capacitor, a distributor and easily a half-dozen grommets, came to $450. $450 which Chrissie gladly coughed up. A bill which, given Yuichi's role in the "sabotage," and the apparent readiness of the American repairman to fight, head-shaking Yuichi had to concede he was in no position to contest.

6

The next morning, during the second massage, Chrissie felt talkative, as if the crisis with the refrigerator had brought them closer, and it was time to share, to build something. Yuichi's episode with the repairman had been instructive and sobering, a man who couldn't see another human being without getting into a fight was not exactly her idea of Prince Charming. But if you thought back, Yuichi hadn't been a wolf at the party, had he? And he certainly hadn't been a wolf at night, nor when he had her helplessly spread-eagled on the floor during the treatments. But what if he were? What if he were actually a wolf? Nobody's perfect, she could live with that. Besides, a little paternally-engendered wolf-streak wasn't the worst thing for a child to have, she thought, her panties becoming instantly wet again. Made a kid stand up for himself, and what was wrong with that?

Actually what she really wanted to know was why he felt he had to wash his hands after touching her. That didn't really make her feel all that great. Did he think she was too passed-out to notice? "You know, I was wondering, what was in that metal cylinder you had with you New Year's?"

"Cylinder?"

"You kno-ow..."

"Ah, a very important document."

"Really? What sort of velly impoltant document?"

"It talks about very important things."

"Like what?"

"Don't know exactly. Never read it." He could tell her that there were three scrolls hidden in Hinomoto Kuni, 3000 years ago. He could tell her about *Ten No Maki*, the Book of the Sky, the only scroll that had been unveiled so far, how it related the era of the gods, and how the ancients had left orders thousands of years earlier for it to be unveiled when there would be two suns in the sky, and the Emperor would become human. And how this had come to pass with Hiroshima, and the end of World War II when Emperor Hirohito renounced his divine status. He could tell her about *Chi No Maki*, the Book of the Earth, the scroll he had been trying to give to the

UN, and how it related the history of the various regions of the world. He could tell her about *Jin No Maki*, the Book of Man, the final scroll which could only be unveiled once *Chi No Maki* had gotten where it was supposed to go. *Jin No Maki*, in which, at last, the names of the gods were inscribed in their right order. But what good would it do? What would it matter to her if he told her that the true history of the world differed from what she had been taught? What would it matter to her that the gods' names were in the wrong order? So what if this was an era of darkness, if our third eyes were shut and our sixth senses clouded, if for untold thousands of years, symbolic truths had been presented to us as the literal Word of God? So what if everything were *Tendo-Muso*, inside out and upside down?

No, there was no way to share insights coming from such an entirely different dimension, such an entirely different way of perceiving the world, and no point either, really. Still, Yuichi thought, clumsy though her attempt at conversation might be, her curiosity was a sign that things were already moving inside her, blockages breaking up, imbalances beginning to turn around. In her own interest, in the interest of her return to health, this demanded reciprocation, it was only right. "Have you ever heard the story of Izanagi and Izanami?"

"No..." God, his English was atrocious. She really was going to have to get to work on that.

"It's a Shinto myth."

"Uh huh."

"Shinto: ancient Japanese religion."

"I'm not stupid," she said, which suddenly seemed like a stupid thing to say, since she was a terrible liar and if he had let her venture a guess, she would have ventured that Shinto was a type of mushroom, and now she was sure the lie was written in neon all over her face.

"Izanagi and Izanami were two of the earliest gods, many thousands of years ago," Yuichi continued as if he hadn't even heard her. "Brother and sister who were ordered by the Heavenly Deities to give birth to the drifting land of Japan. Standing on the Bridge of Heaven, Izanagi churned the ocean with his lance until it began to solidify. From his lance fell a drop of ocean which became the island Onokoro. The two gods made their home on this island, setting up a sacred column. When it was time to couple, Izanami walked to the right of the column, and Izanagi walked to the left until they met. Izanami, the sister, spoke first, telling Izanagi he was a likeable and handsome young man so that he answered, saying that she was a likeable and pretty young lady. But when they coupled this way, the fruit of her womb was the dwarf Sukuna-Hikona, whom they set adrift on a raft of reeds. Again they tried, but this time Izanami gave birth to the Island Awa (which some people called Awaji). These births are called Hiluko and neither is counted as their children."

"I'm listening..." Chrissie said.

"Looking for some explanation for the strange births, Izanagi decided to consult the Heavenly Deities. They told him that after walking around the pillar, it was necessary for Izanagi to take the initiative, that it was not proper for Izanami to speak first."

"OK, interesting..." (Now wasn't that just too-typical male bullshit? Adam and Eve, only with slanted eyes, hold the ribs.)

"Turn over on your stomach, please," Yuichi said, focusing on her kidneys, pressing the heels of his hands into her back perhaps a little more roughly than necessary, isolating blockages that had come to the surface since the first session.

"Oh..."[1] Chrissie exhaled. ('I'm not a man,' that was a hoot, he wanted a zombie wife just like all the rest. Well sorry cowboy-san, wrong number, this is the nineties.) "Ouch..." The pain was excruciating. "OW!"

"Forgive me..." Yuichi purred. That she should not grasp the esoteric nature of the story, the hidden explanation of the Word of God, of the sound-rhythm structure of energy was only to be expected. That she should not know that Izanagi represented the yang, expanding energy, and Izanami the yin, the concentrating energy, that she should interpret it as a love story, as another pillar of the dominant-male mythology was neither terribly surprising, given the era and the culture, nor probably terribly serious. But it certainly didn't inspire him to continue.

"So?" she said.

"So what?"

"So what happened?"

"Well..." Yuichi sighed, and moved down to her left foot to begin the massage of the backs of her legs, bladder meridian, where the energy had stagnated. It took him all the way up to her left buttock, then down partway on the right hamstring, before he felt like resuming. "Once they understood the proper way of doing things, Izanami and Izanagi went on to spawn fourteen islands and 35 gods. But tragically, the 35th god was Ho-Masubi, the Deity-of-Fire, and when Izanami gave birth to Ho-Masubi, she was so sorely burned that she divinely retired."

"It's sad," Chrissie said, sincerely touched.

"Turn over on your back," he said, starting in on her stomach when she had complied. Touching her emotions wasn't the point of the story either, but Yuichi noticed that he didn't press quite as hard on her stomach as he had on her back. "Stricken with grief, Izanagi wept long and hard before he

---

[1] "Oh:" the sound that the kidney energy makes automatically, just like "Ah" is the sound of the liver, "I" (said "ee") is the sound of the heart energy, "E" (said "Ay") is the lung energy, and "U" (said "Ooo") is the sound rhythm of the stomach meridian.

buried her. But it was not long before he missed her so much that he absolutely had to see her. And so he descended down to Yomi, which is the underworld, Hades, or what the Christians call hell. There, in the darkness, he finally managed to find her. 'Our work is not finished, you must come back to the world again, you must leave here and join me back in the light,' Izanagi said.

'I would like nothing better,' Izanami answered, 'If only you had not waited so long to come and get me. Now what you ask is impossible, for I have eaten bread from the furnace of Yomi, and I am no longer free to leave.' Once more, Izanagi was terribly sad."

"It is sad..." Chrissie said, cut short by an exhalation of pain. "Ah, ah!"

"Seeing Izanagi's distress, Izanami offered to go to the Palace of Darkness to discuss the problem with the Deities of Yomi. 'But one thing,' she warned 'You must promise not to look at me.' And so saying, she disappeared inside the palace of darkness, where she stayed for a good long time. Such a long time that Izanagi, unable to control his curiosity any longer, finally determined to go after her.

"And there, by accident, lighting the end of his comb like a match in spite of her admonition, he gazed upon her and instantly fell back in horror. Never had he seen a sight so vile: the flesh was rotted and covered in maggots, the caverns of her body had become home to the eight thunder deities."

"Jesus!"

"Furious that Izanagi had ignored her request not to look, humiliated that he had seen her in her nakedness, Izanami sent the eight Ugly-Females-of-Yomi forthwith to chase him down and slay him.

"Holding his sword behind him, Izanagi ran for his life, but the women were not afraid of the sword and they pursued him. He tore his wig off and threw it on the ground where it turned into grapes. The women picked the grapes up and ate them, but this too failed to distract them from their pursuit. Desperate, Izanagi threw down his comb. And to his relief, from its teeth there instantly sprouted bamboo shoots, a patch so thick that the hellions could not pass. Her furor undiminished, Izanami ordered the eight thunder deities and their 1500 warriors into the chase, but by the time they finally caught up with Izanagi, he was already at the gates of the underworld, the place where darkness becomes light again. Taking three peaches from the special peach tree that grows there, he beat his pursuers so badly that they had to retreat. Only one option remained for Izanami, and that was to slay him herself, but Izanagi, seeing her intent, grasped a rock so big that it would take a thousand men to move it, and placed it over the mouth to Yomi, closing Izanami in..."

"So he didn't really love her after all, did he?"

"That's not the point."

"No?" (That is the point. That is precisely, exactly, always the point. And wasn't it typical that he would say monstrosities arose when the woman took the initiative, wasn't it typical that the woman had to go to hell, while the man got to go away scot-free?) (What was Yuichi trying to insinuate with such a strange, sick story? Was he trying to hint that he found her grotesque? Or was this just some form of sicko-Shinto kinkiness, he wouldn't be the first man she had met who, because of AIDS and condoms, couldn't keep it up without inventing all kind of pervy stuff. If that's what he needed, why not? She'd play along. What if she were Izanami and he were Izanagi? Could be fun...)

Now when the monk massaged her gut, it didn't hurt Chrissie nearly as much as the day before. Or even fifteen minutes before. It hurt, but not as much. Except rather than see this as an indication that her body was responding to his healing, and that blockages were beginning to dissolve, she was sure that he had decided to go easy on her because he was beginning to develop some sort of tenderness for her. She forgot all about the hand washing thing. Her heart filled with compassion and her eyes filled with tears. The terrible struggle that must be raging inside him, the vow of celibacy he was sworn to versus the possibility of real flesh-and-blood love: it must be brutal. She never realized how much she hated religion before.

"Are you OK?" he asked, noticing her tears.

"I OK. I understand what you going through," she said, smiling sadly, sympathetically.

"Ho?" he said, continuing to knead her stomach.

She closed her eyes. A little song ran happily through her head. "The moment when you suddenly realize..." The delay in consummating their relationship made her feel giddy and full of anticipation, a promise of future sweetness which reminded her, funny, she hadn't thought about that in a long time, of how she used to feel when they first discovered about AIDS, that was when people still used to play tennis, and everyone was being careful, and you'd wait till the third or fourth date when you knew someone a little bit better before taking the risk of catching his disease.

7

By Monday, when Chrissie Luna was supposed to start back to work, she had promised, and forgotten, to get a key made two more times. To which Yuichi had responded by unscrewing the light bulbs in both freezer and refrigerator. To which Chrissie had immediately counter-responded by ringing AAAAAAppliance, a call which would end up costing her $550 this time.

This time "Wade" wore a much cleaner pair of overalls with the name "Wilbur" stitched over the pocket. This time his fingernails were even clean. If he had learned anything in his years as an appliance con-man, it was that you didn't want to overdo the rube stuff, that there was a fine line between American-original and disgust. "Sometimes you'll get people just have bad luck with an appliance for a short hwhile and then she's done," "Wilbur" said, throwing a discreet wink Yuichi's way, figuring the guy just *had* to be an ally.

"Well I hope it's over now," Chrissie laughed her too-loud laugh, then asked him if possibly, maybe, on his way out, he wouldn't mind taking a quick look at her answering machine. The damn thing still hadn't recorded a single message since the party, still remained resolutely, insultingly, on zero. "Wilbur" pressed a few buttons, ran the tape back and forward, said a few enthusiastic words about the wonderful world of digital answering machines, and how she might want to look into that, then called the shop and had them call back. A message clear as a bell, test, test, test. "Not a thing wrong with this puppy, sad to say," he said with an unnecessarily loud laugh of his own. "Tell you what I'm gonna do," he said picking up the phone. "I'm gonna program the number for AAAAAAppliance on the speed dial, no extra charge. And...there...you...go." He hung up the phone again and smiled, then put on his coat, making sure to come back to Yuichi and slip him a $20 handshake as a token of his appreciation. "You got any problems, don't hesitate all right?"

"All right." As she walked him back to the door, Chrissie caught herself wondering how much a man like that made a year.

"Bye. Bye now," she said.

"See you soon," he answered, laughing even louder to show that he didn't really mean it.

"Hope not!" she fired right back, drowning his laughter out with her own testosterone-special, to show that she didn't really mean it either. "Bye."

As for the answering machine, of course! Now that she thought about it, it made sense. No doubt her friends thought that she and Yuichi were cocooning. There were no messages because they wanted to leave her alone. They didn't want to disturb the trysting season. Oh-wouldn't-it-be-sweet to have a real reason to prove them right? As for work, to hell with work, she owed herself some time off, and what better time than now to take it?

Trying her best to flatter Yuichi, Chrissie adopted his rhythm and schedule. She awakened at 5 a.m. without music or The Breakfast Show, she did his exercises with him, north, south, east and west. She ate what he cooked, all the terrible seaweeds, daikon radishes, tofu, mung beans and whatnot he made her buy, then she washed it down, as he did, with the absolutely vile-tasting *ume* plum tea he brewed for her not once, but six times a day. She built a little altar to her ancestors, just like the one he built with its picture of O Sensei, then lit incense sticks and pretended her very best to pray, to think about her ancestors just as he suggested, and to express gratitude for their sacrifice. Like him, she tried to see herself as just one more link in a line from distant past to distant future, with responsibilities to both. At night, by 11, she slipped into a special nightgown on which she had had the word Izanami silk-screened and fell into bed exhausted, no thought of night life, no late-night TV documentaries, not even the opening monologue of the Tonight Show. (As for the dishes of ice cream she sneaked when he wasn't looking, well, what he didn't know couldn't hurt him, could it?) If she woke with clear head, and with ankles feeling almost supple, she attributed it more to the just-out-of-dreams euphoria of possible-love than anything else.

In fact, the meter of possible-love fluctuated all day long. Some hours she accepted that it would never happen between them, accepted and even admired his shining devotion to his "vows." Some hours, during the massages especially, she was almost sure love was imminent, but other hours his attention seemed to wander, and his focus seemed to shift to god knows what. But that did not mean she gave up. She lit aromatic candles of every fragrance, ylang ylang, opopanax, olibanum, patchouli and cinnamon roll, until the apartment looked like a fog bank. She locked herself in the bathroom and tried on all her sexiest, slinkiest, skimpiest clothes, practicing various looks and finally settling for one that she thought communicated the proper mix of sincerity and Geisha-submissive slut. The thing was, she didn't think she looked so bad. Her skin looked more healthy, her eyes looked clearer, her aura was bright, and even the corners of her mouth which had begun noticeably to sag with the weight of the years, now seemed to have risen on their own. So what was it? Maybe it was all her fault? Maybe, she had lived alone too long and she couldn't tolerate the presence of anyone else in her nice tidy realm? Maybe she had made him feel like an intruder, an irritant, and maybe he found that to be a turnoff? Or maybe, now that she was forty, men in general would no longer be interested, and she would just have to get used to that?

In fact, why should he be seduced by her? She was nothing but a makeup salesperson living in an apartment bought by her father's life insurance. Why should he be seduced? There must be millions of better catches in the city, and she hated every one of them, hated their walks, their real estate, their self-assured way of smoking and holding themselves, and tossing their heads back when they laughed as if the future were their friend. She pulled at her hair and screamed into the toilet bowl in frustration, hoping it would muffle the sound, but not caring that it didn't. She felt worthless, she felt like she was disintegrating, she wanted to die. But who the hell was he? Who the hell did he think he was? When it all boiled down, what exactly were they talking about here? Five, six inches, max? He couldn't share five inches of himself? Not to dwell on the way he still washed his hands after massaging her as if she were some kind of dirt!

On Thursday, black Thursday, it started to snow, and Chrissie Luna forgot to get a key made three more times. Once because she had happened upon the National Enquirer at the Grand Union supermarket checkout, (which led to her seeing the story about the Oriental One-Man-Vigilante-Army, which led to her having a good laugh with Celestina, the store astrologer, about how the paper said it was Bruce Lee, resurrected, when The Star had insisted it was Jackie Chan) and twice for reasons she couldn't remember.

At lunchtime Chrissie's mother called to chastise her for forgetting to wish her happy birthday. "It's like your birthday is the only one that counts," she said then slammed down the phone.

"She acts like she's Martin Luther King," Chrissie said after slamming down the phone herself. She hadn't forgotten King's birthday, nor would she forget Lincoln's and Washington's birthdays, Feb. 12 and 22, and how many people in the country could you say that about now that they had turned George and Abe into a long weekend? Or astronaut birthdays, she could reel off thirty of those without a hitch. Her mother had this attitude as if Chrissie had left her gray matter at the maternity ward 40 years ago. And she had this not-too-subtle way of hinting that there must be something terribly wrong with Chrissie's boyfriends and employers, like they must be more than a bit slow-in-the-head themselves if they chose to associate with such a worthless scatterbrain.

Stewing in bilious possibilities, Chrissie took a pot and threw some rice into it, covered the rice with water a knuckle deep, just like Yuichi had shown her, and put it on a high flame. Maybe she did tend to get a little distracted in her personal life, but so what? Was it bad to be human, to follow your emotions? Did that make her evil? Does it make a woman evil to think about other people more than herself? How dare her mother criticize her boss or her work! Raj Mikkelson, her boss, would be more than happy to testify on her behalf, and why shouldn't he? Chrissie was the most successful salesperson in his entire force. That's what Chrissie ought to do, set up a meeting. Then her mother could ask Mr. Raj Mikkelson outright what he thought about her performance, ask Raj Mikkelson how many diamonds and fast cars he had managed to buy because of Chrissie Fucking Luna.

And then Chrissie remembered. "Shit! Shit! Shit!" Raj Mikkelson! Her stomach sank into her feet. She raced to her pocketbook, fumbled for her agenda and hastily turned to the right page to confirm her fear. "Shit!" Her meeting with Raj Mikkelson had been this morning, at ten o'clock, and she had missed it!

Mortified, but trying to mask it with a smile for Yuichi's sake, Chrissie dashed to the phone and hit the speed dial, praying that she would be able to repair the damage, intending to tell Raj Mikkelson there had been a problem, it wasn't as if people didn't have problems from time to time. She smiled at Yuichi again, giving him the sign that she wouldn't be long, turned the flame down a bit on the stove, rearranged the pencils in the pencil cup, then turned all the dots on the "i's" on the accusing agenda page into little daisies while waiting the three eternities it took for them to answer.

"Samsara Cosmetics." Usually it went straight through to his private line, but sometimes it didn't, no cause for worry.

"Raj Mikkelson please," Chrissie said in a voice that came off surprisingly confident for someone whose guts felt like sour herring soup.

"May I say who's calling?" The woman on the switchboard had the digitalized synthesizer voice of a computer.

"Chrissie Luna."

"OK, let me see if he's available... I'm sorry, he's in a meeting."

"I'll just hold then." She drummed her fingers on the telephone and smiled at Yuichi again as he left the room.

"Suit yourself."

Thirty minutes she waited like that, cradling the cordless phone between cheek and shoulder while she ran the sponge over the kitchen counter, turned on the living room lights, then went into her bedroom to plump up the pillows and hang up some shirts she hadn't gotten around to hanging up. Thirty minutes of the computer-woman saying "He's still in a meeting, would you like to keep holding?" and Chrissie managing to keep up the cheery facade, "Yes I wou-ould," in spite of her clammy armpits, in spite of all the black thoughts squeezing her brain. One missed meeting, what was that? It's not as if Raj Mikkelson hadn't missed a meeting or twenty with her in his life. She had forgiven him, nobody was perfect. Was it so much to ask for a little telephone confirmation that he had forgiven her?

"Still in a meeting..." the switchboard robot interrupted again, this time sounding to Chrissie like she was almost gloating.

"Still ho-olding," Chrissie said right back to her like it was almost a joke, but she had to begin to wonder. Raj Mikkelson keeping her on hold for thirty minutes didn't make sense. Raj Mikkelson in a thirty minute meeting didn't make sense. What if the woman manning the switchboard really was a computer, and there was a glitch in the software? Or... what if she was a real woman, but was one of those jealous Samsara employees who had never quite managed to swallow Chrissie's success and her special relationship to the boss? What if she was getting even by making sure not to put her through, and Raj Mikkelson was all alone in his office, so concerned that something terrible might have happened to her that the entire operation had ground to a halt, he had started sniffing cocaine again after being clean for three weeks, and it was all her fault? What if... Chrissie had only *begun* to go off the deep end, when a siren went off in the living room, scaring her so badly she thought her heart had stopped. The smoke detector screaming at her: she had forgotten the rice.

Waving her hand through a cloud of black smoke, she beat Yuichi to the kitchen by two paces. "I never burn stuff," she said, furious with herself. "Bastard!" She grabbed the broom and batted at the howling ceiling alarm to get it to shut up. Once, twice, three times she swung, leaving long scrape marks on the ceiling before finally connecting, silencing it once and for all. "Son of a bitch!" She yanked the pot off the stove, and slid it across the counter into the sink under the cold water, where it popped and danced, setting off a cloud of steam which flattened her hair. She removed the phone from between cheek and shoulder and slammed it back down into the charger, to hell with Raj Mikkelson. "What are you looking at?" she snapped at Yuichi, and marched out of the room, she had been making the rice for him.

Left standing in the wake of the hurricane, Yuichi blinked and shook his head, wondering if Chrissie really was his only solution, wanting nothing more than to flee. Quickly he said his sounds, an abbreviated version, to try and come back to center, first in AIUEO order, centering on the *tanden*, next in AOUEI order, centering on the third eye and expressing gratitude, which felt good, and last in AIEOU order, centering on the heart which felt like coming home. Then he took a deep breath, turned on the stove fan, and walked to the living room windows to let in some fresh air. This was no time for self-pity; it was time for drastic action. He closed the living room window again, marched back over to the kitchen, opened the drawer next to the stove and hunted through it until he had located the ice pick. From the bedroom he could hear Chrissie storming around, screaming, "I can't take this anymore!" Clutching the ice pick grimly, he squared up to the refrigerator like a gunfighter at high noon and opened the door. But then, all of a sudden, the fan went silent, and the lights went out.

"Oh my gahd!" Chrissie spat from her bedroom, on the verge of a what-else-Lord nervous breakdown, this really was not her day. "A black-out!" is what she thought at first, except where were the sound of sirens and looting outside? "Probably just a fuse or something electrical like that," she said, trying to sound reassuring and in control.

The building superintendent appeared almost before she had put the phone down, holding his hand as usual behind his back like some kind of speed skater. Once inside the apartment, he muttered, poked at the shattered smoke detector with his toe and tried to keep a serious face on when Chrissie asked him if he thought that might be the problem, then shone his flashlight around for over 20 minutes just for the form of it, before concluding what he had suspected all along, that it wasn't the fuses at all. Quite simply: once again, like the three other times a year, she had forgotten to pay her electricity bill.

She laughed, way too loud once again, gave the super a fiver which she noticed he looked at like it was dog squat, then wrote a check out to Con Edison on the spot and went straight downstairs to mail it. When she returned she put fresh-bought candles all over the apartment, and even lit a nice wood fire. All of which produced a nice romantic mood that caused her to burst into tears. She ran back into her bedroom and buried her face in the pillow, sure that after this latest gaffe, Yuichi-wise, it was already too late.

The next day, Friday the 21st of January, year 2000, brought more cold and bad weather but with wind gusts that blew away the clouds in time to bring a mass of frenzied people out onto the streets at night to celebrate the first full moon of the "new Millennium." To see if the dire predictions of various innumerate crackpots would come true on the 21st day of what just about everybody believed was already the 21st century. Only for Chrissie Luna, blood boiling, hope dwindling, still locked in with a resolutely-resistant monk, did Sister Moon remain less than full. When she stared up at the fat orb, all she wanted to see were the twin eyes of the Sea of Fertility and the Sea of Serenity staring back, was that so bad? And all she got was a terrible sneer stretching from the Sea of Vapors to the Sea of Crises and Seething Bay. The only consolation was that with the full moon, unexpectedly, she got her period. She left the tampon box out next to the toilet, in the hope that Yuichi would notice, in the hope that it would explain at least some of the moodiness of the last few days.

The weekend was even more difficult. Yuichi wasn't really different, same schedule, same big, no-problem laugh, same menu, but to Chrissie he seemed distant and dark and she was convinced he was just counting the hours until Monday and his day in court. She thought about throwing another party, the electricity had come back on, but then thought better of it, knowing she would never be able to pull off the pretending. Instead, she spent the whole time cleaning the apartment, aggressively chain-drinking Skinny Cows (Diet Coke with a scoop of vanilla ice cream, sweet milk of amnesia) right in front of his nose. Japanese men, American men, when all was said and done, what was the difference? A whole week since she had brought this man into her life, a whole week of trying her very best to be exactly what he wanted. She had gotten up with him at five in the morning and done his stupid exercises, she had said a bunch of dumb prayers to her dead grandparents, whom she never liked in the first place, excuse me for living, she had eaten enough seaweed to choke a whale, abandoned any semblance of a social life, put her career completely on hold, barely stepped outside at all in fact, and been in bed five nights in a row at 11 pm, alone. Not To Mention: the small fortune she had spent virtually cleaning out the religious music bins at any record shop she could find, trying to find something to weaken his resolve and loosen his belt. Not To Mention II: the $1000 she had coughed up to repair a refrigerator that had never failed before, as if that were a coincidence. And for what? For some tweezer-dick, agoraphobe tease with absolutely zero taste in clothes. Which, incidentally, she fully intended to mention.

8

On January 24, the day of the hearing, Chrissie Luna finally began to feel better about herself. Like every other day, they awakened at 5 a.m., Yuichi as usual on the couch, she as usual in her bed, but as soon as she had brushed her teeth, and before he could start his exercises, grabbed him by the arm and marched him into the bathroom, turning on the TV with the remote on the way: ice storm in the Southeast had shut down schools, but New York should be OK, low of 16 and a high of 36, perhaps a bit of ugly weather due sometime Tuesday, but nothing too bad just yet.

"Now, I'm going to work on you," she said, pulling out a stool, grabbing him by the shoulders and sitting him down on it. "You can't say no! OK?" she said, and without waiting for an answer reached into a drawer for a little metal device shaped like a hand, with electrodes in the fingers and wires running to a small computer connected to a Polaroid camera. "Hold sti-ill..." She turned a few knobs, looked through the viewfinder, squinting more than necessary, snapped the picture. When the camera ejected it, she began to wave it around as if that would help it dry, then decided that she didn't need to, that she wasn't nervous, that with her makeup there in front of her, she was on home ground, that for the first time since their meeting, *she* was in control. "Only be a minute." She wished she had thought of this a week ago.

As mentioned, Chrissie made her living with cosmetics, but not like some cackling, rouge-caked department store hen selling Hope! brand makeup by the pail-full. Hers was a new, very special branch of cosmetic science involving the use of the client's aura to determine his or her cosmetic needs. Scientific cosmetics adapted to the energy you gave off, ecologically friendly and specifically designed to compensate for any birth challenge or other imbalance which might unfavorably skew the impression you made on others in this dog-eat-dog-world. "You know how you talk about balancing inner imbalances?" she said, "Well this is designed to balance outer imbalances."

"The machine?"

"The machine is called an aura-meter," Chrissie went into her speech. "Or aurOmeter, some people say it aurOmeter. It measures the electric resistance between the acupuncture points of your left and right hands."

"Ho?"

"Yes. Then the computer measures the electrical field and translates this into a color around your head, so you can see for yourself. Red means you're very angry, very hot energy field, etc..."

"Ho..."

"I think maybe the problems you've been having on the street?" Chrissie didn't want to do more than hint but by now she had trained herself to see auras without the machine, and she pretty much knew how the photo would come out already. "Well I think I can help. Probably with the judge too... Don't want to leave something so important to chance, do we?" If she saved him from jail, wouldn't that demonstrate once and for all the extent of her caring, of her devotion to him? After all, great hands or no, Mr. Holy Moly, Mr. I'm-Not-A-Man, Mr. Everywhere-I-Go-I-Start-A-Riot couldn't argue the fact that he could use a little assistance in the domain of public relations and social presentation. It wasn't as if she were the one being attacked on the street by anyone who passed. "See?" She showed him the Polaroid. "Just as I expected." There was an almost entirely white crown around Yuichi's head, like the Dalai Lama and some Yoga freak they had also brought in when first testing the machine. Small wonder Yuichi inspired the ire of just about everyone he ran into.

Like a mad alchemist, Chrissie set to work, extracting dozens of bottles from the drawers in her vast makeup closet, spraying clouds of essence over his head, juggling the makeup brushes so that they clicked and danced through the air, sometimes to the tune of "My Way:" "And-uh now..." Three hours later, three hours of meticulous application of the subtlest of shades of foundation sienna and ochre and ultramarine, of scent number two to make him more sexy, and scent number three to mask the spiritual side and emphasize the earth, the physical, Chrissie Luna thought she had her man. She swiveled the stool towards the mirror so he could get a look at himself.

"Ho!" Yuichi almost jumped in fright. Staring back at him from the mirror was the spitting image of a movie star, peach-skinned and radiant. All that was missing was the final touch, the sunglasses, which Chrissie materialized post-haste, a pair of round John Lennon glasses with gray lenses, that accidentally, on a whim, she had just happened to pick up on the night the lights went out. As if that didn't show intuition! As if any other dead-celebrity design line was even half as appropriate! (George Harrison didn't really wear glasses.)

They only needed to step out into the street for the high level of her artistry to be confirmed. For though Yuichi was tense and prepared for combat, stepping into the icy gutter every time they came within ten yards of any of his usual nemeses, this time his passing caused nary a blink. "You see?" Chrissie said, heart swelling from her good deed.

No, this time it was not the thrill-seekers who attacked, this time it was the women, and by the time Chrissie and Yuichi had walked almost all the way to the Bowery, looking for a cab, there were hundreds of them, whispering quietly, unmistakably smitten, trailing right behind the Chinese love god and his servant, 50% convinced they were seeing Jackie Chan, 50% convinced it had to be Bruce Lee.

A more objective soul might have blamed the shift in attentions on the tabloids or even on the moon, but Chrissie was convinced it was the makeup, and as they got out of the cab at the courthouse, where any number of women were already waiting, the same women as on Lafayette or others, (who could tell?) she was as proud as she'd ever been in her life, and greeted their clamor for him as if it was for her. No other woman in New York City had thought to bail out the poor Japanese monk, no other woman in the *world* had such skill with makeup as to turn a complete pariah into a movie star in three short hours. And as it turned out, even the judge at the preliminary hearing, who just happened to be a woman, thank you very much, was quite helpless to resist the makeover.

To explain the judge's leniency, her cursory inquiry about the scroll, her decision to throw out the 245 GBI, and give Yuichi six months suspended for unauthorized prophecy, and a promise of something much stiffer next time, a more objective person might have cited prison overcrowding, or the careful review of the incriminating TV and UN security tapes. A more objective person might have cited the increasingly dangerous army of chanting women pressing up against the police barriers at the bottom of the courthouse steps, or even the pathetic display by the wired-jaw Mormon who, instead of acting meek and wounded, played a scripture-blaring tape recorder to which he mimed along like a cheerleader, pointing his finger at Yuichi every time the tape said the word Satan. But a more objective person wasn't available on such short notice, not a one within miles.

And so Chrissie got her bail money back and Yuichi, with a great sigh of relief, got his scroll. Bowing his head and closing his eyes he thanked the ancestors of the five races for their infinite wisdom, for the angel they had sent to try his patience and test him, for the scroll itself which he intended to place in the right hands as soon as possible, for the chance to return to the safety of the Land of the Rising Sun. Only the surging crowd of women outside stopped him from hopping a cab straight to the UN and getting it over with right away.

"My bank is only a few blocks away?" Chrissie the angel said sweetly as they checked out the crowd through the courthouse doors, a statement presented as a question which unfortunately showed, in spite of the monk's de facto exoneration, and thus the confirmation of her intuition, how insecure she once again felt.

"Ho..."

"If that thing is so valuable..." (The rest of the thought was so obvious, Chrissie couldn't help but be a little irritated. *Now* who was being dense?) "Maybe you'd like to deposit it for a few days?"

"Hai..." Yuichi nodded, it sounded like an eminently wise suggestion. After 24 days delay, one more day hardly mattered... if the scroll was safe. Besides, Yuichi thought, it would give him time to purchase his return ticket. What better end to this overlong story could there be than to deliver the scroll and hop a cab right back to the airport?

The bank formalities took no time at all, the only problem was that there were so many women trying to follow Yuichi into the vault, and so many more waiting outside, that the bank, fearing for its windows, had to call the cops. The cops, who pulled up looking relaxed, laughing, as if the whole thing were just a big joke, were finally obliged to call in support and use tear gas to beat back the crowd, but even that didn't work for long. It was the police's idea to send Chrissie Luna out the front of the bank and have her spread the rumor that Yuichi had slipped out the back. They hoped that by keeping Yuichi an extra half-hour, even the most hardy disbelievers would finally disperse.

"I'm a very happy lady, you know that, don't you?" Chrissie said, squeezing Yuichi's hand warmly in the bank vault, one last touch before parting. From down, she had come back to way-up again, she felt liberated, confident as never before, and strong. She looked forward to a well-deserved little victory celebration. "I'll make you a key this time, I promise. And then who knows? Maybe the world..."

...Or maybe not, because although Yuichi left the bank as soon as the coast was clear, and the cab he took arrived at 226 Lafayette without delay, Chrissie was nowhere to be seen, having completely forgotten him and run off for a quick fling in Atlantic City with Jim O'Brien, whom she had bumped into by chance at the Grand Union.

Hemmed in by yet another fresh horde of lust-crazed females, faces set in unmistakable sign of their willingness to sacrifice almost everything for a rebellious, nasty, all-night fuck, Yuichi waited for an hour, an hour and half, then two, head-faking, giving hope, then taking it away, playing one off against another, and pushing the buzzer next to Luna every so often, just in case. Time enough to outlast some of the octogenarians in the group, time enough for Yuichi to ask the spirit of O Sensei just what the hell he intended by sending him to this place at this time and asking him to deliver the scroll on a Saturday! Was he dreaming or out-of-his-mind drunk on sake? Time enough, finally, for Yuichi fully to assess the situation, to yawn, stretch innocently, and saunter off the stoop like some big movie star putting it on for his fans, winking casually left and right, not the least bit concerned, towards a part of the crowd which was slightly less dense. At which point, from a dead stop, he broke into a full sprint, running for his humble healer's life.

9

The last ten years had been difficult for Karl-Heinz Retter, not that life before had ever been easy for the dwarf, one time chief overseas operative for the Swiss secret service. No need to dwell on the hardships, the transformations, the thoughts as a man looks at himself in the mirror and watches a once-proud goatee turn gray, watches hairs sprout from his ears (so fast and Rapunzel-thick that without extreme tonsorial vigilance, he might almost consider braids), watches an already large ugly head grow larger and uglier from worries, watches bandy legs grow bandier from carrying the weight of the world, watches himself grow a proud little gut from eating his way through the two million francs in his savings account back in Switzerland. No doubt at his funeral there would be voices raised, Swiss voices, calling him spendthrift, profligate, prodigal, or whatever other epithet their small minds could conjure on the spur of the moment. As if his blood, his morality, were less Swiss than theirs! But such jealousy, such ultimate calumny, would only be further proof of his greatness, greatness of vision and execution.

When your mission in life is greatness, you can't listen to the squawking of chickens, the bleating of sheep, the lowing of bottle-fed veal, because different rules apply. No doubt those same small minds as would have the effrontery to sound off at his funeral would be constitutionally incapable of seeing the strategic straight-line in his decade of apparent drifting. No doubt they would fail absolutely to discern the tactical brilliance of his latest stratagem, his seemingly anodyne occupation walking the dogs of the Big Apple's rich and famous. But that's why the President of Switzerland himself would be delivering the eulogy at the funeral, telling them, because they would be unable to figure it out for themselves: that world hegemony sometimes comes in stealthy, small packages, and that at certain times in history, the best way to get at the hearts and minds of the movers and shakers of this earth, is to get at the hearts and minds of their dogs.

By nightfall, Park Avenue and 52nd Street, Yuichi the humble healer, gasping for air, lungs burning, sweat streaming down his brow in the frozen air, makeup ruined, looking like anything but the picture of collected serenity, had managed to leave behind all but the hardiest eight of his pursuers. All but two aerobics instructors, the astrologer at Chrissie's Grand Union grocery, a tri-athlete, a heavily-pierced bicycle messenger with two flat tires, a rich woman in fur, a young dancer and an apprentice in the mail room at the William Morris Agency. His ruined makeup, his frazzled appearance, the scores of city blocks left behind: nothing seemed to diminish their tenacity. Through the great steam clouds from his frozen breath, he could see them gaining on him, their faces etched with such grim determination that no matter how tired he was, like Izanagi the solidifier in the story, he had to keep running. Lucky Izanagi, who knew how to make bamboo shoots sprout from his comb. Lucky Izanagi, who had the good fortune to be in hell, rather than New York City in the middle of winter where peach trees, symbol of life and hope, just don't grow. Lucky Izanagi, forget the peaches, Yuichi the pacifist would settle for just one banana peel lying on the sidewalk, or an oil slick or patch of ice; if his feet were to slip out from under him thanks to some external cause, he could probably, accidentally, dispatch the last eight she-devils in no time flat.

Lucky Izanagi, finally, who could toss a few peaches to save himself all by himself, without anyone's assistance, who didn't have to turn the corner at Park and 53rd and run smack into two rows of five dogs apiece held, like a team of reindeer, on leashes leading to the small iron fist of one Karl-Heinz Retter. Sent flying like bowling pins were: two Yorkshire Terriers owned by the Countess of Effington and Vulgargrad, two poodles named Fluffy and Light owned by Roberto (Bunny) Sella, the famously obese stockbroker, a Doberman and a dachshund owned by Wella Balsam, the movie actress, and a Labrador, two cocker spaniels, a Lhasa Apso and a Pekinese, owned, in order, by the publisher of the New York City Clarion, by the heir to the Colgate-Palmolive fortune, by a dentist named Goldberg, and by the wife of the Austrian consul who called her little Peke "Monsieur" and used him as a flat-nosed sex toy in the noble tradition of the empresses of the Chinese court.

"Sukuna-Hikona!" Yuichi exclaimed, terrified by the sudden apparition of the waist-high troll, the spitting image of the *Hiluko* dwarf in the *Kojiki*.

"Idiot! Imbezil!" Sensing an insult, Karl-Heinz Retter reflexively lobbed an insult him right back, adding a "Sow-brain!" for good measure, so outraged was he by this most unexpected intrusion, this naked aggression, this violation, this infamy, this chaos of tangled leashes, of scrambling, yelping, discipline-less dogs and base brainless humanoid. He raised the *Neue Zürcher Zeitung*, the newspaper that he always carried tightly rolled up in his hand, ready to bring it down upon the imbecile's head. But that was before he noticed the fine Austrian tailoring on the fine Austrian Loden coat, before he noticed that the poor panting man tangled in his leashes trying to get up, was actually Japanese (a race he had always admired for its stoicism in death), and before he noticed the eight breathless women who came to a

halt just outside his little confused canine circle, sporting that unequivocal look which he always found so uberly-attractive, the look of lust.

"Are you OK?" he asked Yuichi in a high voice, instant outrage turned to instant solicitousness, lowering the newspaper as if the act of raising had been nothing more than part of the dog walker's routine early-evening-stretch. Kick, kick, a Lhasa Apso and a poodle went flying, as Karl-Heinz Retter cleared a space for the poor unfortunate to stand. Swat, swat, the Doberman and Labrador earned a shot to the ass apiece to teach them a little respect, to teach them how to act in the presence of someone who just might be the key to future sexual favors. "Without respekt: anarchy. *Ja?* Retter, Karl-Heinz," the dwarf introduced himself, ostensibly holding up his little gnarled hand to shake, but in actuality calculating the social trigonometry in an attempt to discover exactly what the Japanese man's connection was to these women, and what percentage of them might be amenable to betraying him in exchange for the opportunity to experience every woman's greatest secret fantasy: intimate gymnastics with a Swiss dwarf.

"Yuichi..."

"Gesundheit. Retter, Karl-Heinz, I repeat..."

"Yuichi..."

"Gesundheit." Very strange manners, this refusal to introduce oneself, not once, but twice, a most extraordinary display of rudeness. Karl-Heinz Retter would allow the Japanese man to keep the bicycle messenger with the ring through her nose, serve her right if she caught his cold, but the rest the dwarf would take care of, no problem, especially the woman in furs and the young woman next to her, in whose increasingly-attractive eyes Retter espied the nascent light of recognition.

"Billy Barty!" the young woman finally spit it out, her mouth moving like an absurd flounder's.

"No, that's not me. He's dead." People always thought they recognized dwarfs, why was that? The Japanese man could keep her too. Now that Retter looked more closely, he saw her complexion was as spotted as a leopard's.

"Hervé Villechaize," said the second aerobics professor, a virtual anencephalic, the headband over her forehead obviously there only to insure that what remained of her brain not fall out.

"Dead too!" Retter glowered, instantly putting a third woman in the Japanese camp, the camp of those he wouldn't touch in a million years. He doubted she would even notice the impoliteness of his address, the sentence without a pronoun. A teacher of calisthenics! One more he would gladly abandon to the Japanese man, and no regrets.

"No, no. I got it. You know who it is?" said Celestina, the astrologer at Chrissie's Grand Union. "It's Johnny Woops!"

"Ah ha! A woman of intelligence, I see!" Retter said, nodding respectfully, gallantly, even tipping his little felt hat so that the pheasant feather drew a little exclamation point in the air. Fifteen-odd years ago, back in Hollywood, he had indeed played the eponymous hero in the movie "Johnny Woops," and that did not come without perks. This said, where was the pleasure in slaking one's lust on a conquest already conquered? Where indeed? He gave her the eye and mysterious-seductive smile, just long enough to make sure she had warmed fully to his charm, then instantly shut it off, *Ja!*, ceding her to the Japaner as well.

Ready to move off for good, Retter slapped the newspaper against his right thigh once, so that ten dogs fell instantly back into two straight lines, then thinking twice, smacked the paper on his left thigh so that they executed a neat semi-circle shuffle, aligning them nose-to-*Aschloch* on either side of the "monk" so that even if Yuichi had wanted to he could not have escaped. "If my very honorable friend would care to join me for tea? It might help his cold..." Retter said with a bow. Actually, always three moves ahead, for Retter the point was not so much to invite this complete stranger to tea, as to show the women, in the most subtly subtle manner, that they were *not* being invited.

Difficult as it usually proved for Karl-Heinz Retter not to have at least a modicum of affection for a fellow whose acquaintance, carefully cultivated, might still land four new women directly in a little man's love nest, as seconds turned into minutes, Retter began to find Yuichi positively vapid, with a sort of fishy scent wafting off of him, carp, or albacore... no: carp. And the way he refused to give his name? This bordered on the intolerable... Still in this dark world where a man's word was less-and-less a man's word, it was important: what was said, must be done. The money for a teabag was a small price indeed to pay to stem a global tide of hypocrisy.

"Ja!" The dwarf waved his newspaper like a riding crop, as if winding it up, then ran it up and down his inner thigh. The dogs responded instantly, lifting their legs, right-side column lifting right legs, left-side column lifting left legs. Ten seconds exactly, micturition pause over, legs down. "Shall we?" Retter pointed his newspaper down 53rd, smiling his most cheese-melting smile as the dogs broke into a dignified high-headed trot, in such tight ranks that even if Yuichi had not been thirsty for tea it would not have mattered, he could not have slipped away. No need for Retter to waste even a single word on Nose-Ring and friends: superiority demonstrated, target destroyed, change of location, change of subject.

"People always want to know what it's like being a dwarf," as soon as they had moved five yards away, Retter started in, pretty much the opening he used every time he and the dogs captured someone, any of the rock singers, movie stars and politicians to whom Karl-Heinz Retter, every so often, felt compelled to give a piece of his mind. "They pity you. Idiots. *Ja,* isn't that just like human beings? So vain, so self-important. *Zum Beispiel*, for example, *Ja*? Crowded sidewalks? Look at your long legs, you think you could beat me in a footrace from here to the corner? Of course you don't. I can see you are no dummy. I would beat you by half a block, zoom, zoom," he said, his hand weaving its way through imaginary biped slalom gates, "Right through the legs. And what about the rest? What is it that makes one man better than another? Right, the nose: sense of smell. Now I'm not saying that my nose is all that much better than anyone else's, in all humility, but look where I am, at perfect olfactory height! You want to know who a man really is? You smell him, right in the bull's-eye: that's the giveaway. Just like a dog, dogs are very very smart. In case you were wondering, I only walk male dogs, purebloods..." He tickled his inner thigh again so that the dogs came crashing to a halt, lifted their legs again, and let fly, left to the left, right to the right. "Dogs like a regular schedule," he explained the brief interruption, then smacked his thigh so that they got underway again. "The only difference between me and a dog, smelling-wise *natürlich*, of course, is that I don't have to get on all fours. I am already here." Retter had to admit he had been wrong about the nameless Japanese man. He was a good sort after all, quiet, a good listener, not one of those types who always feels obliged to open his mouth to say nothing at all.

Unable to get a word in edgewise, from the slight detour to drop off Countess Effington's Yorkies, the only two day-campers, all the way back to Retter's apartment on Park and 41st, Yuichi had risen about as high as it was possible to rise in the dwarf's estimation. "Fifth floor..." Retter let him push the button in the elevator, knowing somehow that he would understand without being told that the fifth floor was where Retter lived by choice, and not because he was too short to reach the button for a higher floor on his own. "A meeting of the minds is a rare thing. But I don't suppose I am learning you something, ha-ha." When you were with an equal, a comrade in *Schadenfreude*, it was such a so-fantastic pleasure. Thoughts were understood, no need even to speak. Retter smiled at Yuichi, and Yuichi smiled back in such a way that Karl-Heinz Retter almost confessed right then and there his intention to write a dog training book someday, a massive tome, a monograph, 1000 pages at the very least. Except *nein*, it wasn't quite yet time for such familiarity. If premature familiarity wasn't one of the seven deadly sins, it certainly ought to be.

Retter's apartment was the one with the armored metal door that looked like a bank vault, a doormat big enough to handle 40 paws at once and a discreet Swiss flag decal glued on the doorjamb, not quite high enough to cover the place where uneven paint showed the previous tenant had placed a mezuzah. "Here we are," Retter said, withdrawing an enormous key ring, dozens of keys, from deep in his *Lederhosen*, while the dogs lined up low-to-high and wiped their feet. The door key was the one right next to the brass shield of the Bernese Oberland. Retter found it without looking, waited for the dogs to finish wiping, then opened the door, setting off an electronic eye which caused the first few delicious bars of the William Tell Overture to sound. The dogs quivered with anticipation in front of the open door, but even after he had removed the last leash, Retter made them wait, holding his hand out, showing them off for Yuichi's benefit. Then, with no warning at all, he slammed the *Neue Zürcher Zeitung* on the door jamb, a sound like the crack of a whip. Set free, the dogs virtually exploded into the apartment, and headed for their room, barking and nipping at each other, claws clicking and skidding out on the waxed hardwood floor.

"The littlest dogs are always first," Retter said with quiet pride, as if this confirmed yet another biological, universal, verity. "Please..." he very graciously held his hand out for Yuichi to enter ahead of him. "Allow me to take your coat." He wondered what the monk would look like committing suicide, stripped to the waist. Wondered if he would have the good taste to wrap his abdomen in one of those wide white bandages to keep the guts from leaking all over the floor once the terrible-beautiful act was done. Wondered about that moment when the blood would come out, and how it would probably make a stain which for a while would look like a Rorschach, a perfect little road map which would give you true insight into the real, inner quality of a man.

In the placid safety of his castle-keep, Karl-Heinz Retter was the picture of poise and etiquette. When laid on the Retter-height coat hook, even doubled over, Yuichi's coat still hung down to the ground, but there was no danger of dust in this apartment so Retter simply shrugged his shoulders, ha-ha, a gesture he intended to be self-deprecatory, then raised his hand to show his height compared to the Japanese man's just in case the shrug wasn't self-deprecatory enough. "Make yourself at home, please!" Retter said, steering Yuichi into the impeccable living room, and over to the couch by the window, the smaller of the two couches. "You are not from here I think..." he opened the politenesses while drawing the heavy blood-red velvet curtains.

"No, Japan," Yuichi answered, with a polite bow of the head.

"Really?" Retter pretended to be pleasantly surprised, drawing out the "really" so that it gained an extra syllable or two in the middle. Did the monk think Retter lacked eyes to see? (Japan? *Na ja*, I would have guessed Saudi Arabien...) Or did he intend something else with his insolent answer? Wasn't that the way it always was? You try to be polite, and your only reward is ridicule. Just for that, he would make the tea extra hot, that would show him. "The tea, *Ja!*" Retter laughed again. "Please excuse me?"

Retter slipped into the kitchen, and, model of efficiency, filled the tea kettle and put it on the stove. Then he got out a silver tray and, with an eye to proportion and geometric good taste, leaving a hole in the middle for the tea pot, carefully placed two fine china cups and saucers on one short side of the rectangular tray, three different sugar bowls with three different kinds of sugar, brown, white and crystal on the opposite side, and two unopened boxes of special Swiss jam-filled cookies along each of the long edges. Normally, at this point, he would rejoin his guest for the four minutes and twenty seconds it took the kettle whistle to sound, which should be just enough time to talk about the costumed fellow with the telescope in the apartment across Park Avenue who spied on him day and night, and how, in Retter's opinion, a real apartment was one where you could scratch your balls and pick your nose without anyone looking at you from across the way. Not that he would say it in exactly that way, not yet.

Unfortunately, inadvertently, before Retter could tear himself away from the kitchen, he got caught up in a battle of wills with the tea kettle. A sudden, single-minded determination to demonstrate, contrary to the hand-me-down verities of small minds, that a watched pot does indeed boil. It occasionally came over him, this obsession to prove something as if the fate of the world somehow depended on it and this time it kept him in the kitchen a good four minutes longer than was truly polite, even by less-rigorous New World standards. An opportunity which eight dogs did not intend to let pass by, slipping quietly into the carpeted living room, eager to get a better sense of just what manner of misfit they had dragged home this time.

As strict a taskmaster as was the dog walker, as absolutely punctilious on matters of hospitality and decorum, he was not so authoritarian and bullheaded as to be totally lacking in understanding of canine psychology, nor to eliminate all possibilities for dogs to be dogs. So while out-and-out swarming a guest was indeed frowned upon, if the guest happened to make the first move, well, that was another matter entirely... To this end, trial and error had shown that where "humans" were concerned, a genetic weakness, there was apparently nothing quite like the irresistible, naturally-seductive effect of a young Labrador laid out on the ground, head between paws, expectant eyes looking up showing just enough white to seem mournful. And so it was that, playing his role, the Labrador lumbered innocently over to within two arms lengths of where Yuichi sat on the couch, and gave him the full treatment: the black-velvet puppy eyes, and the tail wagging ever-so-slowly, thump... thump... thump. A demonstration completely lost on Yuichi, absorbed as he was in head-shaking review of today, and ominous thoughts about tomorrow.

"Wag harder you big pussy!" said Fluffy the poodle.

"Yeah, what are you waiting for, dick-licker?" The other dogs joined in, voices thick with mockery and condescension. "Hurry up!"

"Blow me!" the Labrador answered, but did their bidding anyway, creeping forward, inch by invisible inch until he was only one length away, and thumping his tail against the coffee table, such a racket that Yuichi, helplessly, predictably, pathetically "human," finally stuck out his hand to let the Labrador sniff his knuckles. At which point, the dog, just as planned, gave a quick, friendly lick, averted his eyes, and inched back, so that, to actually make skin-to-fur contact, Yuichi was obliged to stretch out further, then further still, until he was in knee pushup position on the carpet.

Legs trembling, the other dogs focused on the kitchen door, waiting for Retter to appear, to witness this provocation first-hand and give them the license they needed. But given the temptation, and Retter's continuing absence, they could hear him in the kitchen jumping up and down and taunting the tea kettle, it was not long before resistance broke down completely. They rushed forward, poodles first, then the rest, surrounding Yuichi, licking his fingers, his hands, his wrists, snuffling, snorting, tickling.

Laughing, Yuichi retreated to the couch, but, aroused by his strange, exciting scent and energy, the dogs did not break off. Instead they crowded in even closer, licking his ankles where the white linen robe left the skin exposed. Yuichi snorted and tried to move his feet out of the way, simultaneously pushing at the dogs' noses to keep them at bay. But this little bit of resistance only emboldened the dogs, inflamed their tongues and fired their hips, aroused them to the point where they did not even notice the return of the victorious dwarf, red-faced and panting from his efforts with the tea-kettle.

"*Sofort!*" Retter thundered, "At once!" brows furrowed, slamming the tray down on the coffee table and pointing an imperious finger in the general direction of the dogs' room. Those with tails tucked them in between their legs, those without lowered heads below shoulders, and looking contrite as possible, casting exaggeratedly doleful looks, slunk away.

"*Ja,*" Retter resumed, furor melted instantly away, charm turned back on like a water faucet. "And so what you are doing here?" He poured the tea into two china cups. Wouldn't that be just like Pachinko-boy to look down upon him, to laugh at him, or laugh at his tea, just because of the genetic advantage concerning suicide. "Cream?" Did he imagine just anybody could be a dog-walker? Did he imagine all dog-walkers were the same? Just let him find a dog-walker in New York City with such an elite clientele. Sure, Retter once looked down on dog-walkers too, a long, long time ago. But that was before he had learned, before seven years of sidewalks and Central Park, in all kinds of weather.

"Cream? No thank you."

"No cream? Really? Hmm..." Stocks, show business, the press, industry, Jewish dentists, politics, Retter had covered every base, selected every dog perfectly to cover the power spectrum. What other dog-walker in New York City operated like that? What other dog-walker in the whole of the five boroughs had such rigorous standards for his clients? What other dog-walker in the entire *United States* had the stature, the seven years experience, the references, the authority to command $35 a day per dog, rather than a plebeian $30? "Go on, I'm sorry, I interrupted you. Your purpose here? Business or pleasure? I hope you don't find me too forward. Maybe it's both, ha-ha, ha-ha. Here..." Retter handed Yuichi his tea, and proceeded to sit down opposite him on the (slightly more imposing) couch of his own, wearing a big smile which, this time, meant "go ahead, I'm listening."

"Well..." Yuichi began, but he did not make it even to the end of the riot at the UN before Retter decided he really wasn't hearing anything new, before Retter's rapier-sharp mind had begun to hatch a so-fantastic plan. Speaking of the UN, the Japanese ambassador to the United Nations owned two ugly Sharpeis which Retter had been eyeing for quite some time now and perhaps the Japanese monk could help him with an introduction... Ha-ha, ha-ha! Two more dogs would make twelve in all: three lines of four, or even more pure, four lines of three. How jealous would they be then, seeing such an ideally compact physical specimen steer so much dogpower, four rows of three dogs each? Of course that meant he would have to work out some kind of system so that the dogs didn't spray each other when they lifted their legs. With only two rows, he had trained both to piss to the outside, but with four, hmm... "Please excuse me?" Retter removed a pad and pen from a drawer in the coffee table and made a quick note to himself, a heading in large capital letters: *"NICHT VERGESSEN RETTERLI!"* then below, slightly smaller, *"Hund,* 4X3, the elimination question." Retter pulled out the handkerchief from his breast pocket and coughed into it so as to conceal the smile at the corners of his mouth. Inspiration would come when inspiration was called, about that Retter had no doubt. "More tea?" What he liked most about himself right now was the hint of condescension in the use of the diminutive after his name. Retterli! As if he were some kind of mentally-deficient gnome, ha!

Three more pots of tea it took while Retter tried ever-so-subtly to steer the conversation away from the monk's account of his forgetful, forever tardy, sex-crazed host and all manner of other subjects completely devoid of even the most rudimentary insights, and around to the very delicate subject of the Japanese ambassador and his Sharpeis. Three times Retter had to excuse himself to boil water in the kitchen to freshen the tea pot, so as to avoid simply bursting out and saying "Stop now *du Aschloch,* do you take me for a fool?" Three different occasions for eight dogs to sneak back out of their room and subject the poor Japanese healer to their increasingly bold libidinal impulses, provocation or no. "You must try these cookies..." Twice Retter had sent the dogs scurrying back to their room, even snatching up the Austrian Loden and throwing it into their room for them to play with to their hearts' content. The third time he had to figure that canine love was what the Japanese man actually wanted. That perhaps in the interest of hospitality, and the longer-range interest of the Japanese ambassador question, Karl-Heinz Retter should just let the dogs and the monk enjoy each other as they saw fit.

"They seem to like you..."

"Yes." Struggling to keep from succumbing to absolute, paralyzing laughter, Yuichi summoned every little trick he could remember to retain self-control: breathing from the belly, chanting under his breath, even imagining the consequences of the failure of his mission. But tongues were darting higher and higher, the two cocker spaniels held his arms in an iron grip, humping away with a vacant look in their eyes, and the Pekinese had crawled under his robes, where he had begun to probe the most sensitive reaches of Yuichi's inner thighs, a feeling which not even the most painful memories could suppress forever.

Like water breaching a dam, Yuichi's laughter finally just erupted. Great, uncontrollable cascades of mirth which bared his gums and squeezed his knees together, ejecting "Monsieur" the Peke from under his robes like a lemon pip, and shooting him spread-eagled across the coffee table where he barely missed the tea set before landing flat on his back with a yelp. Freshly inspired, Laurel and Hardy, the cocker spaniels, shifted their little pelvises into double time. Fluffy and Light, the poodles, pounced on the right ankle while Adolf the Doberman grabbed a thigh. No room left for a frontal attack, Duffer the Labrador bounded around to the back, and in no-time-flat had wrapped his legs hard around Yuichi's head, over the eyes, thumb claws sticking into his forehead, humping as well for all he was worth. "Very ticklish," Yuichi said, but now that the laughter had started, he couldn't stop it to save himself.

"Tickerish, yes..." Retter didn't even flinch, not a crack in the facade, but inside, his mind raced with derision at the pathetic spectacle. Look at the suicide genius, giggling like a silly *Wurst*-vendor! *Ja, ja*, the Japanese demigod had marched into his apartment, all haughty, and the simple Swiss dog-walker had served him tea. But when reality struck, look at the result. "If you're going to start them up, you must finish them off," Retter wanted to say, but managed to hold back yet again, purely out of respect for his Honor the Japanese Ambassador. Don't worry about the dogs, Mr. Sneak Attack, Karl-Heinz Retter will finish them off later, as soon as you hand over the information about the ambassador and take your leave.

"Sofort!" Retter barked once again, but this time to no effect. *"So ist es?"* The dogs wanted to play? He snatched the rolled-up newspaper from the ground, slammed it so hard on the table that the tea tray jumped, then swatted a few rumps on the backswing as well. "Lack... of... respekt!" He herded them out of the living room and back to their room, slamming the door hard enough to make the large living room crystal chandelier tinkle. "That should be that!" Retter returned, rubbing his hands. No, not just anybody had what it took to be a smooth-talker dog-walker, Mr. Pearl Harbor. "More tea?" Retter pasted on his most disarming smile. Maybe the Americans had forgotten Pearl Harbor, but Karl-Heinz Retter, chief overseas operative for the Swiss *Militärabschirmdienst*, most certainly had not.

"No thank you."

"Sure?" Now that the dogs were gone, there didn't seem to be much to say.

"Sure."

"Certain?"

"Certain..."

"Positive?"

"You have many dogs," Yuichi said, feeling a trifle guilty that the dogs had been punished because of him. But by this point, Retter had drunk so much tea that the water had risen into his ear-drums. The monk's words sounded like they were coming from the bottom of the ocean, and his accent seemed to be getting stronger by the minute.

"That's right Papa-san, many dog, but in this country dog not for frying pan, sorry to ruin appetite," Retter wanted to say, but managed, most impressively, to control himself in time yet again, in case his guest's opening turned out to be a roundabout prelude to finally talking about Mr. Ambassador. "Yes, many dog. And every one owned by a very important person..." At this point, the only admirable quality Retter could see in his guest anymore, was his most magnificently impressive bladder, which even after all that tea did still not need to be emptied.

"Ho?"

"Part of a little strategy I have..." Perhaps the monk was refusing to urinate as a sort of contest? Perhaps in Japan, that's what they did, the last one to piss wins.

"Not your dogs?"

"No me dog?" Retter bristled. What was this for an insult? And with what kind of insolent smile? "Ach, not my dogs?" Retter laughed, relieved, *alles klar*. If the Japaner thought he was the only one who could throw on a strong accent... "*Ja! Nein*, not *mein* dogs. Dogs people pay me to valk und keep." By now, Retter had already pissed five times, but then again he came from Switzerland, where it was the amount of piss a man voided that showed his valor, not the capacity to retain it. Defecation? *Ja*, of course, that was another matter entirely, shit was to be held in at all cost. But piss? Piss was meant to flow.

"Ho? What kind of people?"

"Vat kind people? *Ja*, ze vay you are talking sometimes is very funny. Vat kind of people? Vat kind of people? Very important people who vant have dogs but have not time for taking care of zem. So zey leave zem viss me. Zat vay, zey know zey have dog, so zey feel good to have pet, but I take care of all trouble, zey never have to see it if zey no vant, and most them don't. 365 days a year time $35 equal $12775. Per canum. You find cheaper maybe, but you don't finding better. If I am in it for ze money, I probably chooss somesing else more lukrativ, but as it is, vell..."

By nine o'clock, after two plates of microwave *Rösti*, and any number of tumblers of different cherry spirits which Yuichi refused, but Karl-Heinz Retter knocked back, getting completely drunk in the deliberate attempt to display the virtues of Western hospitality, the monk, in spite of an accent (to Retter's tin ear) getting thicker by the second, had still not gotten around to topics ambassadorial. Not a single breach in his defenses, nor the slightest opening either for Retter to broach the subject himself in a natural and potentially successful way.

Not only that, but when Retter looked at his watch as was his habit, (one of the few habits he allowed himself) his guest took it as a hint, smiled, nodded politely, and got up to bid adieu. Retter, playing along, went so far as to hunt for the mysteriously-missing coat before asking whether Yuichi did not think it might be a good idea to phone his hostess first, "given her clearly capricious nature, *natürlich*," to confirm that she was actually prepared to receive him. "*Ja*, no point going all that way for nothing..."

Nine thirty, ten, ten thirty, consistent as ever, Chrissie had apparently still not arrived home, or at least that's what Yuichi supposed since the answering machine answered every time, which he was almost certain would not be the case if affection-starved Chrissie were home.

"Still nothing?"

"Nothing." Yuichi shook his head.

"Thoughtless, completely thoughtless!" Retter, voice shooting even higher than usual, pretended to be outraged, thinking that a little taste of modern Swiss neutrality was exactly what this moony woman needed. "And she told you she would be home? I will talk to her for you." Karl-Heinz Retter was about to mention that he was thinking seriously of writing a book on talking to women, but held back at the last second, just because.

Although Yuichi's bladder said it was clearly time for the "tea" to come to an end, time to leave the excitable little man alone with his dogs, Yuichi's gut said that heading downtown to Chrissie's on the off chance that she was home but had simply decided not to pick up the phone was probably not the best idea. The prospect of being locked out and having to spend the whole night walking around New Sodom was less than alluring. With all the violent, clutching, needy souls, it had proven to be perilous enough by day; by dark of night he feared it could well be fatal. "Perhaps you know a hotel, not-too-expensive, not-too-far?" Spending his limited resources on anything other than a plane ticket back to Japan was sheer folly, but first things first. If he were to die before delivering the scroll, a flight home would be the least of his worries.

"I am no hotel? Ach, you vant hotel? Nonsensz! For sleeping? You stay here man. You sleep in ze dogs' room, zey von't mind."

For predictable, canine-related reasons, it took forever for Yuichi to fall asleep, but the same was true of Karl-Heinz Retter, so awash was he in visions of future glory, so exhilarated was he by the way things were going, by the smooth way the Japaner had fallen directly into his trap. The ten dogs he already took care of had given Retter a foothold in American finance, in entertainment, in publishing, in hygiene products, in diplomacy, and thanks to Goldberg, the Jewish dentist, in the biggest growth industry of all: healthcare, Jewish healthcare. The Japanese ambassador's Sharpeis meant diversification, an expanded power base, access to state-of-the-art technology, to a temporarily depressed but potentially vital economy, and to a disciplined work force. *Ja*, for example, when was the last time anyone had heard of a Japanese jazzman? That pretty much proved the point. What more did you need to know? At Retter's funeral, the President of Switzerland would have to extend his speech by half an hour at the very least to include every last inspired detail of the dwarf's tragically too-short life. Tomorrow morning, first thing, without fail, Retter would make the shifty Japanese monk spill the beans. Trick him, or twist his arm, but make him arrange the meeting with the Japanese ambassador to the UN at once.

Tomorrow morning... All night long, dog upon man upon dog upon dog, Yuichi also thought about the morning when he would be able to take his leave from this latest mad angel the ancestors had sent to help him. Tomorrow morning, when he would have liberated the scroll from its prison at the bank, when he would be free to leave this nightmare, this New Yolk City, this temple to violence, greed and lust. Tomorrow morning when he would once again be free to focus completely on helping to save the world from destroying itself.

"Everything OK?" The dwarf checked in two or three times just to make sure, and each time, hearing his steps on the creaky wooden planks of the hallway, the dogs stopped their humping and stretched out, heads between paws just before he opened the door, the picture of innocence.

"Are they always like this?"

"Bitte?"

"You know that too much ejaculation is not healthy..."

"Ejacuration..."

"Yes, too much ejaculation weakens the constitution."

"Too much ejaculation? *Mensch!* You must be joking!" Now Mr. Fresh off Boat Person was an expert on dog-jizz as well. Or was this like that everything-is-linked fable about the butterfly that waves his wings in Peru, producing a hurricane in China? Oh yes, a dog who ejaculates in New York City weakens the Constitution, can't wait to see you prove that one, Rising Son.

"Never mind..." Yuichi waved Retter off, and put his head back down on the dog-smell pillow. How could the little man possibly see it? The dogs weren't doing anything their human counterparts in this tragic era weren't doing. "You know why dogs lick their dicks? Because they can!" Isn't that how the American joke went? Defying authority, letting animal instincts run wild just because they could.

So it was even in Japan. God, church, government, teachers without wisdom, experts: the people had begun to see through every last one of them, and they tried to get away with as much as possible, just to show the authority that it had no hold on them. But they were still children, they were foolish, they had not evolved enough to take responsibility for themselves. The breakdown of morals, the predominance of the physical, the animal, the culture of excess: it was all part of a terrible but necessary gestation period. A period of transition until the life-will reasserted itself, until it once again found itself at the center of human preoccupations. Until then, until human beings took responsibility for themselves, until they became their own authority, one had to be strong and patient. And sometimes one had to catapult a flat-nosed dog clear across a room.

10

Yuichi did not manage to fall asleep until 4:30, which meant that instead of waking at five as he intended, as was his habit, he finally pried his eyelids open at eight, feeling heavy-headed, groggy, dog hair in every orifice, and looking in little better shape than his poor spackled Loden coat. It took him three sneezes to remember where he was, but as soon as he did, he wrenched himself free from the bed, and pulled on his robe. No time for exercise, no time for ablutions beyond a little water on the face to try and clear fur from nostrils, mouth and ears, no time even to consider what new and strange hazards might be awaiting outside, he dragged eight coat-attached growling dogs down the slick wooden hallway to locate Sukuna-Hikona, express his gratitude, and bid him adieu. The bank opened at nine, and Yuichi was determined to be first in line.

He found Retter in the dining room, putting the last touches on a silver, crystal and starched-linen *Ovomaltine-Eier-Muesli* feast for two and dog-chow feast for eight at whose sight eight dogs instantly loosened their jaws and started a yipping, growling, biting scramble of a race to be first to their respective bowls.

"Good morning!" Sukuna-Hikona was in painfully good cheer. Cheeks and ears freshly shaved, he whistled the William Tell Overture as he poured orange juice from a crystal pitcher into two long-stemmed glasses. "Please." He held his hand out, palm open, inviting Yuichi to take his place, then climbed up onto his own chair, snapped open his large, razor-creased napkin, and tucked it into his collar, repeating his hand-invitation for the monk to follow suit.

"Thank you very much," Yuichi said, bowing. "I must go now."

"Must to go? *Mensch!* Are you crazy?" He nodded at the window, outside of which all was white, snow flying by horizontally. "Six inches since last night, they even closed the schools. Sit, eat."

"Very sorry... Thank you for everything."

"Go now? Alone? *Ja*, that is, without protection?" He held his hands out on either side as if to say 'What is this for nonsense?'

"Thank you again..."

"OK wait." Retter almost fell off his phonebooks and tripped over his napkin in the rush to get into his weather-most-foul gear. Trying his best to retain some measure of dignity, he race-walked to the front door to grab the leashes and an old copy of the *Neue Zürcher Zeitung*, then race-walked back, hitched up the dogs and tore them away from their bowls with a mighty heave. In the Berner Oberland there was a certain kind of pinched-face smile you could smile which could kill a man on a distant peak, and that's the smile he focused on the monk, not that he had much hope that such high-mountain nuance could possibly get through to this fishlander. Wouldn't that be just like a Japaner to try and sneak away without spilling the information? Retter thought. "Where is your bank? Ah ha, yes, I see. Can we just pass by and pick up the other two dogs? It's on the way," Retter said. Which wasn't true, but where was it written that you had to be honest when confronted by Japanese deceit of such high order?

At the bank it took four people thirty minutes to explain to Yuichi that he couldn't have his scroll back. It wasn't the white spots on his coat, it wasn't his sunken eyes, his rather desperate demeanor, nor the remnants of yesterday's unwashed makeup. It wasn't the turbulent *Lederhosen*-clad dwarf with the ten dogs, it wasn't the fact that Yuichi had virtually closed down the bank half of yesterday afternoon, what with the crowd of women outside, and that it looked like the same scenario setting up again this morning. It was simply that the safe-deposit box he had signed for yesterday had a co-signer, a Ms. Chrissie Luna, and that without her here, or at least her signed accord, there was simply nothing they could do.

"Ho?" What about the crucial importance of the scroll? The possibility that what it contained might help save the world?

"Of course, this is not our problem..." one banker said, with a shrug of his pin-striped shoulders.

"It's just a security measure..." said the one next to him.

"In your own interest..." said a third and so on...

"Put yourself in our position..."

"You wouldn't want someone else coming in here and..."

"Violating time-tested procedures..."

"If we make an exception for one person, we have to make exceptions for everybody..."

"Come back later today with Ms. Luna and we will be most happy to be of assistance..."

"More than happy..."

"Until then..."

"There's just nothing we can do..."

"Try to understand..."

"Nothing personal..."

Incredulous, Yuichi looked them straight in the eye to make double sure this wasn't just the American sense of humor again, then, face grim, shoulders set, turned around and marched to the door.

Putting on the John Lennons to hide his eyes, Yuichi stepped through the revolving door and onto the sidewalk, intent on hailing a cab to take him straight down to Chrissie's. To hell with the expense, to hell with plundering the savings with which he hoped to get back to Japan, it was time to get this over with.

Out on the sidewalk, the sea of female admirers engulfed him, touching, pulling at his white linen robe, rubbing his crew-cut head, pinching his soft-as-peach cheeks, gaining courage with every second, until parted once again by eight tired, moody, hungry dogs, plus two fresh-as-the-morning and very-jealous Yorkshire terriers and a Swiss-German dwarf who decided it was time to open another line of inquiry. "Excuse me, but what exactly is in this so-called scroll?"

"Don't know," Yuichi answered, walking up to the cross-street and scanned the traffic in both directions. All was still relatively quiet, snowplows and salt trucks, and only an occasional taxi crawling along down the center of the blind streets, struggling through the oatmeal.

"You don't know. Of course..." What kind of fool did this Japanese man take him for? Again! The non-existent scroll, the unconvincing gibbering at the bank, the sex-starved hostess who was never home: did the Japanese man think Retter was retarded? Retter should have known the Japaner wasn't trustworthy right from the start when he refused to give his name. And why, which was really the point, why all this impossible secrecy about the Japanese ambassador? There could only be one reason, did he think Karl-Heinz Retter was too dense to figure it out? The sneaky back-stabber wanted to set up a dog-walking business of his own, starting with the Ambassador's Sharpeis. Ho, ho, ho. Of course! All those seemingly naive questions about dog-walkers, all that pretend-pretend. So that's how they paid you back for generosity in the land of the Yellow Bellied...

When an empty yellow cab finally stopped to pick up the yellow man (synchronicity, *Mensch!*) Retter piled right in behind him without even asking. The taxi driver, a Ghanaian who could hardly speak any tongue known to man, let alone a language as artless, as fatuous, as English, tried to explain that he didn't want ten wet-smell dogs and a dwarf in galoshes in his cab, but Retter hardly gave him a choice. "Drive now, you!" The cab could be driven by the whole of Africa and Islamia combined, Karl-Heinz Retter didn't intend to let this deceitful little Japanese man out of his sight for one minute.

From 9:45 to 3:00, while Yuichi paced back and forth through the slush in front of "Chrissie's" wearing an almost comical worried look, Karl-Heinz Retter humored him, hands-on-hips, foot tapping indulgently, an ever-so-slightly cynical tilt to his smile and felt hat. Mind you, not that Karl-Heinz Retter wouldn't love to lay eyes on anyone with such a preposterous name as Chrissie Luna, but how long did Fishworthy intend to keep up the pathetic charade? "Excuse me, do you know Chrissie Luna?" Yuichi stopped anyone who went in or out of the building at 226, "Have you seen Chrissie maybe?"

"Clissie Runa? Never heardofer." "Asshole." "Who wants to know?" "Fuck you," they answered him, small surprise. Retter wondered if they even had acting schools in Japan. Not likely. The thought of all those banzai guys on the suicide airplanes during World War II crashing into American battleships with the wrong expressions on their faces made Retter almost laugh out loud in scorn. That would be one of the first subjects he would take up with the Japanese ambassador. Once they had put the problem of world hegemony behind them, they could probably make a killing starting up a chain of acting schools.

"Excuse me, but you wouldn't possibly happen to know the name of the Japanese ambassador to the UN?" Retter threw it out, feeling suddenly bold enough to toy with the monk, like even if he asked him straight out, it wouldn't matter.

"Japanese ambassador?" Yuichi scrunched his face up, trying to synthesize the question. Hilarious! If a Swiss actor ever acted like that he would be exiled to Turkey for life, no parole. Or even Yugoslavia, if those people could ever keep a country together...

"No, ha-ha, of course you wouldn't know..." No, "pathetic" was the only word that really fit! Pa-thet-tic! Karl-Heinz Retter could wait all day if need be. You didn't become the chief overseas operative for the Swiss *Militärabschirmdienst* without patience and endurance; and a certain wannabe dog-walker was about to find out just what that meant. "You wouldn't mind keeping the dogs, while I get them something to eat, would you?" Let him see how easy it *wasn't* to keep ten dogs in line. "You don't mind if I go buy a sandwich, while you wait for her, do you?" Ten different personalities, ten different cardinal priorities, ten different sets of different-sized bladders and intestines. "I was thinking of getting a Coca Cola, would you like one too? Or perhaps you would prefer some RAW FISH?" Ha-ha, there would be defecation all over the sidewalk. And then? And then? Then: bang! One phone call from Karl-Heinz Retter, and the police would swoop in and deport the amateur on the spot, so huge would the mess be. People always underestimated the dwarf just because he was small. One little phone call to the INS... The Japanese man couldn't even begin to suspect how much his destiny hung in the balance of Karl-Heinz Retter's good graces. "Are there many Japanese ambassadors to the United Nations? Only one, right? And we still claim we do not know his name? OK, OK. You want to play games? We'll play games. Any luck with your Chrissie? Oh, she's not back yet? Don't worry, I'm sure she'll show up, any time now." In a pig's ass she would. In a pig's ass...

Unfortunately for Yuichi, neither in a pig's ass, nor the next day did Chrissie Luna appear, no matter how early they arrived on the spot (in a special limousine paid for by Retter), no matter how diligently Yuichi invoked the ancestors of the five races, (who seemed completely to have abandoned him) nor how thoroughly he pounded the pavement, pacing back and forth between 226 Lafayette and the travel agency with its cruel reminder: Tokyo, $1250. $1250 which he no longer even had.

At first, Karl-Heinz Retter distracted himself by timing the monk on his Swiss chronograph. After that he tried to wring some pleasure out of haranguing the half-dozen fresh hot-house peach, hot dog and souvlaki vendor parasites who had rolled their carts up to service the assemblage.. Then Retter turned his attention to the flock of female admirers still grouped around the monk, looked them over until he was certain there was neither *Valkyrie* nor child actress in the lot, and amused himself for two good hours watching the dogs capture and release, capture and release the ones his nose told him would be most marked by the experience. Giving so much attention to such obviously non-tumescent women was only further proof of his fundamentally altruistic nature, Retter thought, allowing himself a brief gloat.

And perhaps that was his mistake, for suddenly, inexplicably, as if infected by the idleness and absence of routine, oh Satanic hubris, the dogs started letting him down, casting sideways looks of affection at the monk instead of at him, and putting on a performance that was much less than satisfactory, much less. No one else noticed legs held up at 89 instead of 90 degrees, no one else noticed heads tilting and jowls hanging loose. But then, no one else's bandy thighs sported bruises from being beaten by an angry *Neue Zürcher Zeitung* reduced to pulp, and no one else had to cross Spring to the little drugstore/news stand and suffer the impertinence of the Zoroastrian upstart who told him that the last copy of today's edition of the Swiss paper had been snapped-up a half-hour earlier by a dog-walker just like himself, and proposed instead a Swedish paper called *Expressen*, buzzing with cheap, idiot-attracting four-colored type. "Swiss? Swedish?" he said, in that tongue-glued-to-top-of-palate way, "What's the difference?"

"What's the difference? What's... the... difference!" Retter had never had much sympathy for the British, that pasty-skin race of beer-soaked fornicators, but for the first time in his life he understood just what they must have gone through trying to hold an empire together on the Indian sub-continent.

With a big grateful smile, Retter actually went so far as to accept the Swedish paper, until he felt certain the Zoroastrian was convinced he was about to make a foreign-paper-sized profit. Then, at the last moment, Retter blindly reached out for a copy of The Star, (which this week had both Bruce Lee and Jackie Chan on the cover) and tossed the Swedish paper right in the shopkeeper's face. "Terribly sorry, good fellow," Retter said, flipping three quarters at three different parts of the counter, so that the curry-worth was forced to scramble in the most hilarious way to rake in his ill-gotten harvest. As for The Star, well, it didn't roll up nearly as neatly as the *Neue Zürcher Zeitung*, but, at least for a while, it sure helped the dogs keep their eyes straight.

By three o'clock, with the so-called monk still showing no sign of flagging, Retter, toes numb, fast approaching absolute boredom, began again to smell that familiar fishy smell. Briefly, charitably, he tried to convince himself that it was a blocked sewer, a burst pipe somewhere or even an ill-wind blowing in from the Fresh Kills dump, but it was no good, the stench was definitely coming off the monk. Maybe he didn't exactly smell bad, and in this situation, without instruments it was impossible to be absolutely scientific, but the very idea that the monk had spent at least two days in that same white linen robe, and *Gottinhimmel* knows how many more before then, gave off a sort of mental stench, which if anything, smelled stronger than the real thing. For the life of him, Retter didn't understand why Yuichi didn't just commit suicide right away, on the spot, end of headache, end of strife. And if that meant he took his little diplomatic secret to the grave? Well then too bad, Retter would just have to find his own way to the Japanese ambassador, wouldn't he?

Except wait just a second! The rival dog-walker scenario still made perfect sense, but suddenly Karl-Heinz Retter saw what had previously been hidden: that it was only a cover for a cover. Observing Yuichi out of the corner of his eye, observing the whole pathetic Zen act, the terrible costume, and the Austrian coat maculated with god-knows-what, there could only be one possible conclusion: Yuichi was a spy. A deep, deep, deep undercover member of Japanese Intelligence. Sure! It made perfect sense. The strange questions about dog-walking in his incomprehensible English, "No you dog?" "What kind people?" A transparent attempt to destabilize. Oh what a fool Retter had been, what a distracted fool, even going so far as to invite the viper into his very own apartment!

And yet, now that Retter thought about it, maybe not such a great a fool as all that, friend, for hadn't the viper been exposed before loosing its terrible green-yellow bite? The President of Switzerland would be speechless, how else to praise Karl-Heinz Retter for unmasking this most brazen attempt to infiltrate Swiss Intelligence? But hold the aphasia *Herr Präsident*, the job was not done yet, not by a long shot. The bird was still in the bush, the horse on the other side of the river, the cow not quite over the moon, the grass on the other side of the fence not even fertilized yet. Extreme delicacy would be required here, tactics, patience, subterfuge, intrigue and heroism of a sort rarely seen in modern times. And discretion, *Ja*, more than anything, discretion: Retter must not let on about what he knew, not under pain of death, not if they stuck bamboo slivers under his finger nails, not if they tried to brand his tongue with a red-hot branding iron, or cut it out to sell as an aphrodisiac for some limp-banana loser in Korea. Karl-Heinz Retter had his work cut out for him, this he could see. His mind raced, he would have, single-handedly, to reinvent the profession of viper-trapping. Now that he had his fish, no question of letting him out of his sight for even a second. Now, more than ever, he must hold Yuichi captive, follow him everywhere to get the irrefutable proof. Let him slip up just once, then bang, a sharp blow to the back of the neck and that would be that: redemption, triumph, angelic trumpets. "Don't worry about her," he said jerking a disparaging thumb at the imaginary apartment of the imaginary strumpet, Chrissie Loonah. "*Ja*," Retter said, as if an idle idea had just come to him, "If you don't have any place to stay again tonight, you are most welcome to stay with me, as always. No problem."

In the limousine on the way back to Park and 41st, Retter just happened to glance at the devolutionary newspaper in his hands, at the ridiculous cover story about the Chinese movie actor everyone claimed to have seen. Such garbage, such fodder for helpless souls. He snorted, he chortled, then, right there in the limo, looking through a forest of canine legs, seeing the monk with the Peke on his face, he had another so-fantastic idea. People were so gullible, it would probably be no problem at all to get them to believe that Yuichi was in fact the movie star they were looking for. And Karl-Heinz Retter would be his agent!

The future was beautiful indeed, Retter could see the whole scene with cinematic 70mm clarity. He would dress in livery, with von Stroheim pants and riding crop, and he would walk the dogs down Broadway where capturing all the choicest directors when they came to town for premieres would be child's play. Here was the biological proof that generosity pays off. A bag of tea given in perfect innocence, and now he was all set to be the agent of a movie star.

Which did not for a second mean that Karl-Heinz Retter intended to forget either about dog walking or about Yuichi-the-spy. Once he was a film agent he would have stature enough to walk twenty dogs minimum, power enough to hire as many dog walker's assistants as needed. As for the latter, *Ja*, well, what with the legion of women that movie stars were practically obliged to have sex with, Retter should easily be able to slip in just one crafty little Mata Hari of his own. Then, one unguarded word from the monk, and Retter would have his viper. One little word, that's all that would be needed to trip up Mr. International Spymaster, to get the goods, to wrap up the package, and seal the deal. And, while collecting 10%, that was the best part. Ha-ha, ha-ha.

They would need three Sikorski helicopters to lower his sculpted marble mausoleum onto its site on the gentle, verdant southern slope of the Jungfrau, and the noise would be so loud that the President of Switzerland would have to wait an hour to give his speech. Then he would have to wait another half-hour while they played an all new version of "Requiem" written to order by the Protestant great-great-great-grandson of W.A. Mozart himself. Plenty of *dies irae, dies illa* but easy on the *Kyrie eleison Christe eleison* and the rest of the Papist mumbo-jumbo.

11

There was only one immediate problem with Karl-Heinz Retter's precise calculations: the next morning, while he renewed the dance with the Zoroastrian across Spring Street, purchasing a copy of "Variety," a little reading in order not to appear too uncultured when he ventured back into the film biz, a little problem arose with the arrival of a sound truck carrying a certain wired-jaw vengeful Mormon in a wrinkled white shirt and equally vengeful Mister-Mack's-of-Salt-Lake-City, Mormon-blue suit and tie. A sound truck blaring scripture from the Writings of Abraham: "Nevertheless, the wealth of this great city was built upon sin for the people served many idol gods and offered upon their altars men, women, and children after the same manner as the Egyptians. And they had numerous slaves who were kept down in bondage and poverty and were driven like dumb beasts to provide the luxury in which their masters dwelt. Behold, the inhabitants of the city did delight in whoredom and adultery and murder and all manner of evil, whereby they might get gain. And the anger of the Lord was kindled against them. Nevertheless, he did let them go on that they might be fully ripened in iniquity before the fullness of his wrath should fall upon them. All of these things did the Lord God show unto me in a dream on the night before we entered into the city of Ur; and He said unto me, Abram, this city is vile and corrupt, but in it are some few souls who have not bowed the knee to their idol gods and it is because of their prayers that I have brought you here, that they might be taught to worship the true God after the order of heaven and be led out from wickedness and bondage..."

Words which, once again, Yuichi would be hard put to impugn, glorious words which, unfortunately so transported the Satan-starved Mormon, that he could not bear to still his restless legs and remain in the safety of his truck, but had to get down and repeatedly poke the Japanese "devil" in the chest. At which point Yuichi, slipping and sliding on the mess left by the dogs, just trying to regain balance, connected a front kick to Mormon chin and an elbow to Mormon temple which laid the righteous fool Mormon out once more in no time flat. Fire engine sirens from the paramedics just down Lafayette, police sirens in the distance, and here we go again.

Retter crossed the street and pushed smoothly through the crowd, advantage #2439 of being a dwarf, not that he was counting. But once he had taken in the situation, his high spirits received an instant ice bucket shower. What perfidy! What insolent perfidy! Going to jail: wouldn't that be a sneaky viper trick for getting away? With a lick of the lips, Retter marched over to the Mormon's prostrate form, nudged the kneeling, first aid-giving monk aside to open up the target, and with a cruel sideways look at Yuichi, cocked his foot and let the Mormon have it, once in the gut, and once, in case anyone had missed the first blow, right in his polygamist balls. No Japanese monk in a fishy smelling white linen robe was going to escape him that easily! If Yuichi was going to be arrested, Karl-Heinz Retter intended to be arrested right along with him. And the dogs? Well the dogs would just have to fend for themselves. In the Bible, did it say that animals should dominate men? Of course not! Quite the opposite as a matter of fact, quite the opposite.

And then the police arrived, five squad cars screeching to a halt, and reason returned, so that when the cops asked to whom the dogs belonged,

Retter, despite the stack of black pooper-scooper bags tucked neatly into his belt, pointed to the Mormon and slipped off through the crowd, zoom, zoom, zoom, slapping the copy of Variety on his right thigh so that the dogs would follow. What would the dogs do on their own? He couldn't possibly abandon them. How would that look if he did? How would the planet spin on if even Karl-Heinz Retter succumbed to base betrayal?

As for Yuichi, poor Yuichi, the police cuffed him and loaded him into a squad car, forcefully, indelicately enough to give him a sizeable bump on the crown. And that night, what do you know, but he was in the holding tank with 24 other fractious scofflaws, back behind bars, January 27, year 2000.

"Officer Murphy! How's yer mothuh?" "Eh, let me get the window!" In the holding tank it seemed like most of the inmates were repeat offenders, it was like a giant reunion, everyone seemed to know everyone else. And while Yuichi wasn't exactly jovial, he wasn't really all that sad either.

Twenty seven days since he had arrived here to accomplish an apparently simple mission: go to New York City, deliver scroll, leave New York City. But did Yuichi worry about this? Did he wonder about the ancestors and their tricks? Did he think about the scroll? Did he reflect about poor distracted Chrissie Luna or the true nature of Sukuna-Hikona, his suspicious, irritable little homunculus host? Or did he wallow in shame and hang his head thinking about 27 days of futility, convinced he must already have failed? No, plenty of time to address all that later, right now he was simply too tired. After three days of pacing and she-devils and three full sleepless nights servicing the hounds of hell, he simply stretched out on the holding tank floor and went to sleep. Even peach-tossing Izanagi himself might be ready for a bit of rest.

12

Chrissie Luna walked in the frozen Atlantic City sand arm-in-arm with Jim O'Brien until she could no longer feel her toes. Chrissie Luna ate Atlantic City hot dogs and Atlantic City pretzels and Atlantic City toffee that stuck in her molars, and took her tongue hours to dislodge. Chrissie Luna matched Jim O'Brien (Irish) whiskey for (Irish) whiskey, and Chrissie Luna neglected to remember Yuichi for four full days.

She wasn't much of a gambler, a bucket of nickels was all she really cared to invest, but *he* loved the adrenaline of it, and with her there, for some reason, the dice were rolling his way. "Come on, come on... Yeah! Fuckin' ay!"

They kept it going for 48 hours straight. He called her his lucky charm, laying on the Irish accent doublethick, and she called him O'Brien. From this mismatch-made-in-heaven magic had sprouted, and when they weren't gambling or going for walks, they were in bed, curtains closed, sleeping, watching TV documentaries and making love with the sound of the waves piped in from below over the sound system. That's what it was, Chrissie was sure, not sex, but making love.

Maybe for the first time in her life, Chrissie Luna knew there was a difference, and that difference was that she had been able to let herself go, just like you were supposed to be able to do. And although she told herself to be patient, she just felt obliged to cast him an appreciative glance every so often, to show him that she was glad to be here with him, just so he would know it, because men are so insecure.

On Thursday morning, while O'Brien was out gambling on the greyhounds, Chrissie Luna took a bubble bath then went back to bed. She flipped through some magazines, (an elevator at the Empire State Building had plunged 40 floors down, but the two people inside had not been hurt) played TV Keno every time the mood came over her, and checked the news (the Republican debate for the New Hampshire Primary had turned particularly nasty, and a poor little Cuban boy who had washed up in Florida had been visited by his grandmothers). She watched one documentary about Greenpeace and the French nuclear test at Mururoa atoll, a second about the upcoming opening of the International Space Station, then a third about the design and testing of a new drug by Reaper Pharmaceuticals, a drug expected to neutralize at least some of the effects of *prion* diseases, aka transmissible spongiform encephalopathies, aka Mad Cow. She thought about how the symptoms of the disease, irritability, aggressiveness, fatigue, insomnia, amnesia described just about everybody nowadays, but as usual the TV made her drowsy, so she made a vague resolution to stop eating beef by next Jan. 1, and didn't really pursue it beyond that.

A nap would be the height of complete sinful idleness, she thought, but while surfing through the channels just to make sure she wasn't missing anything, she came upon The Mid-Morning Snack Show news, where they broached the New Year's suicides, as if that was the kind of topic you talked about to start a day! "When reports were made earlier this year about a New Year's suicide wave there was much hand wringing and told-you-sos," said the painted hairdo in her most authoritative news-speak, "But official statistics revealed today show that visions of traffic jams on the Golden Gate Bridge might be just more millennial hysteria. According to Center for Disease Control numbers, arrived at after detailed examination of coroners' reports which for the first time take into account, not only the ages, but the prior condition of the deceased, only 17000 total years were lost by the 2000 or so alleged suicides. A figure which CDC officials said was equivalent to less than a third as many as the years lost by a worldwide television audience during a simple Super Bowl Sunday."

For some reason, after hearing this, Chrissie Luna began to cry. She didn't feel sad about the suicides, or even the time wasted on Super Bowl Sunday, it wasn't that, or at least she didn't think so. The strange thing was that Chrissie Luna didn't really know what it was other than an overwhelming sense of hopelessness, of futility, of being forty, of years passing and life extinguished just like that, snap of the fingers. "Gilligan's Island," "Josie and the Pussycats," "MASH," "Saturday Night Live," Elton John, John Lennon, Paul McCartney, you lived through half a dozen dance fads, hems rose, then dropped, then rose again, you got four inches taller with platform shoes, then four inches shorter when styles changed. And in the end would anyone remember you? And if they did would they have anything to say about you even remotely resembling who you were? Not to be negative, but sometimes it was just overwhelming.

By lunchtime, when O'Brien returned, even though the blues had not left, Chrissie reckoned she had pretty much managed to pull herself together, except for the red eyes and the swelling and the smile she pasted on which she wasn't sure was entirely convincing. But just her luck, O'Brien wasn't in a good mood either, she knew it the minute he stepped in the room and slammed the door. Apparently, the dogs had eaten much of his new-found wealth, apparently he didn't care to be consoled...

"This isn't exactly helping..." she couldn't help but inform him.

"Fuck's wrong with you now?" he answered in a tone as if she had been the last sane person in the universe, and now she wasn't anymore.

"I'm sorry," she mumbled, and shook her head, forget it. She was just upset about the suicides she told him when he insisted. She had to tell him something.

"Silly cow," he said on the way to the throne. "Two thousand more, two thousand less," he strained to add through the thoughtlessly open door, "Fucking good riddance, that's what I say." And then he took a shower and without drying off at all, dripping wet, just like that, took her without even asking, right there on the deep-pile shag carpet, aptly named.

Chrissie Luna finally got completely fed up with him the next morning which was right about the time she discovered that she'd won $21,534 on a Keno ticket, an explosion of good spirits which Jim O'Brien, who had lost all but $12 of his windfall back thanks to a clique of overfed, velvet-pawed dogs, one-eyed *Jai alai* players and criminally imbalanced dice, failed to share. Which, coincidentally, was also right about the time the mid-week special room he had rented for their little fugue at the Trump Taj Mahal, turned into the more expensive weekend suite.

"Oh my godddd," she said, "Yuichi! Oh shit, oh shit." While O'Brien watched her, hands on hips, wondering what manner of nonsense this was now, she turned the room upside down collecting the torn and soiled sartorial mementoes of the mid-week fling from under the bed, from between the sheets. "Quick, I gotta go, OK?"

"When it rains it pours," he said, but ironic-like, ironic enough anyway to stop her in her tracks. Him losing the money and her winning at Keno had nothing to do with it, it just helped him realize how he really felt about her. He didn't like the way she acted like they were going to spend their whole lives together after only three days in fucking AC. The way she looked at him, the way she held herself, everything. It made him feel important, and when a woman made him feel important it turned him mean. No, he preferred women who were slightly disdainful, or so downright evil-nasty that you never knew which way was up, kept you on your toes.

Actually, now that O'Brien thought about it, it wasn't that either. Really the problem was that ever since the news about the suicides, she had not been able to stop crying. "I'm sorry," she said, and probably meant it, but still it made it difficult for him to come without thinking of a half-dozen other things like buggering choir-boys, or pushing some pale-skinned, blue-eyed, black-haired gi up against a doorjamb like he used to after last call in Dublin, hiking up her skirts and giving her what for right there with a finger up her arsehole, before sending her home to her parents. You could forgive a bird many things, but when she made it hard to blow the load? That you couldn't forgive. Not that, never that, blow the whistle, Ref.

"I don't suppose you could lend me a little money, could you Lucky Charm?" he said, stopping outside the bus as if to suggest that if she didn't make a little gesture and cough up a small sum she would be riding home by herself.

"I hate you!"

"Come on," he persisted, head bent, wiping his nose with the back of his hand as if "pathetic" would make him seem more deserving. "Round it off..."

"Round it off?" she said a bit too loud, outraged, then looking around in case anyone was listening, and lowering her tone. "You are a bastard."

"Yes."

"Say it."

"I am a bastard."

"OK then," she relented, as he knew she would. "But on one condition..."

"What's that?"

"You never try to pay me back."

"You mean never try and see you again?" It sounded too good to be true, but O'Brien managed to keep his smile in check. He wiped his nose with the back of his hand again for pathetic-good-measure. "Jeez."

"Deal?"

"OK, deal..."

It was a long bus ride home, during which Chrissie wondered just how it was that she continued to collect one loser after another, continued to have such bad luck in love. A question shrouded in mystery, a painful fog comprised of a crazy selfish mother unable to give affection, of catastrophic initiations into the world of sex, affairs that came to abrupt ends for no reason she could fathom, of admirably-idealistic remnants of various egalitarian concepts which made her absolutely unwilling to consider the cause and effect of base male psycho-biology, disinclined as she was to play the traditional duplicitous game. Except that she played the game anyway, debasing herself to the level of the men she chose, (who, because of her lack of confidence, were never prime material to begin with) giving them everything so that they would love her, and hanging around long after her dignity had evaporated just to make sure to receive the last kicks she knew she would get.

And yet the crazy thing was that she still believed in Prince Charming, believed 110 percent. But what if he only appeared once she was sixty? She certainly didn't intend to spend the next twenty years without sex.

"There's logic for you," said Chrissie's mother, the only time Chrissie made the mistake of sharing her thoughts on the subject. "Prince Charming? You wouldn't recognize Prince Charming if he sat on your face."

13

In the *Kojiki*, the "scripture" of the Shinto religion, the story is told of how, long after the creation, Izanagi, the-male-who-invites, gave birth to three gods and assigned them their places in the world. To the goddess Amaterasu-o-mi-Kami, whose symbol is the sun, he gave dominion over the plain of high heaven. To the god Tsuki-yomi-no-mi-Kami, whose symbol is the moon, he gave dominion over the night. And to the god Susano-wo, whose symbol is a star, he gave dominion over the Sea Plain.

As befit their nature, the first two gods obeyed their father and went dutifully to the places to which they were assigned; but the third god, Susano-wo, also called the impetuous male, resisted his father's dictate and began to weep. He wept and wept, until his eight-grasp beard reached to the pit of his stomach, wept until his weeping had withered the green mountains into withered mountains and dried up the rivers and the seas.

At long last, Izanagi bestirred himself to find out what might be wrong, saying, "How is it that instead of ruling the land whose dominion I entrusted to you, you wail and weep thus?"

"I only weep," Susano-wo answered, "Because I wish to depart to the nether world to visit Izanami, my mother."

Furious, for what Susano-wo requested was quite impossible, Izanagi said, "If that be so, then you shall not dwell in this land." And so saying, he expelled Susano-wo forthwith.

"If that be so," retorted Susano-wo in turn, "Then I will do as you say and depart. But not before bidding farewell to my sister Amaterasu." And so, with this purpose in mind, the impetuous male at once made his way up to Heaven, but with such a noise, and such heavy footsteps, that the mountains and rivers shook, and the earth quaked.

Alarmed by the racket and convinced that, as befit Susano-wo's nature, the impetuous male's intentions could only be impure, that his real purpose in visiting her was to wrest away her land, Amaterasu hastily made ready for battle and confronted him. But crafty Susano-wo was prepared. He swore that his intentions were pure, that he had only come to bid her farewell and that if she still refused to believe in his sincerity, then their only recourse was to hold a contest to see which one of them could beget the most gods.

As it turned out, after many births, Susano-wo did indeed manage to produce more gods than Amaterasu, which, divine logic, not only testified to his sincerity, but confirmed that he was the more powerful. Flush with victory, eager to celebrate and confirm his dominance, Susano-wo proceeded to lay waste the land, to break the dikes in the sun god's rice fields, to fill up the ditches, and even to spread excrement in the palace where Amaterasu ate.

First Amaterasu discovered the damage to her dining palace, but this she merely attributed it to Susano-wo's impetuous nature and left it at that. "Perhaps," she said, "the excrement is something my brother vomited through drunkenness." Next she discovered the broken dikes in the rice paddies, but again she forgave him, saying: "It must be because he begrudges the land they are on." But, finally, Susano-wo, the impetuous male, flayed a piebald horse backwards and threw it into Amaterasu's weaving hut. An act so horrifying, so revolting, that Amaterasu could no longer find it in her heart to forgive him. With that, she locked herself up in a cave, saying if this was the way it was going to be, then from now on, all would be darkness below.

Operating by the light of the stars and moon, priests and scholars, living proof of the ossification that occurs when an oral tradition is codified, had, over the centuries, offered any number of arbitrary interpretations of this tale, had turned symbols with esoteric meanings into vulgar totems for worship, had even preached a god in man's image. But the inner truth remained for those given the key, those with eyes to see. This was the aftermath of the hiding of the great knowledge: Susano-wo, the star god, the god able to create the most gods, was the dominant current in the modern world, the current of science and lucre, of filth spread over the earth, of lakes and oceans fouled. Tsuki-yomi-no-mi-Kami, the moon god, was the current of art, intuition, imagination, religion and love, those things that give solace, hope and meaning: truths in the weak light of the moon. Intermediate fixations to be jettisoned when the time was right. And finally, Amaterasu-o-mi-Kami, the sun-goddess shut away in a cave: this was another form of Izanami, the knowledge which had been hidden away starting ten thousand years ago, the knowledge which the Westerners called "Word of God", or "Messiah," the knowledge which, Yuichi was certain, infused *Chi no maki*, the Book of the Earth. Knowledge moreover, which, since the destruction of the planet was not part of the Great Design, would certainly return when Amaterasu was good and ready.

Perhaps, Yuichi had failed the test so far. Perhaps at the UN, because of the jet lag, he had demonstrated a lack of vigilance, perhaps he had failed to read the signs, perhaps he had made a mistake accepting Chrissie's hospitality, and a second mistake putting himself at the mercy of Herr Retter. Or perhaps, ho, this was all just a symbolic replay of the ancient myth: Retter was Susano-wo, Chrissie Luna, woman on the moon, was Tsuki-yomi-no-mi-Kami, and Yuichi, or the scroll rather, was Amaterasu, who could only fully become what she was, could only come out of the cave, when the others recognized fully their blindness, the error of their way, the superior vision provided by the light of the sun compared to the light of the stars and the moon.

14

Just because Yuichi was in jail didn't mean that Karl-Heinz Retter had abandoned the idea of turning him into a celebrity. To the contrary, dear friend, with Yuichi out of the way, on ice, it would give Retter a chance to get the head start he would need, to circulate unhindered, to set things up without interference according to pure reason and infallible laws of marketing. It wouldn't be easy, no project worth devoting time to ever really was, but it shouldn't be overly difficult either. Had Retter not, at one time, been the head of a studio out in Hollywood, making Swiss-themed shows for a Swiss-mad world? Sure it was a volatile industry, and sure he had slipped from sight, but there was not a doubt in the dwarf's proportionally overlarge mind that the name Retter, Karl-Heinz, would still make more than one suntanned, blow-dried, captain of culture quake in his lizard-skin boots.

On the other hand, no sense rushing things. The best schemes demanded planning, meticulous planning. Even a rank neophyte knows that to clear a hurdle of any consequence, you have to move back a few steps so you can take a run at it. Does a soldier go into battle without preparation? Did Hannibal cross the Alps without elephants? Of course not! Absurdity incarnate! And elephants needed food, and water to drink and bathe in, someone had to take care of that. That's what people never thought about. Why were the Arabs who came to Switzerland today all on welfare? Oh no, Karl-Heinz Retter was not afraid to ask the questions no one else dared! Did Hannibal go on welfare? Of course not. And why? The answer was simple: planning, meticulous planning.

Just to prove how much in control he was, to prove to the gods and his nosy, prying neighbor-with-the-telescope across the way that there was no need for haste, which everyone knows makes waste, Karl-Heinz Retter spent the whole first day after Yuichi's arrest in exactly the same way as he did every day, starting off, once he had collected the Yorkies, by taking the dogs to the park.

There, as a sort of warm-up, he let them run free while he sat back on a bench, hands behind head, the picture of leisure, clucking at the various pathetic specimens and their children. Watching as they pretended to enjoy themselves chasing balls of all sizes and shapes. This was one thing he would never get over about America. Chasing balls left and right was an exercise intended to be character-building, but all you had to do was look at the result: the greedy little freckled mongrel bastards in their up-to-the-minute $200 sport shoes, and their only dream to grow up good enough so as to throw balls for money. As if this was a dream worth dreaming! Which one of the junior legends, which one of the little tyrants, even on Karl-Heinz Retter's worst day, the days he was crippled with gout, could beat him in a footrace down even a moderately crowded city block? Not a one, of that he was sure, not a one.

'Help us, jolt us back to life, turn us back into truly functioning democrats, teach us to dream real dreams, please Mr. Swisserland,' they practically cried out with every wobbly spiral and each hanging curveball. But Karl-Heinz Retter did not get off his bench for all that. Did he look like a man in the habit of giving alms to the poor? Did they take him for one of those low sorts, one of those unspeakable ruffians who gained personal solace from distributing pity?

No, he was just a man looking for temporary diversion, and although there was little unexpected in the exercise, it gave him no end of pleasure, from behind his newspaper, to watch his dogs break up the games of catch and touch football, to watch the way they ran off with the balls, shaking their heads, savaging the leather or plastic, digging the canines in as deep as doggedly possible. As for the way the players laughed happily, the way they got down on all fours and growled at the dogs as if that or their "Here fellas" would get the cherished sphere back: it was only further proof of exactly how beneficial ball-throwing was for the rational faculties.

And then of course, if the dogs actually bit, which was what, in certain extreme circumstances, he had trained them to do, *mein Gott*, there was always such a circus of running around and self-righteous fathers squealing, putting on the hard-and-manly act. "Who does this dog belong to?" they invariably said, then stormed around putting on faces intended to look fierce and outraged, as if a finger-puncture were some great tragedy, some sort of *casus belli* crisis, forgetting that even in times of crisis good grammar need not be abandoned. That the *Dativ* case still exists even if little Adam the prospective homosexual, or Sylvia the neurotic accountant-to-be, or Dougie, the future crybaby lawyer, should lose the fingers of both hands and a couple of toes as well. "To whom does this dog belong?" said Karl-Heinz Retter merrily under his breath, getting up from his bench and smacking a certain Swiss newspaper on a polished-shiny *Lederhosen* left buttock with a loud crack which made ten very different dogs come running. "Why don't you just guess, Mr. Smith. It'll be good training for the election this Fall. Which candidate is the best? Just guess, Mr. Jones. Ha-ha, ha-ha."

To throw off any would-be pursuers, spies, fifth columnists and sex addicts, Karl-Heinz Retter took a circuitous route to Greeley's Western shop, a horse-riding equipment place near Macy's where he intended to purchase his costume. A route so circuitous, (involving, by pure chance, ten full passages in front of the Japanese ambassador's residence), that the stock of little black plastic pooper bags on his belt dwindled to a perilous few. (Had he been there, the ambassador would have been treated more than once to a nifty display of Retter's unparalleled scooping technique, hand in bag, catch the nuggets as they fall, before they hit the pavement. Who else had such a height advantage as to be able to pull this off? What other dog-walker managed such an enormous savings in Kleenex and dignity? Who else had such scientific feeding methods as to guarantee nuggets from the dogs, and never slush?). A route so circuitous that he arrived at the riding shop after dark, just as the hired hand was closing, a process which the impertinent lummox, the walking intestine, the Kindergarten failure, did his best to assure Karl-Heinz Retter was absolutely irreversible... Until the wee man from MAD, very calmly, very quietly, opened up his charm, full bore. "Dear friend. Do you think the Koreans close their shutters and go home when opportunity knocks? Dear friend. Do you think the Koreans decline a chance to make money when one presents itself? Dear friend, is it possible that you not be versed in the very wise dictum to the effect that the client is always right, dear friend, or are you just part French? Do you think a client, dear friend, would be inclined to return to your insignificant and quite out-of-the-way shop when treated so rudely? I ask you this, dear friend, do you want a Korean in the White House?" One to five, rat-tat-tat, more pure reason under whose charm the pimpled throwback in question, base clerk that he was, finally could not help but fall. Aided, one might add, by the geographical panic and confusion created by the mention of *two* foreign countries virtually in the same sentence, and by the fact that each enunciation of "dear friend" was accompanied by a general showing of fangs on the part of two Yorkshire Terriers owned by the Countess of Effington and Vulgargrad, two poodles named Fluffy and Light owned by Roberto (Bunny) Sella, the obese stockbroker, a Doberman and a dachshund owned by Wella Balsam, the movie actress, and a Labrador, two cocker spaniels named Laurel and Hardy, a Lhasa Apso named Euripides, and a Pekinese, owned, in order, by the publisher of the Clarion, by the heir to the Colgate-Palmolive fortune, by a dentist named Goldberg, and by the wife of the Austrian consul who called her little Peke "Monsieur" and used him as a flat-nosed sex toy in the noble tradition of the empresses of the Chinese court.

Picking out the costume was no problem at all, Karl-Heinz Retter knew exactly what he wanted. A new pair of von Stroheim-esque Little Man riding pants with the Jodhpur hips, another Western shirt with fresh pearl snaps shiny enough to blind a man at ten paces and an out-of-the-box pair of Little Man knee boots with shiny leather so exhilaratingly fresh you could almost hear it moo. But did he rush through his choice? Did he pick the chosen items off the shelf and hurry to pay? Not likely. He made the ill-mannered clerk bring him a dozen things he didn't want before even deigning to point to the things he did want, which was not only just, but the best way to lower the price. He tried each boot on, fluffed each Jodhpur hip to view from every possible mirrored angle, polished each pearl snap and held it under the spotlights until the impudent clerk reeled dizzily. Now was the time to hint that the transaction *might* be possible if the proper pecuniary considerations were applied. A point which the poor dense fellow was apparently constitutionally unable to grasp.

"My dearest Bobby, do I resemble the sort of person who pays retail?" Retter brought his fist crashing into the side of the counter. If there was anyone who looked less Jewish than Karl-Heinz Retter, Retter would like to meet him, but in front of the uninitiated, pretending to be a member of the tribe had often paid off for him. "Perhaps you'd like to try again, my dear friend, Bobby."

"Bobby" tried and tried, but by the fourth time ringing up the bill, he finally lost it altogether, insulting the cash register as if its missteps were not his fault alone, then, even worse, the last straw, double-checking himself by counting on his fingers in that most unpleasantly silly way Americans had. Not starting with the thumb like any normal human being, but starting with the index finger, then the middle finger, ring finger and pinkie, then, at last, the thumb. As if the number five and the number one were identical! A display so emetic that Karl-Heinz Retter had no choice but to inform him: under no circumstances did he intend to hand over good money to such an impertinent little pimple-squeezer, and who did he take him for, dear friend? The world was overrun with charity cases who thought they were owed something, and overrun even more with stupidly-sympathetic souls joining in on the conspiracy, this plot against humanity and all that was noblest. But Karl-Heinz Retter did not intend to go along for one minute, not one nanosecond, and so what if he had to return to the shop tomorrow or the next day? He would return as many times as necessary to make his point, no compromise. With ten virtually identical, if not quite so fresh, outfits from past campaigns, he could afford to be as patient as necessary. And if the Japanese monk, or even the Japanese ambassador had a problem with that, as they say, then to the devil with them too. Who was the Japanese ambassador anyway but a slanty-eyed hypocrite with a cocktail smile like all diplomats? Need Retter point out that the middle syllable of ambassador was "ass?" And Sharpeis? Karl-Heinz Retter laughed out loud in scorn. What were Sharpeis really other than a poorly-planned excuse for a dog? All that quite useless skin like a New York City socialite before plastic surgery, a genetic error, a breed recognized world-wide only thanks to sinister cabal, and back-room-manipulation by various Zionist-leaning kennel clubs. A shameless drool factory kept from extinction only by horrendously severe misunderstanding of the word "cute."

In the fresh, crisp, new copy of the *Neue Zürcher Zeitung* Karl-Heinz Retter managed to find downtown, a minor miracle, the lead headline was *"Selbstmord Tragödie,"* a headline so large and enticing, "Suicide Tragedy," that Karl-Heinz Retter just had to read the article on the spot. It was the same news that Chrissie Luna was to hear two days hence in Atlantic City, but delivered early, thanks to various moles at the Center for Disease Control in Atlanta. Swiss moles working for Swiss Intelligence, (what a mellifluous phrase that was: Swiss Intelligence!) and for various Swiss pharmaceutical companies, in the interest of getting a jump on the competition for the treatment of any new disease that might come down the road. That little head start which meant the difference between financial health and ruin. As for the word "tragedy" in the headline, any fool with even half-a-European sensibility would understand it was not intended as a trick to stimulate the morbid sentimentalism of the potential news buyer. Even the most random, doddering *Gymnasium* dropout would grasp instantly that the word was intended in its purest, most precise philological sense, referring to eschatological inevitability in a decaying culture, rather than anything to weep or wail about.

Apparently, according to the Center for Disease Control, the real number of New Year's victims was closer to 10,000 than 2000, but the rules about suicide were quite strict: coroners were not allowed to count deaths as suicides unless explicit verbal or nonverbal intent to kill oneself, or implicit or indirect evidence of intent to die, had been demonstrated. Which meant that Johnny not only had to figure out a way to kill himself but had to remember to share his intentions as well, which, big surprise, *Ja*, was apparently quite a bit more than Johnny could manage.

But while this certainly made for messy statistics, Karl-Heinz Retter was not one to look a gift-horse in the mouth. A gift-horse! He laughed happily, inadvertently slapping the newspaper on his thigh at his so-fantastic pun. Ten dogs came screeching to a halt, ten legs lifted in perfect symmetry, ten bold streams coursed out in the middle of rush hour ankles, whose owners, once again, tried their very best to show outrage and anger. Not that Karl-Heinz Retter chose to notice. Let them commit suicide too if they weren't happy -- pathetic, anonymous, pointless, statistically-unverifiable suicide. Which one of them could even understand a bilingual pun like *Gift*-horse, let alone be able to come up with it all by themselves, and not only while walking faster than anyone in the five boroughs, but steering ten dogs as well? "In German, *Gift* means poison, dear wet-ankled friends," he announced in his most condescendingly didactic voice, pulling a dwarf-handful of quarters from his watch pocket and throwing them carelessly into the air. "Buy yourselves some tissues, *Ja*?" he snorted, dismissing them with a supercilious, impatient backhand wave as if to say, 'now, please, out of my sight.'

Ten thousand people killing themselves in one night? Karl-Heinz Retter tried to calculate how many similar nights it would take to produce a planetary cleanup worthy of the name, to effect a proper pruning of the human tree. To cull the last of the pimple-squeezers and thumb-suckers, the body-piercers and drug addicts, the Sodomites, welfare parasites and wrinkle-nose laughers...

15

Chrissie Luna hopped off the bus at Port Authority, and with a very business-like stride distanced herself from Jim O'Brien and the hand-job he had insisted she give him on the bus, looking for a cab while trying her best to appear like was not carrying $21,534, or even a rounded off $20K in her purse. She half-hoped that Yuichi would be waiting outside her door so that she could apologize to him immediately for leaving him so high and dry, and half-hoped that he was dead, which would be sad, but would certainly make her life easier.

Inside the cab, she had almost managed to convince herself, feminine intuition, that outside her door was exactly where Yuichi would be, but when it turned out that she was wrong, that he was nowhere in sight, she decided that it was only because he had managed to sweet-talk the super into letting him in to the apartment. First she would give him a good tongue-lashing for invading her privacy, and only then would she apologize for abandoning him. But a tad less volubly, that was sure, and without quite so great a show of contrition.

When even that scenario proved to be wishful thinking, no lights on, no sign of life whatsoever, neither there nor here, Chrissie Luna let out a big sad sigh "Ooohh." "He's not even enterprising enough for that," she said to the empty apartment, trying to shift the blame, but it wouldn't stick. The door clicked shut behind her, and she just stood there, overwhelmed by the heaviness, bag in hand, rooted to the spot, unable to think of a single reason to move, wondering if there wasn't something seriously wrong with her. Twenty thousand dollars in her handbag, just ready for the bank, and she didn't feel any better than this. "You've blown it again, girl," she said. Atlantic City, Jim O'Brien, her whims and defective intuition, shit, shit, SHIT, she tried to cry, but what was the point when you didn't have anybody, not even a cat or a goldfish to see your tears?

It was then that she noticed the furiously blinking red light of the answering machine on the wet-bar. "Ha!" she snorted, a laugh meant to sound sardonic but that didn't quite come out that way. Eight messages! So the machine was working after all. She dropped her bag and followed her index finger across the room to the "playback messages" button, resigned, ready to take the chastisement, the punishment, that someone as evil as her truly deserved.

"Hello Clissie?" The first message was from you-know-who, sounding so cheery and composed it made her grimace with embarrassment.

"Sorry," she said to the machine when the second and third messages also turned out to be from Yuichi, which made her feel even more guilty and rotten, causing a complete, abject confession: "I'm the most awful person who ever walked the face of the earth." A confession whose hyperbole she regretted when the next three messages turned out to be hang-ups, doubtless also Yuichi, which made her feel even worse than before except that you couldn't really say that you were the most rotten person who had ever walked the face of the rest of the universe, since, aside from the moon with the astronauts, she wasn't altogether sure that people in the rest of the universe even had to walk and it was completely meaningless to say that you were more rotten than the astronauts who had walked on the moon because, like, who wasn't?

Casting murderous looks at the answering machine, wishing she had never gotten it fixed in the first place, she wondered how hard it would be to pulverize it once and for all and even started looking around for an appropriate electronics-smashing device. All of which gave her enough time to hear the last two messages, which weren't from Yuichi at all, but from her work. A cryptic, but very real sense of urgency hinting at terrible problems. Big trouble which made her instantly forget all about Yuichi and his trivial, me-first predicament, his obsession about finding a place to lay his little freeloading head.

16

In the latter part of the 20th century, two megalithic cosmetics companies had divided up the world, making two men, ugly, vicious little trolls with padded shoulders and pony tails, very rich. In the business of disguise, Chrissie's company, Samsara Cosmetics, with its very exotic use of the human aura as a diagnostic tool to ensure the proper makeup, had quickly captured imaginations and markets in much of North America plus Northern Europe, those industrialized countries where the conditions of luxury, the poverty of culture and the generalized climate of boredom gave people a longing for the exotic, the erudite, the esoteric, regardless of how alien these were to their heritage.

The second company, Nigel Forsythe Cosmetics, which marketed a cheaper line of makeup called "Hope!" had adopted a tactic deliberately aimed at those excluded by Samsara, men and women in the developing world, and discount-class department store shoppers in the First World. The advertising made heavy use of supposed-to-be-classy English accents and galactic-caliber American movie stars, and suggested, subliminally (but not terribly subtly), that the use of Nigel Forsythe Cosmetics was the surest path to heaven on earth. A heaven of appliances and dazzling cars under endless fiery-red Hawaiian sunsets, of cocktails with parasols and fruit in them, of diamonds dripping off of ample ear-lobes, and pearls cascading down firm but infinitely soft, welcoming, modern cleavages. An image which apparently worked well on the target audience it was designed for, but which was so lacking in sophistication that any half-self-respecting user of Samsara was most unlikely ever to switch brands.

Between Willi Roth, the German owner of British-sounding Nigel Forsythe Cosmetics, and Raj Mikkelson, owner of Samsara, there was little love lost. As soon as their commercial rivalry had played out, as soon as the world had been divided up, customer allegiances had been reinforced, and fluctuations in profits had become no longer the result of anything that could be influenced by human hands, the rivalry had to move to new ground.

At first it was the women. Willi Roth fell in love with a beautiful Somali girl he noticed on one of his publicity safaris, and he showered her with diamonds and cars, treating her as the Hope! mascot in a way, until Raj Mikkelson was seen in public with a Sudanese model who was not only half an inch taller than the Somali girl, but had had two French *Vogue* covers and three *Elles*. Not to mention sufficient quantities of diamonds and cars from previous suitors, that Raj Mikkelson could actually save money on her, instead investing his love-dollars in public relations junkets to the Bahamas or Zihuatenejo so that the press could report to the world about just how enduringly happy and intimate Raj Mikkelson's love really was.

Willi Roth's feelings for the Somali girl flagged and finally disappeared altogether on the night he met a Danish film star named Vibeke Hansen. Not only was she half an inch taller than Raj Mikkelson's Sudanese "love," not only did she have bigger Danish breasts, three covers of People Magazine, one cover of Playboy, one cover of Time and about half-a-dozen TV Guides, but he had to lure her 42D breasts away from a rock singer with a 16 inch tattooed cock. An act of folly which gave Willi Roth an aura of virility so potent that two continents away Raj Mikkelson suddenly discovered he could no longer get it up. "My Somali girl was sweet, but she was just too young," Willi Roth confessed in a People article of his own, "With Vibeke it's different. We can talk..."

Raj Mikkelson tried for a month to call in favors and get the Sudanese model enough magazine covers to recapture the public's imagination and envy, but apparently even two *Vogue* covers, four *Elles* and two *Mademoiselles* could not compete with the powerfully seductive symbols of a 16 inch tattooed cock in Vibeke Hansen's past and the breasts in her present. So Raj Mikkelson gave the Sudanese model her pink slip and set his sights on a German model with so many magazine covers you couldn't count them. They were married in an enormous jet-set wedding on an island belonging to the late Aristotle Onassis, and they lived happily ever after, at least until the divorce, which was even better publicity than the wedding. "I can't help it," Raj Mikkelson's exclusive confession appeared in 60 different magazines worldwide. "I just get bored."

It was at the 1997 Cannes Film Festival, the 50th Anniversary, that the competition between Willi Roth and Raj Mikkelson moved from women to ships. Willi Roth leased a 120 foot yacht moored in the new harbor, inspiring Raj Mikkelson to pay a fortune for a 121 foot yacht to moor precisely in the neighboring berth. Willi Roth responded immediately by trading in the 120 footer on a 122 foot model with a helicopter pad and helicopter on top. The very next day Raj Mikkelson traded his yacht in on a decommissioned mine-sweeper measuring no less than 150 feet long, plus three PT boats which he decked out in Samsara colors and anchored in the bay in case Willi Roth and his ratty discount pony tail should decide to take a cruise.

Willi Roth responded by actually buying *"L'Espoir,"* a French Navy destroyer whose old engines were still young enough to propel the ship at a healthy 35 knots, if necessary. The bash on board the destroyer the night before the end of the festival was the best party in Cannes that year, more expensive than anything the Studios did. The decks were stocked with innumerable lovely long and lean ladies rented from any number of Parisian modeling agencies, the buffet tables groaned with lobster, caviar, Spanish fly and condoms, champagne corks popped until well after dawn, mega-watt movie stars reeled drunkenly, taking their clothes off and diving from the highest levels into the freezing water below. The fact that none of the geniuses died conking a head on a floating champagne bottle, or being mangled by a propeller belonging to the destroyer's busy tenders was nothing short of miraculous, and only contributed to the reputation of the party, to the salubriously Bacchanalian image of Hope! around the world. Some people said there hadn't been a party like that in the whole fifty years of the festival, not at the Hotel du Cap, the Moulin de Mougins, the castle at La Napoule, nor anywhere; the press said it was the return of the Great Gatsby. While this was not necessarily meant as a compliment, and the press coverage wasn't likely to have any appreciable impact on cosmetic sales one way or another, Raj Mikkelson, Mr. Samsara, was still livid, inconsolable, more broken than Humpty Dumpty himself. Vibeke Hansen left the party with a Sylvester Stallone-lookalike whose true identity she didn't discover until a good three weeks later, but even that bit of good news failed to put Humpty Dumpty together again.

The next two and a half years were a cold war during which both cosmetics companies acquired huge fleets of ships which circled the globe, ostensibly on promotional tours, but in reality caught up in a huge game of alliance-building and naval chicken. Up until last Wednesday this had been essentially without consequences other than to empty bottles, to decimate entire crustacean populations, to fill various government coffers and unload containers-full of surplus, free cosmetics. And then Time Magazine printed a cover of Willi Roth's new Belgian girlfriend, Betsy, with a title "Sexiest Woman Alive."

Two days later, Wednesday, January 26, off Dakar, Senegal, in the middle of another fabulous party, a large explosion left a jagged hole in the stern of the flagship of Nigel Forsythe cosmetics, *"L'Espoir,"* sinking it and the wife of the President of Senegal within minutes. An act followed mere hours later, quite a coincidence, by a Stinger attack on the helicopter attached to Samsara II, in which Raj Mikkelson was supposed to be flying but wasn't, thank God. A day of carnage by whose end, four Samsara ships had been rammed by Filipino freighters, and a full half-dozen Nigel Forsythe vessels had been taken over by pirates in the South China Sea, their crews and guests machine-gunned and the ships scuttled. All of which was only discovered because when the Thai Navy caught the pirates the next day, they found videos that the pirates had shot of themselves raping and shooting, loading crates of champagne onto their powerful launches and smoking Marlboros as the six ships gurgled, hissed, bubbled, tipped up, then slipped quietly below the waves in the background.

Disastrous though Chrissie Luna's personal life might be, her work, which she kept rigorously separate, was another story entirely. With a painter's natural sense of harmony and eye for color, and with her sincere conviction that Samsara makeup could truly help the rich-less-fortunate in this harsh world where appearance mattered so much, she came across as erudite, serene, Pythian, with vast control over a mysterious and important craft. The loud business voice which, in a social situation, made her seem so ill-at-ease, at work made her come across as the voice of authority and knowledge. The forgetfulness? No problem. Her agenda remained scrupulously up-to-date, not only with appointments but also customers' preferences, names of children and pets, and subjects discussed during each session. It was this ability to subordinate herself, to be truly interested, to ask questions which made people feel important, which virtually guaranteed that her customers not only swallow the makeup-by-aura fiction whole, but come back time and again. Gladly, they volunteered referrals, happily, virtuously, they opened their pocketbooks to purchase whatever new Amazonian potion or ecological skin cream Raj Mikkelson thought to peddle.

In a social situation, such was Chrissie's history, that she could never quite get beyond the sense that friendship or love could end instantly, for no reason whatsoever, and certainly not because she would be the one ending it. In her work, she knew they wouldn't fire her in a million years: Chrissie Luna, social misfit, was Samsara Cosmetics sales' biggest star.

When Chrissie finally got someone at Samsara on the phone, it was so much like a spy movie that she could not believe her ears. "Take a cab to 55th and 5th, you will be given further instructions when you arrive..."

"Excuse me?" she said, with an intonation of outrage, and a hint of "would you care to repeat that?" Were they trying to intimate that there was something wrong with her impromptu vacation? Did they think their star salesperson didn't deserve a bit of R&R? Or was this about her missed meeting with Raj Mikkelson. That would be interesting! After all she had done for Samsara, all the money she had poured into his pockets. Raj Mikkelson himself would certainly never complain about just one little missed meeting, not after all the meetings he had missed with her, but there were jealous assistants aplenty who might try and bend his ear. "Does this have something to do with..."

"No questions, just do what you're told. Put the phone down now, understand?"

"This isn't funny."

"Understand?" the voice said one last time, hanging up before she could answer.

Five cab rides to five different locations, 55th and 5th, 44th and 4th, 33rd and 3rd, etc... it took her before she finally ended up at the right place, an abandoned night club on the Hudson, where it seemed like everybody she had ever met in the company was already gathered, some looking somber and some just looking plain glum. Even Raj Mikkelson himself was there via live satellite feed, pony tail untied, ratty, greasy hair falling over deathly pale cheeks, cocaine-trembling hands clutching the wooden lectern while he collected breath and wits. A long pause which Chrissie was certain was only for her, Raj Mikkelson waiting for her to be seated, and not begrudging her in the least the meeting she had missed whenever that was. No wonder everyone was looking at her. Let them look, she thought taking doubly-long to be seated, brushing off the folding metal seat with a Hermes silk scarf, and lowering her posterior ever-so-delicately. Did any of them have as good a sales record as her? Did any of them have full license to take off to Atlantic City with a hot Irish stallion whenever they wanted, and for as long as they wanted?

Raj Mikkelson looked right at her, and no one else (why didn't that surprise her) waiting patiently for her to get good and comfortable. "Three words for you," he croaked, "This... is... war..." Winded, beleaguered, he opened his mouth again as if to add something, then shook his head, and stepped back from the dais, almost collapsing into the arms of his nurse. Chrissie Luna still had not the foggiest idea what this call-to-arms could possibly be about, but everything about the forlorn, broken figure on the screen, her boss, the visionary who had created Samsara Cosmetics out of nothing, screamed of pain and treachery, of a world spinning dangerously out of control. A feeling so powerful, so gut-wrenching, so overwhelming, that a sudden, involuntary sob escaped from Chrissie Luna's throat and she had to bite her lip to keep from bursting completely into tears right then and there. If Raj Mikkelson needed soldiers, he could count on her, in the name of everything that was decent, in the name of American initiative, in the name of human dignity, in the name of human values, she would show him she was worthy. He had waited for her to arrive before beginning his speech, he had looked right at her. She would not let him down.

17

They warned Chrissie Luna to be extra vigilant, to screen new, and even old, customers mercilessly by asking for their phone numbers and calling them back, once, twice, thrice, until she was sure as sure could be that they were who they said they were. They told her to keep makeup and makeup brushes under lock and key in a safe place to prevent tampering and they told her to purchase an electric stun gun to ward off potential assailants, because there was no predicting to what level the psychopaths at Nigel Forsythe Cosmetics might stoop, no telling when naval battles in far-away seas might evolve into guerilla warfare, urban sabotage, or direct targeting of Samsara employees and clients in New York City itself, company headquarters.

Such a picture of tension and imminent violence did they paint that Chrissie Luna almost didn't sleep that night, brow knitted and jaw locked from the torment of phantoms, heart racing from the hint of moving shadows, stomach knotted from the roar of moth wings a hundred blocks away. So shaken, so obsessed was she that the next morning, which looked no less normal than any of the other 14644 mornings of her life, she didn't even dare go outside to shop for stun guns nor take her Keno wad to the bank. And at lunchtime, when the super rang her doorbell to inform her, in the usual Minnesota-Scandinavian Brooklynese, just how many problems a certain Chinese fellow had created in her absence, Chrissie Luna wouldn't let him in the apartment but held the whole conversation through the door, her eye glued to the peephole.

"I'm not really feeling too well," she said.

"Yeah, lot of that going around."

"Yeah... Really?"

"Uh hmm. Yeah, you know, your Chinese fellow there, boy, he kept asking for you," he said as if it didn't even bother him not to talk face to face, as if he were used to talking to doors. "But I didn't let him in, no sir. He was furious! You let one of them in, they invite the whole family, next thing you know you got a sweatshop situation. And the sidewalk! Golly, you shoulda seen the sidewalk with all those dogs! Guy like that deserves to be in jail!" The super paused as if this were always the moment in the Chinese freeloader story when they opened the door. And indeed, although it looked like the super, the way he held his left hand behind his back, speed skater-style, and this see-what-I-done-fer-youse way of beginning to angle for a Christmas bonus even before Groundhog Day could not really be anyone *but* the superintendant, Chrissie Luna, still fully caught up in epistemological paranoia, could not be sure enough that it was the super to actually open the door. And even if it was the super, for instance, how could she know for sure that Nigel Forsythe monies had not already diverted his allegiances? How could she know for sure that behind his back he did not hold a long butcher knife just ready to stab her in the heart? Or else a huge baggie full of that red rat poison he was always spreading around, and which he would force feed her once he knocked her flat on her back, straddling her chest and cramming the little red pellets into her mouth until she couldn't help but swallow? Which, she thought, after a week or whatever in Atlantic City with Jim O'Brien, was honestly even less appealing than the knife. "I'm really not feeling too well..." Chrissie Luna said, hoping he would take the hint.

"OK, well, hope you feel better then," the super said, shrugging his shoulders. "You need anything, you just let me know, OK?"

"Will do..." Chrissie Luna looked through the peephole long enough to see that he wasn't, in fact, carrying a butcher knife in his behind-the-back hand. But that didn't mean anything. It could be tucked inside his belt, or fixed by a garter to his leg, his pockets could be overflowing with rat pellets or anthrax. Or nerve gas, small and odorless, you could inject it under a door and flee in no time flat and no one the wiser. Nerve gas! Chrissie Luna clutched her throat with both hands and began retching. "Air!" she said, gasping, like someone waking up in the movies might say 'Coffee!' "Air!" she croaked, falling to her knees and crawling to the window. "Air!" she squeaked, raising her arm as high as possible and lunging for the window handle, just in time to discover that she didn't feel so bad after all.

As for the bruises on her neck from the auto-strangulation, a little Plum No. 2 base and some light blush would take care of it for all but the most discerning, sharp eyes. And as for the sharp-eyes, well, too friggin' bad, get a life, you didn't go to Atlantic City on an outrageous Dublin-or-nothing love-week extravaganza without collecting a love-bite or two! She picked up the phone and called the super, letting it ring and ring until he finally picked up, out of breath. Yes she was feeling much better thank you, yes it is quite miraculous, the powers of recovery of the human body, yes probably is the weather, stranger and stranger nowadays, but what was I going to say? Oh yeah: what was that about the "Chinese" fellow? Back in jail? Uh huh. Um hmm. No, just curious. Any idea where? No, no, just wanted to make sure. Can't be too careful, can you?

18

In the *Kojiki* it is related how, after Amaterasu locked herself in the Heavenly Rock Dwelling leaving all in darkness below, eight hundred deities appeared in the Plain of High Heaven to attempt to entice her back out. They placed a large mirror in front of the cave, then proceeded to sing and dance, such a fine noise that Amaterasu could not help but become curious, as they knew she would.

"Why do you rejoice?" she asked from inside the cave.

"We rejoice," they chorused, "Because there is a deity more illustrious than Thine Augustness." And they showed Amaterasu her image in the mirror. Astonished at this sight, Amaterasu, who had apparently forgotten what she looked like, forsook the cave in the attempt to get a better view. And when she had gone out far enough, His Augustness Grand-Jewel quickly drew a rope across the mouth of the cave behind her, saying from now on she must go back no further than this.

Back in the holding tank after the arraignment, grateful for the prospect of a little time to reflect, to take stock, a little bit of life reduced back to the austere basics, a promise of an unvarying routine and no subtle tyrants with hidden agendas to adapt to, Yuichi thought about O Sensei telling them the story of Amaterasu time after time, offering it, like the tale of Izanami, as a symbolic account of the actual historical event: the occultation of the Great Knowledge, the sealing up of the Word of God inside a cave. Except for the part of the story where Amaterasu came out of the cave, which O Sensei insisted was meant as prophecy, referring not to a historical fact but to an event in the very near future. Eight hundred odd lunatic deities dancing in front of the United Nations, each of them praising a more powerful god had not brought the sun out, but sooner or later, one way or another, Amaterasu would come out of her cave, the scroll would have to be delivered, of that Yuichi was sure. Such a vital bit of knowledge could not possibly be kept from the human race much longer. It was as apparent as the stars, the moon and the sun.

The only real question now was one of timing. Why could Izanagi not look at Izanami, and why did she seem putrescent when he did? Why did the Bible call Jehovah a masked god? Because the truth of things must remain hidden until we are ready for it, until we are truly worthy. When the time was right, Amaterasu would come out of the cave, and there would be 800 deities dancing and raising their voices in praise to a more illustrious god. There would be a rope stretched behind her, a rope made from the strands of the world's dreams and prayers. And there would be the mirror at the mouth of the cave, the wisdom of the heart, imperfect, two-dimensional, but already rooted enough outside to lure Amaterasu out. Maybe the "Book of the Earth" was only the reflection of the Great Knowledge, the mirror with which Amaterasu would believe she was already outside, but whether it was Amaterasu herself, or just the reflection, Yuichi was once again certain he would get it where it had to go.

After 28 days here, true, the only thing he had really managed to accomplish was to leave the scroll lying comfortably in a vault at the Susano-wo City Bank, but no need to worry. Perhaps he had been too passive up to now, or not smart enough, perhaps, in the attempt to show his hosts, his angels, gratitude and humility, he had overdone it, he had not asserted himself enough. Perhaps he had failed to listen to the lesson they were trying to teach him: that Susano-wo, the star god, didn't respond to gratitude and humility. Not to worry, as soon as he got out of jail, he would take care of everything, not a second wasted.

But did Mr. I've-Been-Too-Passive have a plan for getting out of the joint? For paying the $20,000 bail the arraignment judge had ordered as a recidivism surtax? No, no other plan than patience, and the conviction that a solution was sure to be provided sooner or later, when the time was right.

A bit of illogic sure, but we all have an Achilles' heel, and Yuichi wouldn't be the first to demonstrate that too much concentration on matters celestial is not always the best preparation for Western philosophical rigor. Let alone the realities of New York. Furthermore, illogical though Yuichi's tactic might be: what was the alternative?

Of the 800 saviors arrested New Year's Day, the prisoner on the bottom bunk, Reverend Y, the flat-knuckled, anvil-fisted ex-boxer and head of the Church of Apocalypse, Profanity-Allowed, had better reason to be paranoid than most. Ever since he had heard the call of the Lord, hung up the gloves and begun to preach about the upcoming War of All Against All, the New York City Clarion, needing a focus for a subscription-boosting crusade, had rolled the dice and chosen him as the prime incarnation of end-of-century malaise and frustration. At 6'5" and 260, the ex-boxer was a big, seductive target, no doubt easier to hit than most of the more anonymous malcontent visionaries running around hawking similar apocalyptic visions.

At first, the Clarion merely mocked him, satirizing his pinch-me-if-this-sounds-familiar notion of the cleansing virtue of future conflict, his retread vision of the new world in which past injustices would be redressed, in which the downtrodden and the righteous would finally rise to their appointed place. But if irony and satire, tools apparently too subtle for a new Millennium, helped swell Reverend Y's flock, attracting fight fans, people of color, the homeless, just about anyone who felt that the labels downtrodden and righteous might apply, irony and satire did nothing to increase sales.

It was the paper's conservative columnist who finally hit the nail on the head, dubbing the ex-boxer "Reverend Hate," and turning him from just another lunatic into the scripture-spouting vulgarian that White America would probably be obliged to eliminate if ever it hoped to sleep well again. An illusory threat, a looming shadow, which not only achieved the desired goal as far as the paper's circulation was concerned, but soon, predictably, in time-honored fashion, fired the imaginations of every anonymous, self-pitying racist in the lower 48, every sorry soul for whom the crusade against the monster offered sudden purpose. The more cowardly sent hate mail, and made anonymous phone calls; the more daring slashed his tires and spray-painted death threats on the walls of his Harlem apartment. But it was when one of the yahoos firebombed a church meeting in Providence, Rhode Island, killing one person, and leaving third degree burns on six others, that the FBI finally got involved.

Badly in need of a public relations boost after a number of dry years and embarrassments in the changing crime landscape, they set up a new religious surveillance branch at the Bureau. To outsiders, including the liberal columnist at the Clarion, the news that there were now guards on duty around the clock to protect Reverend Y, was confirmation that America worked after all, government by and for the people. But you didn't have to be poor or Black and you didn't need a PhD in conspiracy theory to understand even before New Year's Day, that the sun glass Boy Scouts in the last row jotting down the more rabble-rousing, seditious passages the black man quoted from the Book of Revelation, were not in attendance either to protect Reverend Hate or for personal inspiration, so much as to get the goods on the big bad nigger so that when the time came he might be properly lynched in a court of law.

Until New Year's Day on the North Plaza, they couldn't touch him, not for tax evasion, not for draft resistance, not for rape, not even for jaywalking. And the more The Man tried, the more the Clarion horn blew, howling for his head, the more the simple folk, the hungry and the dispossessed lined up, saying things like, "If it's true, it's true, ain't nothing you can say," and "It's gotta be true, otherwise why would we be here?"

But then came New Year's and the riot, and what had been a game for the Reverend suddenly turned serious. Apparently, as he saw it, people in high places had decided that things had gone far enough. High enough places to spare no expense to plant 799 lunatic extras at the UN and bring in a platoon of armored lackeys to crush them. A platoon which, Reverend Y couldn't help but notice, jumped off the goon trucks, vaulted over the whiter targets standing at the front of the plaza, and headed straight for him first.

But they could not silence the truth, they could not hush the prophecy. And even though they had managed to subdue him, and cart him off to their jail, the Lord had veiled their eyes and he had slipped through their fingers, out on bail before they knew it. Except then, a week later, just minding his own business, the same Boy Scouts in sunglasses had surrounded him again, this time arresting him on a trumped-up charge of turnstile-jumping. Although this did little to diminish his paranoia, he could see the Lord's hand here too and did not resist. For clearly, what the Lord wanted was for him to spread the word to the brothers in the hole.

But did he get him a brother for a cellmate so that he could further the holy mission? No, somehow he ended up paired with a Jew. Ninety nine point nine percent of the men in prison were brothers, and he had to end up with a Jew. And not just any Jew, but Nat Gold, the most talkative damn Jew since Jeremiah, including Groucho Marx.

"Oy, oy, oy," Nat Gold started up the minute the cell door clanged shut, climbing up to the top (not the middle) bunk of the triple-decker cell with an exclamation of pain on each rung of the ladder, as if the climb were a walk-on-glass Calvary, an ordeal worthy of the North Face of Everest. "I got this stiff neck, you know? You ever get that?"

"Nah," Reverend Y tried to make the man understand he wasn't in the mood for chit-chat.

"How 'bout carpal tunnel syndrome?"

"You can shut the fuck up now," Reverend Y said, but he was wrong.

Nat Gold couldn't shut up, because Nat Gold had a little secret: up until 20 years ago, he hadn't been Nat Gold at all, but a skin and bones, dyed-in-the-wool Baptist redneck name of Billy Joe DuPre, who, having swallowed a bit too deeply some pissin'-on-the-campfire wisdom about how the Jews ran the world, had decided to move north to Jew York City and become as Jewish as possible himself.

A difficult apprenticeship, which sometimes Nat Gold pulled off better than others. Sometimes the transformation was so thorough, so successful, that there were days when Alabama and Billy Joe DuPre were completely forgotten, days when Nat Gold was even more prone to Jewish-self-loathing than a Yeshiva student addicted to Chinese food. There were entire years when Nat Gold, for example, had the time to invent for himself a colorfully horrific mother and a matzo-ball-soup-cooking wife named Sarah with a loathing for sex and a constant need for plastic surgery. A wife named Sarah, (be careful what you wish for, because it might come true), who one day appeared in (soon-to-be-tucked) flesh and blood to complete his transformation by refining his understanding of persecution. And all, thanks to Sarah's revulsion for anything related to sex, (including sharing the same soap or bathroom) without having to get his own pecker sliced, hold the applause.

And then there were those days, always at a *bris* or a Seder, just when you thought he was gone forever, that Billy Joe DuPre would pop up again, stewed to the gills on Rebel Yell, wearing his yarmulke askew, like Gomer Pyle sings Hanukkah, and say things like, "Puhsonally, ah ratha enjoa be-an eu crastkilluh." Be that as it may, over the last twenty years, "Nat Gold" had become a master of calculation and subterfuge, far more evolved, he was sure, than anyone with the misfortune to be merely born Jewish. Anyone who, by definition, only had one persona to conceal, compared to Nat Gold's two.

Within seconds of walking into the prison cell with the large black man, Nat Gold had pieced it all together, done the math, grasped the situation, and implemented his plan. While he could think of a dozen reasons why, just on principle, Reverend Hate might take offense to him, reasons including being Jewish, being small, being white, being in the slammer for domestic abuse, not being Black, and being Jewish, this was as nothing compared to the two dozen reasons he could summon for Reverend Y to take offense to Alabama Billy Joe DuPre, loose-cannon redneck who might at any moment feel an irrepressible urge to share some insulting peckerwood verity regarding men of color.

After fifteen years of marriage to his Sarah, a woman who turned deaf the minute he came within five hundred feet, Nat Gold was no longer the most talkative man. But he felt instinctively that the only way he might get out of this particular situation intact was to keep up a steady stream of chatter to convince the good reverend how squintingly harmless, weakly insignificant and downright pathetic this being called Nat Gold really was. Not just flashes of Nat Gold, not Billy Joe DuPre *playing* Nat Gold, but Nat Gold one hundred percent and, this time, no mistakes, more Jewish than Abraham, more Jewish than Maimonides, Martin Buber and the Baal-Shem, more Jewish than Sammy Davis Jr. And that's why he couldn't shut up.

"You know what they got me for?" Nat Gold said. Sarah drove him absolutely mad with her demands, then beat him up, called the cops and had him locked up for domestic abuse. He hadn't really intended to mention it, but...

"Do I care?"

"Do you care? Do I care? Does anyone care nowadays? My wife, Sarah, for example..."

"I do not care about your damn fool wife..."

"No you're right, you're right..." Nat Gold scoured his mind for a subject to keep the conversation going. "You know what the worst part is? She had plastic surgery..."

"You want to give it a goddamn rest?"

"And the doctor, he..."

"Maybe you don't know who I am?"

"...messed the whole thing up." If anyone knew who Reverend Y was, it was Nat Gold. And knew not only who Reverend Y was, but Julius Vaughn, which is what Reverend Y called himself ten years ago, back when he was the WBC number three ranked heavyweight contender, a man with such massive, powerful fists that once, as a publicity stunt before a fight in Chicago, he had killed a steer with a punch to the forehead. Nat Gold studied the sports page religiously, Mister, Nat Gold watched the fights on HBO, and even went to the Garden a few times a year. Nat Gold could give you statistics: 15-0 record, 12 knockouts in the first or second round. Nat Gold even knew that when Reverend Y had hung up the gloves to heed the call of the Lord and start the Church of the Apocalypse, Profanity-Allowed, it was at least partly because his shoulders were too sore to continue fighting. Why else had Nat Gold mentioned about his stiff neck, if not, at least in part, to fish for enough sympathy so that Reverend Hate would not simply smash a fist into Nat Gold's forehead and kill him outright?

"I don't think we introduced ourselves. My name's Nat Gold?"

"You ever hear the story of the little white guy who comes into a prison cell with a big black man?"

"No..."

"Black man says, you want to be the wife, or you want to be the husband?"

"OK..."

"And the white man, he thinks it over, and says, well, I better be the husband. So you know what the black man says? In that case, white boy, get down on your knees and suck your wife's dick..."

"Right, well..."

"So shut up, all right? Last warning."

"Last warning, right, OK, gotcha. No problem there..."

It was then that the cell door opened to reveal the newest cellmate. "Yuichi," he introduced himself, bowing low, as soon as the cell door closed behind him.

"Sure," Reverend Y said, casting a murderous look at the upper bunk, then turning around to face the wall, first a Jew then a Jap. And not just any Jap giving him the old 11 o'clock bow, but the same slanty-eyed no account, the very same TV high-stepping, fucky-wucky doofus "arrested" with him January 1st. Not only that, but a Jap named Luigi! If that didn't smell like the FBI, he didn't know what did...

"Sure." Following the black man's lead, but just that much too late to seem entirely credible, Nat Gold took one bored look at Yuichi and, springs-squeaking audibly, turned his back to the door too.

"Ho?" Yuichi said. What was this now? Holding his bedding, standing immobile in the cell doorway, Yuichi, smile-frozen, confidence creaking, tried to imagine a proper response to such an incomprehensible greeting. But what was the proper comeback to such unexpected hostility, such an instantaneous and uncalled-for lack of humanity? A month ago, something like this would not have phased him. Even three weeks ago, he would have taken the affront and let it slide around him, *wakame*, rather than let it lodge in his gut like this. But now... Disgusted, he tossed his bedding onto the middle bunk, and just stood there shaking his head.

Did the ancestors think he needed yet another test, did they think he needed more obstacles in his way? Or were the ancestors hitting the sake bottle with O Sensei and laughing at the earnest little healer as he tried to fulfill his earnest little mission to save the human race? Was a little help out of the question? If he could materialize a castle, materialize a car, materialize a hole in the prison wall and a slide to freedom, these people would follow him in a flash, there would be the material proof of his power, of the truth of his path, proof they could touch and hold, and he would be greeted at the UN with open arms, instantly. But he had no such methods, no physical proof other than an imprisoned scroll in a suspicious hieroglyph. Nothing more than certainty reinforced by unorthodox, esoteric interpretation of a few ancient Japanese myths. And what could such ethereal notions as Amaterasu and a mirror possibly mean to men whose first impulse was to show you their backside?

Without calculation, Yuichi began suddenly to speak, inspiration flushing out self-pity, "One day, the Japanese Zen Master Tanzan was walking with the Monk Ekido when they came across a pretty young woman waiting on the banks of a river and needing to cross. Seeing her predicament, the Master picked her up without further ado, placed her on his shoulder and simply carried her through the strong current until they had reached the other side. There, the woman thanked him and they went their separate ways, the woman up the river, and the holy men downstream. But while Master Tanzan walked on deep in contemplation, Monk Ekido was consumed by dark thoughts. Had they not taken vows of celibacy which prevented them mingling with the opposite sex? he asked himself. What sort of master was this who succumbed to temptation at the very first opportunity? The further he walked, the darker was the cloud over his head. Finally Master Tanzan stopped and asked him what was wrong. The Monk Ekido told him exactly how he felt, and how he was beginning to wonder if Master Tanzan were really a master at all. Master Tanzan laughed as hard as a man could laugh, laughed until the Monk Ekido's ears had turned red. Then, when he had caught his breath, he said very simply: 'I carried her across the river, but you carry her still.'"

"So?" Reverend Y snapped, suddenly turning back over on the bunk. By rights, when a man stood behind your back the way Yuichi had, it was almost an obligation to take him out. But the ploy was too obvious, and Reverend Y had simply waited him out, this was one trap he didn't intend to walk into. First they send in the Jew for sleep-deprivation, then they send in the Jap... to tell bedtime stories? Today's FBI was taking some serious drugs. "What the fuck kind of story is that?"

"Story about anger, really, I suppose," Yuichi said.

"Story about anger?"

"My anger... your anger." Yuichi stretched his hands to the heaven, and brought them back to center.

"What about my anger?" Reverend Y rose to the challenge.

"You are an angry man, yes? Yes..." It was hard for Yuichi to miss: the large black man was blinded by anger, drunk with anger, you could hear it in his words, see the stiffness in his body from the *jitsu* condition in gallbladder and liver meridians. "Anger is good, anger focuses the concentration when you use it properly. But maybe anger is also like the woman in the story, and perhaps some people carry it much longer than they need to..."

"Next thing you know some goddamn Jap is going to be telling me what it's like to be a black man in America," Reverend Y got up from his bed and leaned back against the wall, giving Yuichi the before-fight-stare.

Yuichi reached out, put a soft hand on the black man's left shoulder and pressed so that the big man sat back down on his bunk. A move so smooth, with so much current flowing through Yuichi's hand, that Reverend Y didn't even think to resist. Yuichi shrugged. "We all have our reasons. Only question is, when we carry anger too long, who does it really hurt?"

"You keep talking bullshit, you might just find out who it hurts, bitch," Reverend Y said with a laugh, once again because he had to, but it was like his shoulder felt alive for the first time in years. "Man, you too much."

Now he saw what was really going on here: the FBI had sent the monk in to pretend he was Mahatma Fucking Gandhi himself so as to try and convert Reverend Y to nonviolence. That was their plan, sure, crystal clear. What they wanted was to put his balls in a jar, transform him into some kind of soft-palm Martin Luther King. Cause once that happened it was open season, some jarhead down in Mississippi (or wherever) would take out his hunting rifle and blow Reverend Y's motherfuckin' head off. And nobody would do a damn thing about it, no cities would burn, and there would be no War of All Against All, because all of his followers would be sworn to nonviolence. And if him as MLK wasn't about a fucked up liberal-white-boy-wet-dream, Reverend Y didn't know what was. Nothing against Martin, but the suit just didn't fit.

"I tell you once, you no hear, I tell you again. Carry anger too long, who it really hurt? Too much anger wreck body, make tendon stiff. Japanese medicine say, you want to heal world, first you heal yourself."

"Bullshit."

"I fix for you. You want me fix, you tell. I fix if you help..."

"Is that so?"

"And we fix you too, Misatuh Einostein," Yuichi added quickly, effectively deflecting the black man's resistance.

"My name's not Einstein," Nat Gold protested, but Yuichi was not diverted from his purpose.

"Inside, you laugh at him," Yuichi nodded to the top bunk. "You think you superior. I read you thought and you listen maybe a little. But you too have problem inside and you blaming everybody else. You scared, you tired, and tired make you impatient, someone talk to you, you yell. At night you groan, right? Sadness so deep, is not even tears. Don't worry, we fix..."

"How you know that?" Reverend Y asked, that got his attention. For the most part, Reverend Y had managed to silence his cellmate by intimidating him. But as soon as he fell asleep, Nat Gold did indeed groan, all night long, and the black man was feeling punchy from lack of sleep.

"I just know..." Yuichi answered.

"You can stop him groaning?"

"Problem in kidney meridian."

"You stop him groaning, I'll get down on my knees to you."

"We fix shoulder, you get down on knees."

"OK Mahatma... Let's see what you can do..." Reverend Y said.

"Take off shirt."

"What did you say your name was, Mahatma?" Reverend Y asked, taking off his shirt as requested.

"Yuichi." He gestured for him to sit down on the floor.

"Luigi, right. Tell me something, Luigi..." Reverend Y said, one last thing. "What exactly you in here for? If you don't mind my asking."

"Here for kicking shit on a Mormon."

"Kicking shit out of a Mormon," Nat Gold corrected him, with a little paternal chuckle.

"No, kicking shit on a Mormon, sorry." And so saying, before going to sleep that night, Yuichi treated Reverend Y's shoulder, then moved Nat Gold onto the middle bunk and filled him so full of energy that it silenced his groaning, allowing the Reverend to get his first good night's sleep in ages.

Strangely enough, that night, as if pacified by the truce radiating out from the epicenter, in the rest of the prison, the other inmates also let the tension go down a notch. And it wasn't just one night either, but the next day, and through Super Bowl Sunday with its Apocalyptic showdown between Titans and Sheep. Bit by bit, a semblance of peace began to overtake the overcrowded jail as one after another potentially-volatile situation was defused by hardened criminals and guards slipping into Japanese Ebonics.

"Hey murafuck!"

"You tocka me murfuckel?"

"Daslight Nigloo."

"Don't you be carr me nigloo. You no know who you tocka."

"I'm tocka guy who mama a plostitoot-hore-srut."

"You mama too, onry when I done she feer so good she folgetta chalge me. And nine month raytah, you boln."

19

Karl-Heinz Retter made four exceedingly unpleasant trips to Greeley's Western on four successive days before he finally walked away not only with the little costume he had picked out but with the greasy owner's greasy assurance that the revolting young salesman would be fired within the fortnight, *and* a little chit allotting him a free hem job at a nearby tailor. The free tailor, a most unpleasant fellow as it turned out, no surprise, not only disliked dogs, but acted as if physical contact with a dwarf made him queasy. Karl-Heinz Retter made sure to hunch his back even more than normal while the tailor made the tucks on the back of his shirt which did nothing to improve the fit, but was, once again, a question of principle over petty personal comfort. If Karl-Heinz Retter didn't teach this pin-mouth a lesson, who would?

Back in his apartment, with the costume finally firmly in hand, Karl-Heinz Retter moved the living room furniture to the side, opened the windows wide, and fortified by the cold air, began to rehearse his approach, holding an imaginary phone to his ear and dialing the imaginary Los Angeles number of Hristo Boromirov, the Bulgarian executive producer of "Johnny Woops," the film in which he had starred so many moons ago. No need to go through the "who's calling, please hold" bit with the secretary; he dialed straight in to Boromirov's imaginary private line.

"Hello?" Retter imitated Boromirov's cabbage-choked accent.

"Retter..." Retter imitated Retter, and most excellently, even if he did say so himself.

"Karl-Heinz Retter! Eat me. Haven't heard that name for a while. I thought you were dead..." Retter rolled each "R" mercilessly, made each "H" sound like the hag of Sofia spitting her rotten lungs out.

"Naw, that was the other guy."

"So what you been up to?" the imaginary Boromirov asked, naturally he would be curious. Retter knew the bastard wouldn't be smart enough to see the potential in the monk, but he shouldn't be too far gone to understand that any business proposal coming from the mouth of Karl-Heinz Retter must be taken with utmost seriousness. That if Karl-Heinz Retter had done it once, he could most certainly do it again.

"I'm an actor's agent..."

"Really..."

"...One actor in particular, martial arts, that sort of thing... *Nein!*" Retter fell out of character, slamming the phone down. It was no good, no good at all. It all sounded too forced, too much like desperation, not nearly smooth enough. If you couldn't make them feel that you didn't really care about what happened, that you had only adopted a certain project out of boredom or because you had nothing else to do, they wouldn't listen to you for a second, not even half a second! Not to mention, he had that same neck-crawling feeling that the mongrel across the way was once again watching him through his infernal telescope. Wouldn't he be surprised when Karl-Heinz Retter moved out to a place with no one across the way? When the monk's ascension to Hollywood superstardom would pay for a new apartment in the Empire State Building, or Trump Towers. A place so high up that not even the pigeons could see you, and you could scratch your balls and pick your nose at whatever time of day or night you might choose.

Thus fortified, Retter immediately (but nonchalantly) placed a second imaginary phone call, to Dagmar Zwingli, the director of "Grandmother Heidi," the smash hit TV show which never would have been born if Mr. Karl-Heinz Retter, had not founded a rival to the AC Nielsen television ratings company, the dearly-departed William Tell Ratings agency. A rival with a more Swiss approach to basic values, part of a long-term strategy to spread a more Swiss approach to culture across the whole wide television world. (And in the process, to cut off the tentacles of mindless, anything-goes, improvised, imperialistic-mongrel American culture at the root.)

"Dagmar baby," Retter permitted himself this almost obscene familiarity right off. He knew she had a crush on him, an obsession which he might at the time have allowed her to consummate with extreme sexual violence had he not been otherwise committed to an all-encompassing, consuming fantasy involving Shirley Temple. "Dagmar baby." Surely she would understand and respect one of the rare faithful men left on the planet. "There's something I want to talk to you about. I don't suppose you happened to pick up any of the gossip rags recently? Happen to notice a little item about a certain actor with not-entirely-round eyes? Well..." Click! The imaginary phone connection went dead. The ungrateful hog-washer, the insufferable strumpet. Dagmar-Quagmar hung up on him! She hung up on Karl-Heinz Retter. After all he had done for her. An outrage! Scandalous! Well, she would be sorry, very sorry, he would make sure of that. Nobody treated Karl-Heinz Retter that way. Nobody!

20

Chrissie Luna's decision first to look for Yuichi, and then, once she had determined his whereabouts, her decision actually to make up her mind and invest her Keno winnings to bail him out and bring him back into her life was accelerated by the need to present herself to him before the "hickies" faded completely. An arbitrary deadline to be sure, and she knew it, since at any moment she could easily fake another nerve gas attack and throttle some fresh bruises onto her graceful swan neck, but a deadline nonetheless without which she might never have worked up the courage to leave the apartment. The way Chrissie Luna reckoned, deliberately bruising yourself was a tactic uncomfortably close to self-abuse. And self-abuse, like the TV doctors said, was one of those things that if you did it once, you might well do it again until it became a habit. From there to turning into a statistic, Chrissie Luna also reckoned, was probably no more than a tiny baby step, if that.

Thus $20,000 in, $20,000 out, early Monday morning, January 31, (while the rest of the country wallowed in post-Super Bowl depression, and religious scholars on TV debated the eschatological significance of Titans being beaten by Rams), after only four nights in jail, Yuichi was freed again by the very same impaired angel as before, leaving behind one amazed, grateful Reverend from the Church of the Apocalypse, Profanity-Allowed, whose sore shoulders, thanks to Yuichi's healing touch, felt as good and loose as they had in the prime of his boxing career, and who was about ready to give Yuichi a Nobel for curing the Jewish man of his groaning.

Craning her neck awkwardly to show off the "love bites," Chrissie Luna flopped down on her couch, kicked off her shoes and rested them on her Isfahan rug. Let Yuichi get his own drink this time, let him worry about her for once, do him good. It had taken her a lifetime of romantic setbacks but this time she had learned her lesson. This time things were going to be different. Let him ask her about Atlantic City, and what kind of lover Jim O'Brien had been. Let him inquire about the cosmetic wars, and what it was like to live your life in the shadow of the Grim Reaper, let him know that there were two parties to this deal here, and sometimes in life you have to compromise. $20,000 was $20,000, not that money mattered, but she couldn't wait to see what show of gratitude he intended to muster for twenty large.

"I tried to get the scroll from the bank."

"Nice try!"

"But they wouldn't give it to me."

"Is that so?" On a gratitude scale of one to ten, so far he was at about minus thirty.

"Chrissie, you must understand!" Yuichi snapped, looking ever-so-earnest, so earnest that she couldn't quite stifle a laugh. "I cannot get scroll unless you sign."

"Hmm," she said. That's right, they *had* co-signed the safe deposit box. "Oh I'm so sorry," she said, except that she wasn't so sorry at all. Wasn't this an unexpected windfall? "I think I'd like a martini, you know how to make a martini?" She didn't smoke, but it occurred to her that if she did, this would be an ideal time to light one up and blow great calm smoke rings in Yuichi's direction. "I had a long few days in Atlantic City, you know?"

"Oh, Atlantic City."

"And I was thinking I felt kind of like a massage."

"Ho..."

"On my bed? What do you say?"

Yuichi said nothing, but simply turned and walked softly towards the bedroom, resigned. What was the alternative? Surrendering to blackmail was tricky business, but Chrissie clearly had an advantage she intended to use, and the only question now was how much time he intended to waste before giving in. A month ago he might have worried about the purpose, on a cosmic scale, of this latest complication, but now it hardly mattered. A full *shogatsu*[2] month he had spent here and still not come close to accomplishing his mission. He didn't feel attraction for Chrissie, he didn't feel revulsion

---

[2] Japanese New Year

nor much of anything in between, but he understood that they had evolved beyond "Chrissie, I am not a man." If the way to the scroll passed over the poor woman's body, if he had to carry her over the river, then the time had finally come, so be it.

At first Chrissie wanted Yuichi to be Jim O'Brien because when O'Brien made love to her there was no pretense and no dignity, (what was she thinking, 'made love?' when he just took her, plain and simple), and that had helped awaken her animal side. Making low cat growls, clawing playfully at the back of Yuichi's neck, she followed him into the bedroom, turning off the living room lights as she passed. Unhooking his bag, she slipped it over his shoulder, and when he turned around, she pulled him into a kiss.

"Wait!" he said, pushing her tongue out of his mouth, struggling out of the lip lock and moving her back to arms distance. Turning her around gently, he unzipped her dress and clumsily unfastened her bra, then pushed her over to the bed by the right side, pointing for her to kneel by the pillow, facing him. Which she did, sucking in her gut and hitting the bedroom light switch to plunge them into darkness. "No..." he said, "Lights on." Slipping out of his robe, he walked to the bed by the left side and kneeled down on the foot of the bed, across from her.

"Is this some kind of..." Chrissie was getting nervous.

"Shh. Must find holiness in other. Izanagi and Izanami, man speak first, OK?"

"Go on."

"Love union is like creating the world. Must see the other, the fundamental difference, the one that becomes two which makes the world. Crose eyes..." He waited for her to close hers before closing his own. "Imagine a force that runs from the end of the heavens to the center of the earth. You are this force, this force is in you. Feel the force, feel the energy run through you, the wave. Coming in, going out. From deepest earth to the end of the universe... and back. Feel your feet glow with this force, feel your ankles glow with this force. Feel your calves, your thighs, your pelvis, your sex. Feel your stomach fill with this force, then feel the force in your lungs, your heart, your head. You are Izanami, I am Izanagi. We are holy. We are creating the world here." And saying this, Izanagi moved forward and kissed Izanami softly, ever so softly on the lips.

What if I get pregnant and the baby is a dwarf like in the story? Chrizanami thought to herself, wondering if the few nervous words she had said to him were a few words too many. What if Yuichi turned out to be a wife-beater, or what if he locked her in a cave and didn't let her out? What if it turns out he was sexually abused as a child, and in the middle of the night, instead of getting out of bed to give their poor deformed dwarf baby a bottle, he got up to molest him? Or, what if he were a mole, a plant working for a certain rival cosmetics firm?

"Shh Izanami, I am holy and you are holy. That's all you need to know."

Soothed by his voice and by his hands which he placed on both sides of her pubis, Chrissie finally relaxed and closed her eyes. The warmth of his hands rose into her gut and traveled down her legs, filling her with a delicious sense of well-being, of being in the right place. Her pelvis rose in little rhythmic waves, with an occasional spasm of pure pleasure. Slowly, ever-so-lightly, he lowered his body over hers, touching her nipples with his chest, then running his chest down her stomach before returning. Lightly, just as lightly as he, she ran her fingers down his ribs, grasped his waist, then ran her hands down to his buttocks. Her defenses melted away, her features softened, her lips turned red and soft, she lost for a moment the look of a beaten animal, she gloried in just feeling good: a moment of pure grace crossed her face. So wet was she that when Yuichi finally penetrated her, he slid all the way in to the hilt. She gasped and without even having to concentrate, began to come. "Sacred. You are holy Izanami," Yuichi whispered when she opened her glowing eyes. "Yes!" she whispered back, stretching her hands to the heavens and looking up at him at such an angle that the ceiling light produced a kind of a halo around his head. Yes! It had definitely been worth the wait.

21

Yuichi stepped onto Lafayette just as the first trucks were beginning to rumble by, turned uptown and set his collar against the wind. It was in winter also, fifteen years ago: O Sensei been giving the invocation, when the flame on the altar candle had suddenly gotten very small, causing O Sensei to fall silent. They had all watched as that flame remained that way for five whole minutes, tiny, unwavering, until O Sensei, trembling, had said, "If this is a sign from the ancestors, please let me know," and the candle flame had grown to over a hand in height, before becoming small again, like an eye winking. The weight in the room had been almost unbearable, the tears had flowed from O Sensei's eyes until his cheeks glowed. The ancestors had made their presence known, there was no doubt possible. The ancestors had confirmed, by their presence, by their manipulation of the flame that the path embarked upon was true and right, that the salvation of the world did indeed lie in the medicine, in the guardianship of the scroll, in the direction being followed.

In bed with Chrissie, lying there after the act, Yuichi's body had turned feverish, his blood had started to boil and no matter how he tried to calm his racing pulses, his pounding head, it was no good. He knew he would not be able to sleep there next to her. Waiting until he was sure she was asleep, he got up to take a shower, hoping that might help wash away his anxiety and soothe his troubled spirits. Which it didn't.

His sense of foreboding increasing from minute to minute, he paced for a while in the living room, then tried stretching out on the couch, before finally deciding to slip into his robe and go outside to get some air. If she discovered him gone, she would probably be hurt, but sometimes a healer's got to do what a healer's got to do. Had this union really been necessary? Would what he had managed to touch in her still be there in the morning? Or would there be consequences, an even stiffer price than before to pay? That's what Yuichi had to figure out. He needed to be alone, and he needed to walk.

If, as they say, there is no such thing as coincidence, then call it intuition that as a result of a troubled spirit and insomnia, Yuichi should set out on an aimless jaunt whose path should cause him to turn a corner and bump into none other than his Honor himself, Motowori, the Japanese Ambassador to the United Nations, out taking his Sharpeis for an early-morning run. *"Sumi Maisen,"* forgive me, the two men said simultaneously, proceeding to an exchange of civilities and identities which was virtually complete before the ambassador, whose night-vision was not the best, despite thick spectacles, actually realized this sincere, humble fellow was the very same madman whose televised New Year excesses had caused him such embarrassment. (Specifically, but not limited to, the assiduously-mocking attention of no less-worthy a figure than Marakchi, His Honor the Ambassador to Iraq.) But there was nothing mad about Yuichi in person, and it was hard for Motowori not to be seduced by the earnest look in his eyes, hard not to be infected, as they walked along, by the sense of urgency with which Yuichi explained about the ancient scroll, and his present difficulties with the American woman.

For Motowori, there was no question of making an international diplomatic incident out of this, calling in the State Department, etc... especially since, around the millennium, apocryphal scrolls had been a dime a dozen. Still you never knew, and if a little show of benevolent authority by the Japanese ambassador convinced the Luna woman to hand over the goods, what was the harm? Without even consulting his agenda, the Japanese Ambassador agreed to show up at 226 Lafayette at 8:30 that very night.

22

Karl-Heinz Retter had been obliged, temporarily, to assign his aspiration to be an actor's agent to one of many back burners on his very large mental stove, the imagined rejections on his imaginary phone calls had confirmed that the time was not yet ripe. But did this mean that his interest in Yuichi diminished? Did this mean that he just drew the curtains in his apartment, threw up his hands and got drunk on *Kirschwasser* until he vomited? Far from it, far from it. No, who else did you think was waiting outside the prison in a rented Cadillac with two-way mirrored glass and ten dogs sleeping in the back when Yuichi was bailed out? Who else, wearing the latest Oerlikon headphones, connected to the latest Oerlikon boom mike and cryptographic computer, followed the two of them to 226 Lafayette, and played cat and mouse with the meter maids until the sun went down and then some? Who else waited patiently outside, with the drug pushers, the pimps and the rest of the human refuse passing by, watching the on-off-on dance of lights on the fifth floor, listening to the synthetic speech reconstructed from the vibrations hitting the window panes, and imagining the worst, a miscegenated Kama Sutra tangle of sweating musky bodies, of frivolous passionate nonsense? The answer? Karl-Heinz Retter, and no one else. What do you think?

Ja, as far as the goings-on on the fifth floor were concerned, the animal impulse was not something Retter was exactly disposed to look upon favorably. But men were weak, and he didn't imagine there was any evil intent in such temporary diversion. On the other hand, when the bedroom lights went off, then the living room lights came on and went off again, and Yuichi himself slipped furtively out of the building? When he marched heedlessly, insolently uptown, and more or less precisely bumped straight into His Honor the Japanese ambassador and his two lazy, panting Sharpeis? Absolutely no room for forgiveness remained in Karl-Heinz Retter's perfidy-shattered heart.

O world rent asunder, o inhospitable vale of tears where real men, men of principle, men of standards, no longer had their place. O merciless, self-destructive Gaia determined to swallow her most noble spawn, o empty, friendless horizons. Where was one to turn in such a world? What was one supposed to do in such an endless wilderness, how was one supposed to act, where was a good reason to move at all, rather than just step out into traffic and end this miserable existence for good? To seal oneself below ground, to wrap oneself in the earth's warm embrace, to rest and let the storms and turmoil wash over one forevermore. What a relief that would be, to let mediocrity run rampant unhindered, to let actors and nutritionists become political figures unopposed. To let jazz men deal the cards and sports players and film directors crowd the pantheon, and just to be able to laugh at it all. To be able to laugh and know you had done your part, there was nothing left to do, no more futile striving, no more heart-break, no more grand visions dashed by shabby sorry spirits. A pity there was so little traffic at this hour, a pity that even in moments like these when past and future lay clearly open, pinned in front of the eyes like a worm-dissected, that Fortuna should not even have enough decency to grant a man like Karl-Heinz Retter the means to a respectable, dignified end.

And now? What was this? Dagger upon dagger, not only was Yuichi's conversation with the Ambassador of Rising Betrayal continuing, but they were actually walking off together. Did stoop-shouldered Atlas himself ever have such a load to bear? Could Atlas, noble Titan though he might be, even have imagined what a miserable horde ran rampant over this poor, helpless planet? Could Atlas have dealt with the Sodomites and the Cellulites, with the ocean of people who forgot to take out their wallets while waiting in supermarket checkout lines so that they might be ready to pay and not make everyone wait, with the beggars and the rat-people and the bicycle messengers, and the business-women on their way to work in stockings and jogging shoes as if no one was going to look at them, as if there were no such thing as taste and common-decency?

In fact, when all was said and done, exactly what did Atlas have to complain about with the planet on his shoulders like that and all the nastiness back behind him, out of sight, out of mind? Whiny old Atlas, Mr. Big-Shot Titan, Mr. I've-Got-The-World-On-My-Shoulders-And-You-Don't! How different was he from any of the other Greeks in New York City, the hot dog and *souvlaki* vendors with the hairy dollar-grubbing knuckles? The globe on the shoulders, sure, the muscle flexing, fine. But when practical push came to practical shove, would Atlas be able to stop crying into his hankie long enough to muster even half the wherewithal of the mere mortal, Karl-Heinz Retter? Would muscle-bound, hairy-knuckle Atlas be able to manage something so simple as to shift a rented Cadillac into Drive, fine tune an Oerlikon boom mike, and, with masterful discretion, pursue two baneful reptiles as they belly-crawled away back to a diplomatically-immune cave? Not likely.

Slowly, softly, discreetly, Retter wheeled the rented Cadillac between pothole and delivery truck, using every trick in the Book of Stealth to remain unseen. The dogs were beginning to give that full-bladdered whine, and Retter thought for a moment to let them void themselves right there in the back seat, after all, it was only a rental. *Aber nein!* Caught in the act of sacrilege, Retter slapped himself in the face as hard as he could. Pissing in a Cadillac! What next? What next! What if he had to keep the Cadillac beyond tomorrow, and he had to live with the stench of drying uric acid? What if he were to die in a car crash, and they pulled his body from the wreckage? The American newspapers would have a field day about the homeless gnome living with his dogs in squalid fetor, and by the time the President of Switzerland had managed to clarify the matter, to extract an apology, a retraction, it would be too late, the image of Switzerland would be stenciled indelibly into the collective mind. Oh yes, the sharp slap to the face had done him a world of good, had refocused his briefly clouded brain, his rancor, and not a moment too soon.

The two of them walking along like that chattering happily, and not so much as a hint of suspicion that Karl-Heinz Retter even existed. The quisling and the recreant: there was a pretty picture. Or not the quisling, since that was hardly fair to Quisling, noble Norwegian, poor reviled villain of the winner's history book, rather... What was the proper epithet? *Ja*! The scheming tergiversator and the spiteful fifth columnist with his spiteful, unwashed Sharpeis. And what was this? The ambassador actually handing the leashes of his mongrels to Yuichi? Enough! *"Mensch,"* Retter cried out in involuntary anguish, pounding the horn in a brief lapse of self-control, how much pain was one man built to bear? But even that desperate Klaxon, that anguished cry to the heavens, to Mount Olympus itself, deafening in the empty morning streets, failed to divert the two yellow men for even the tiniest moment from their smug exchange of buck-toothed shibboleths, from shameless duplicity and ophidian collusion, from the ambassador reaching into his breast pocket for his agenda, and artless Yuichi walking the Sharpeis for an entire avenue-to-avenue New York City block.

23

Chrissie Luna awakened around ten, surprised not to see Yuichi, but bearing him no grudge, happy in a way that he was not there to cling to her, the way she had feared he might. Last night when he had left, she had heard him, but she kind of liked him slipping away like that. It showed he didn't care too much, showed that he had still not been tamed, that he was still a hunter, a man. "The sun will not set today without Chrissie Luna getting that damn key made," she vowed. But the sun was not due to set for another six or seven hours: there was plenty of time. Coffee, shower, makeup, she actually caught herself singing, so glad was she that Yuichi had not been Jim O'Brien. She wouldn't go so far as to say his performance last night had been worth $20,000 dollars, but it hadn't been worth a whole lot less either. With hands like that, how could you not be a generous lover? She shuddered involuntarily at the memory of his touch on her thighs, in the crease of her leg, his kisses on her neck, his nipples on her nipples, and it was like he was at her all over again. He had played her like an instrument, made her insides hum, what was she thinking? He had played her like an entire symphony orchestra. Plus she was prepared to bear witness to anyone who wanted to know that what they said about Japanese men being tweezer-dicks just wasn't true, unless of course Japanese tweezers were just simply bigger than the ones she was familiar with.

She looked in the mirror and wondered if anyone else in the whole city felt as good as she did, and decided that no one did, because if everyone did there would be peace on earth instantly, and unless something had changed in the last hour or so, and the Late Morning Show hosts were lying, that clearly wasn't so. She would love him ten times a day if he wanted, she would never pretend she had a headache, she would always be ready when he was. The only thing she wasn't sure about, a very small thing, is that when he had given her all the pleasure she could stand, he had not taken any pleasure of his own, not that she could see at least. But she certainly didn't intend to let that get in the way of her good spirits on a sunny, beautiful, crisp winter morning.

With that in mind, she frittered most of the morning away doing a dozen little things around the apartment she had intended to do for weeks, dusting, watering the plants, scraping the grout in the bathroom, painting her toe-nails, and finally stepped outside to get the key made around midday. Caught up in romantic reverie, she gave not a thought to cosmetic wars; transported by the dream, she failed to notice a vengeful dwarf and ten dogs get out of a rent-a-Caddy across the street and pull in behind her.

Another thing about Yuichi: when he thought she had fallen asleep, he had snuck off to the bathroom, where he didn't just wash his hands this time, but jumped all the way into the shower, as if she couldn't hear the difference. Jim O'Brien hadn't taken one shower the whole time in Atlantic City, he didn't feel like he had to wash her off him. Maybe that's just the way they were in Japan? Let those without sin cast the first stone, she wasn't going to let it bother her. But as for the not coming inside her, that was something else, and for the moment she was working on two hypotheses. One, she didn't turn him on enough. Or two, as the instant shower suggested, even though Chrissie felt confident that she was just about as clean as you could get and still have it be sex, apparently he didn't find her clean enough to even shoot his sperm inside her, which was far worse. If his religion really forbid him giving her his sacred fluid, why didn't he just go to the sperm bank and spoo in a Dixie cup? Or, shit, if His Fucking Holiness found the idea of sperm banks used by normal people degrading, then lock himself in the bathroom and jack off into some Saran Wrap? Was that too much to ask? Was that too much?

Oh yes, he would get his key, no problem, but the scroll? That was something else entirely. She smiled to herself, enjoying a sense of power and control: now she had something far more important to forget.

24

Karl-Heinz Retter knew who Chrissie Luna was the instant she stepped out the door, the Izanami sweatshirt, the unmistakable lust-voice as she said good morning to the building superintendent polishing the intercom panel. He followed her at a respectable distance, all the way to the Grand Union and beyond, to the little sidewalk key maker just on the other side. "Keys? Ha!" Retter said to himself, reining in the dogs as Chrissie stepped in behind the only other customer and pulled out her key ring. The perfect opportunity! Who could get more keys made than Karl-Heinz Retter?

Apodictically, nobody. As for the nameless Japanese monk, he would rue the day he had ever crossed swords with Herr Karl-Heinz Retter, rue the day he had forced a little big man's hand. Sure, conquering another man's lust object was hardly a dignified occupation. Granted. But you can't have your rice-cake and eat it too, it was not as if the monk had given Retter a choice.

Practically oozing charm, but aggressively pretending not to notice the woman with the amphigoric name for a second, Karl-Heinz Retter slid into line behind her, brushing his thigh with the *Neue Zürcher Zeitung* so that the dogs surrounded her. Only after they had worked her over for a couple of minutes, softening her up, licking and snuffling, did he even let her know he knew she existed. "They seem to like you," he said with the most apathetic tone in his arsenal, giving her the love eyes, the raised eyebrow, the indifferent tongue in the cheek, his best little man Lothario look.

"They're cute." She smiled pleasantly, still too caught up in her feeling of well-being and power to react to the dwarf.

"They don't like just anybody."

"Really?" She smiled, pretending to be delighted as a sudden wave of how-could-I-be-so-stupid panic gripped her gut. Was this the result of the coupling last night? A gestation-free manifestation? Or worse, omigod, what if the dwarf were some strange, deformed Nigel Forsythe assassin? It didn't seem likely that an assassin would need ten dogs to do his work with him, that that was the best way to pass by unnoticed, on the other hand, there he was standing behind her in a line to get keys made and not a hint of actual keys on him. Perhaps the assassin's dogs were bionic, with hollowed out fangs dripping special dog-venom which could kill you inside of 30 seconds? If so, she was already as good as doomed.

"Really," Retter answered, pointedly ignoring Chrissie even further, checking his watch, forgetting Target One as he became irritated by Target Two, the key maker, some Spanish-derivate or other, trying his level-best to charm the other customer, a woman he probably only found beautiful because he could not see her too-large calves. And while his little key maker-puppet-show, his finding himself funny, his harmless banter was no doubt in Retter's interest, giving Retter more time to maneuver with *Fräulein* Chrissie Luna, Karl-Heinz Retter was not one to close his eyes to yet another lamentable example of decline in the service industries. Not from a locksmith, which was what? Little more than a licensed burglar, a Gypsy not to be trusted for a second. "He doesn't seem to be in a terrible hurry, does he?" Retter threw the words out casually, keeping his full disdain in reserve.

"No, he doesn't..." Chrissie answered, to be polite, discounting the idea of venomous dogs on account of the 30 second limit having passed, but keeping an eye on the dwarf nonetheless, in case he might be carrying curare-tipped darts tucked into a miniature blow-gun packed in his deformed little cheek.

"Keys are a very important thing," Retter said, glad to discover that they were somewhat on the same wavelength. "You have to be careful with locksmiths," he continued, winking to show that she really didn't need to be careful at all, since he was there. "Sometimes they make impressions of your keys, and follow you home to find out where you live."

"Is that true?" Chrissie smiled, figuring that if the dwarf actually had curare-tipped blow darts in his cheeks his speech would probably be even more slurred than it actually was, figuring that it would doubtless be far more likely for him to wait until she was distracted then whip out some nitroglycerine-ink fountain pen from his breast pocket and jab her in the back of the knee.

Retter just smiled back, as if words were unnecessary to underline how terribly deceitful locksmiths could be. Suavely, wriggling four stumpy gloved sausage fingers like a magician to get her attention, all at once he plunged his entire hand deep into his *Lederhosen* pocket. Chrissie Luna's heart skipped a dozen beats. Her face molded into a look of terror inspiring Retter, misunderstanding the look as adoration, to let the suspense last. A wink and a tongue in the cheek, the Lothario look again, before he finally condescended actually to extract his enormous key ring, jangling the keys as if to say: who knows more about locksmiths than a man with eighty three keys?

"That's quite a key ring," she said, but the sight had not assuaged her in the least. The fact that the ugly little man *did* have keys after all didn't prove a thing. The only people nowadays who didn't have keys were young children, homeless people and probably astronauts too, since none of the short-sleeve knob-heads at NASA could get their brains out of their plastic pencil holders long enough to think to sew pockets into the space suits. He could still quite easily be an assassin, just waiting for her to let down her guard. What, for example, was to stop him from dusting uranium-coating on the keys, then giving her an accidental paper cut and rubbing it in?

"Quite a key ring, yes, well said," Retter fired back, opening his arms as if to say: did you expect otherwise? "Perhaps we should find another locksmith in the neighborhood? One who would appreciate our business a little more?" Retter felt calm, collected, in control of his game, maneuvering her exactly where he wanted.

"Perhaps..."

"Genug!" Enough! Retter barked at the dogs, who had begun to get a little fresher with Chrissie than was really, honestly warranted. A smack on the thigh and they were back in ranks on either side of her, two straight rows of five aligned like steps, high to low, a second smack and they raised their legs, and start-and-stop five times, demonstrating superior bladder

control, gratefully let loose precise jets of urine, speeding up insouciant Miss Splatter-Calves' little flirting session by a factor of ten. "Ha! She never knew what hit her," Retter said.

"Huh?"

"I'm writing a book on dog-training," Retter shrugged, letting slip in all humility, as if to explain how absolutely common-place the extraordinary was in his orbit, then quickly cutting the humility short, now that the coast was clear, and turning his attention to the Puerto Rican locksmith. Retter's work was not done, not by a long shot.

"Do you know when the first keys were made?" Retter challenged the key-making upstart on his own terrain. Let the Spanisher know right off he was not dealing with neophytes here, let him know not to try any of his fancy behind-the-counter Gypsy tricks. "*Ja,* I didn't think so, didn't expect you would, ha-ha," Retter clicked his heels and pivoted away from the locksmith so that he'd know the discussion was closed, and that Retter's attention could under no circumstances, any longer, be diverted from his key-making Guinevere, Miss Chrissie Luna. "What, if I may ask, does the honorable lady do?"

Engaged in conversation about cosmetics, and encircled by the dogs, Chrissie temporarily forgot all about her fear of assassins, allowing herself to be lassoed for coffee, (where Retter got into an argument with the coffee-jerk about the history of mocha java), then lassoed for pizza, (where Retter chastised the waiter for his ignorance about Garibaldi and opera). Lassoed until she and Karl-Heinz Retter found out they actually saw the world in much the same way: that there were people out to get both of them, that it was terrible to be misunderstood, and that the only hope for this poor suicidal planet was the "little guy."

The Cosmetics Wars, her fears, she told him everything, feeling a trifle silly for mistrusting him earlier. He listened carefully, punctuating her lecture from time to time with words like "Fascinating!" and "Napoleonic!" which not only further demonstrated the vastness of his knowledge but sent chills of vindication down her spine and made her want to confess even more.

"I don't sound paranoid, do I?" She hoisted one last warning flag, with a little warning-flag laugh, just in case.

"Ha!" Retter snorted as if nothing could be more absurd. "Paranoid?" he shook his head reassuringly. "In my humble opinion, you're no more paranoid than I am, or than any person with half an eye open. Paranoia is just a word invented by Jewish mind doctors, ha, frightened by people of superior intelligence."

"Maybe so..." The thought that she might be "superior intelligence" after hearing for 40 years that she wasn't, opened the possibility of a whole new world to her. What would it be like to have a good personality *and* be intelligent? What would it be like to be full of self-confidence when you woke up in the morning? To walk down the street knowing that no one could look down on you? Funny that she should think "look down," when this poor Disney dwarf, this bleached Teutonic lawn jockey, this gnarled, deformed little leprechaun who had doubtless spent an entire life being looked down upon, had overcome his handicap to the point where he could look down on others. Such effortless confidence, such rapid-fire resistance to being taken advantage of, such a willingness to stand up for what was right and ethical and pure, such apparently masterful handling of all the uncontrollable events that made city living such a burden. Brief though their acquaintance had been, she had to admit that she already held him in true admiration.

And then there was that little something else, that intangible something that she had always heard about but never felt first-hand: when she was with him, she felt safe. And *that*, especially in light of the last few days, was one feeling she could definitely get used to. In fact, checking the master list of pluses and minuses, as they walked through Central Park, and the pups bounced happily away to play with the children, the only real blemish she could see on the proud wee man, an insignificant, trifling problem, was his almost inconceivable ugliness. Ugliness way beyond the call of duty, a phrenologist's nightmare, a face only a great-great-great grandmother could love. Or perhaps not love, but just barely tolerate if she were legally blind. Ugliness so monumental, an aura so black, an appearance so far from any norm in any culture she had ever heard of, that she had absolutely no idea what blend of Samsara earths, Samsara fruit tones, Samsara facial prosthetics, or Samsara plastic surgery one might use to counter-attack. Ugliness so spectacular that Chrissie Luna's armpits remained drier than the Sahara and the Gobi combined, and, perhaps for the first time in her life, she couldn't even begin to go down that old familiar road of imagining what their children might look like. Which maybe was just as well, for once.

"If I may say something?" Retter said, the picture of European gallantry.

"By all means."

"I must confess: I've never seen such conviction, such intuition, such wisdom in anyone who was neither a child nor a movie star."

"Really?"

"Really. May I invite you for dancing this evening?" He would have to start writing that book about talking to women.

"I haven't held a party for a long time." She decided that ugliness of such heroic proportion could not possibly be his fault. "I'd love for you to meet my friends."

"Excellent idea, couldn't be better."

"226 Lafayette, fifth floor, 8:30, that sound OK?"

"Madame..." Retter said, taking off his hat with a calligraphic flourish of the pheasant feather forming a heart and a question mark, then bowing his head, holding his hand out and backing away as 10 dogs, like Lippizaners, got down on one knee, pointing noses to the ground. "Until 8:30. *Bis später.*"

"Yes, until 8:30..."

At the Grand Union, feeling confident and alive, Chrissie was in that mood where she could easily buy the whole store out, but Celestina, the store astrologer, the voice of reason, intercepted her right by the shopping carts, before she could get fully to work.

"Aren't we in fine spirits today!" That was Celestina for you, perceptive enough for three.

"Why yes!" Chrissie prided herself on being good with signs, but Celestina was tops. No one ever guessed Chrissie's sign, but Celestina had done it right off the bat, the first time she saw her.

"For Capricorns," Celestina said into the microphone so that the whole store could hear, "Today is a day when you don't want to conquer the world. If you're having a party, think wine and cheese."

Celestina was right. A party was all about making impressions, like makeup, every subtle note had an impact and tonight she didn't want to send the wrong signals. Nothing too expensive, some wine, some cheese and crackers, and if the party got going, they could call out for Thai or Lebanese. "Are you free at 8:30?" Chrissie said to Celestina on her way out. "226 Lafayette, fifth floor, last name Luna."

Yuichi was waiting outside on the street when Chrissie returned. She flipped him the key cavalierly, what was the big deal? "Would you mind carrying these?" she said, handing him the grocery bags without waiting for an answer. In the elevator he told her he was inviting a friend over to meet her, and right in stride she answered that was good, because she was inviting a few friends over as well. In the meantime, she informed him that as much as she might enjoy a repeat performance of last night, right now she preferred to be alone. She had to be honest with herself, that's just the way she was feeling. "Meet me at the bank at 4:30, OK?" she said, while putting the kettle on for tea, but she knew even before she said it that she wouldn't be there. And he knew it too.

25

It was an entirely different Chrissie Luna greeting her guests that night, a Chrissie Luna radiating so much confidence and poise that for just a second her mother thought she had come to the wrong apartment. A Chrissie Luna who had put one I'm-too-special-to-share-my-sacred-gism-with-you Japanese monk right in his place.

Celestina Thompson, the Grand Union astrologer, arrived with her boyfriend Jack Bravo, unpublished millenarian novelist who headed directly to the hors d'oeuvres table. Banished Jim O'Brien, staring straight ahead with a sheepish smile, arrived with Chrissie's mom, intending to get her drunk on Black Bush, kissing the cow, as they say, as if to repair the boorish behavior with the daughter. Karl-Heinz Retter came with a bottle of *Kirschwasser*, a kiss on the air above the hand for Chrissie, a sneer for Yuichi and eight very pleased dogs. Motowori, the Japanese ambassador, dressed in a sharp gray flannel suit, successfully concealing his surprise at the unexpected size of the gathering with a diplomatic poker face, came with flowers, a sight so fragrant that Karl-Heinz Retter almost passed out. Never had world hegemony seemed so close. The Japanese ingrate monk had tried to pull a fast one, Retter would trap his viper, put horns on him and laugh all the way to the mausoleum. But no question of rushing things, Karl-Heinz Retter was no amateur. Let everyone else fall over each other trying to shake the ambassador's hand, Karl-Heinz Retter made a beeline for the kitchen, the most-geometrically distant point possible from where the ambassador had apparently decided to set up camp. The kitchen, the obvious power-corner. Retter's tactic? To watch the proceedings from afar and bring the party to him when the time was right.

A deceptively simple tactic only if you weren't Karl-Heinz Retter. For every successful tactic has two parts, the obvious part, und the less obvious. In this case, given the topography of the arena and the nature of the targets, Retter's less-obvious part-two involved gradually, patiently assuming psychological control of the party by using his canine infantry to make diversions and create havoc, to open up various avenues by steering unwitting guests into unwitting negative alliances, which is what you called it when two people were thrown together at a cocktail party in isometric limbo, neither one getting anything from the encounter, but neither able to leave.

Thus, like clockwork, would both Chrissie Luna and His Honor the Japanese Ambassador fall right into a precision Swiss trap. Ha-ha, ha-ha. Taking a deep breath and closing his eyes in concentration for the brief second he needed, Retter began sending telepathic thoughts to each of his canine faithful, who branched out immediately to the four corners of the battlefield.

Monsieur the Peke, the cocker spaniel named Hardy, Duffer the Labrador and Werner the dachshund cornered Yuichi by the stereo, giving him the eye, then with tongues and little nips progressively backing him up to the balcony, baring their fangs menacingly each time he tried to slither away, over towards Chrissie or the Ambassador. Fluffy the poodle, Adolf the Doberman and Laurel, the second cocker spaniel, chased each other, with a mock display of ferocity, through the legs of the dubious specimens fawning and scraping incomprehensibly around the Hong Kong-cheap suit-and-tie wearing Japanese ambassador. As if he were really something special rather than some sort of scrotum-licking testament to political payback not worth a second of fuss. Euripides, the Lhasa Apso and Light, the second poodle, roamed around alternately striking terror at the wet-bar, guarding the open door to screen the latecomers, and generally steering traffic through the first quadrant. A very efficient, streamlined double-tactic indeed, which left Retter free to pursue a number of side-interests while waiting for more serious situations to evolve.

First he telepathically challenged the millenarian novelist with the obscenely self-aggrandizing name to an hors d'oeuvre eating contest, and won, then he argued with him about the mythical Titan Atlas, of all things, whom the novelist insisted, in the original myth, wasn't carrying the earth on his shoulders at all, but was actually condemned to stand on the edge of the earth holding up the heavens as punishment for his revolt against the gods of Olympus. Which anyone knew, Karl-Heinz Retter above all, the other way around being a Tunisian heresy one adopted for the sake of convenience. (Just like, the times being what they were, one used the word "pathos" to mean illness, when the original notion meant anything but, for to do otherwise was to risk wasting a lifetime in pointless etymological haggling.) This line of inquiry, for some reason, led poor proud Jack Bravo (ha! Americans and their names!) to say that he found Retter to be quite negative, as if that wasn't negativity itself! And to follow that with a supposedly insightful little bromide to the effect of "Thought creates form," which Retter straightaway countered with "'Form follows function:' Frank Lloyd Wright," not only leaving the poor mindless aphid scratching his head, but giving Retter the opening he needed to cause the Lhasa Apso to herd the novelist's familiar-looking button-nosed blonde girlfriend over from the balcony to the kitchen, to him, on the off-chance that she turned out to be a higher-quality catch than Chrissie herself.

A possibility which, with a "Have we met somewhere before?" and a "Karl-Heinz Retter at your service," Retter quickly discounted. No, truly, the more Retter looked at Chrissie, smiling happily over by the dining area, queen of all she surveyed, the more he liked her. She wasn't perfection, that was clear, but at his age Retter no longer expected perfection, and thank god. In life, it's not as if one was ever presented five perfect mates to choose from, so that all one had to do was just pick out the one with the most pleasing constellation of beauty marks. No, as soon as others entered the equation, at least where romance was concerned, life became a matter of compromise. With this one you had to overlook a glass eye and a wooden limb, with that one, you had to endure educational lacunae, for example ignorance of social conditions in the Po Valley during the 14th century, with another, whimsical tastes and unreasoned prejudice, with a fourth, incontinence and a love of cats, with a fifth, excess facial hair, an unsightly bulge in the throat and an artificial vagina. That was life...

Whatever had caused Chrissie to allow herself to be seduced by the monk-snake, whatever mind-clouding mix of loneliness and fear had caused such temporary dementia, Retter had to be forgiving. But with the help of Fluffy the poodle and Hardy the cocker spaniel tugging cutely, ferociously, on various trouser legs, Karl-Heinz Retter could make sure that none of the male guests lured her way linger long enough for her to make a similar mistake again.

For two minutes and fifteen seconds, Retter watched people coming in the front door, watched them take off their wet coats and talk about the storm which had come up outside, listened to them discuss the changing weather and the sanitation strike with pitiful, lamentable earnestness. For three minutes and ten seconds, Retter amused himself by causing the four dogs assigned to the Japanese monk to herd him closer to Chrissie then closer to the Japanese ambassador, before herding him back to his spot at the balcony again. For four minutes exactly, Retter tried his best to convince the empty-minded astrologer and her weak-spined novelist boyfriend to bring their obvious mismatch to a merciful end. When this most generous bit of advice proved ineffective, provoking only resistance, Karl-Heinz Retter raised his hands, said "It's your life," which it was, thank God, and backed away.

It was at this point that Karl-Heinz Retter noticed he was beginning to feel a sensation similar to boredom. Not boredom itself, for what was boredom other than a vulgar sensation for distracted souls, but something similar enough so that finally there seemed no reason for Karl-Heinz Retter not to turn on his heel and unveil the real master blow, the technique only the finest-of-the-fine in the spy game had ever even thought of: the so-called triple-tactic. The triple-tactic, with the one obvious part, the second less-obvious follow-up and a third positively-hermetic conclusion, whereby the operative, invoking a certain flexibility of principle, leaves base in the power corner and begins to circulate after all.

Sneaking well below radar, inconspicuously picking his teeth in the Swiss manner, little gnome-hand pressed to tip of no-longer-so-little gnome-nose, Retter glided so softly away from the kitchen that the button-nose and her gloomy boyfriend didn't even notice. But as vivifying as it felt to step away from the kitchen, now that Retter was actually out in the flow of the party, it didn't look so pretty either. Hard to imagine how Chrissie could have managed to assemble a less attractive crowd, or how, for that matter, anyone with a roll of quarters couldn't go down to the Bowery any time of day or night and wrangle-up a better selection than this. On one side, by the open door, where a rotting odor as of garbage wafted into the air, you had a bunch of scythe-kneed newcomers, more weather-talking backsliders and reprobates who looked like they were in competition for the disease-of-the-month poster child. On the other side: the Japanese monk, almost tap-dancing to keep dog tongues from holy yellow feet while laughing that ridiculous laugh. A laugh which, wouldn't you know, once again seemed to lure the moon-eyed bubble-head astrologer right to him. Some choice that was!

To be honest? By this point Retter no longer really cared in the least what the Japanese monk might look like committing suicide. In fact, once Retter had made it through the forest of legs at the entrance, he decided that he could think of a thousand people he would rather see commit suicide than the monk, any number of them at this very party. Like the muscular young man talking with the older lady by the wet-bar, or the Japanese ambassador, or even Chrissie, who would probably look absolutely angelic taking her own life. Unless she decided to hang herself, in which case Retter honestly doubted that a thick, swollen, purple tongue hanging out of that weak mouth, dangling on that feeble chin, would really do much to enhance her attractiveness. *Ja*, which was less the point right now than the fact that the self-evident route through the social minefield, from wet-bar, via balcony (just to show the monk and the bubble-head his backside), to couch, to dining area described a perfect clockwise circle. Outside, rain lashed the windows with renewed vigor, lightning crackled and thunder almost instantly roared. And what other sign did a Swiss man need?

Chrissie Luna was relieved for once not to be thinking about herself, relieved that the open door meant she didn't have to listen to her idiot *"Getting-to-know-you"* door-bell chime, relieved that people were helping themselves to food and drink in a natural way that led her to believe they were truly having a good time, no pretending. What could she say? Everything was perfect. Celestina (Chrissie was certain Celestina would never think to wash her hands after touching her) brought her a glass of champagne then, bless her heart, proceeded almost single-handedly to take over the rest of the practical side of the party. Hippolyte, the French artist, (who she imagined probably never washed his hands ever) brought her a glass of wine, kissed her on both cheeks, introduced her to two French friends he had brought with him, informed her that he had changed his name to God B. Rented, ("Heet's a Fransh pon, *Dieu soit loué*, transleshun: God Be Praised..."), apologized for having insulted her wine last time then waltzed off to take care of the music. One of the freeloaders, who would never have talked to her before, (and who almost made her feel like washing *her* hands) exchanged her wine for a Sloe Comfortable Screw which almost made her gag, and stayed to watch her drink it while they talked about his boyfriend the serotonin junkie who was considering getting a sex change operation, and whether she thought a new makeup strategy might not be a better idea. "Not for my boyfriend. For me!" he said. When he took his leave, the boyfriend in question informed her that he was a musician with an Obscene Rock group, handed her a coconut daiquiri, and gave her an a cappella rendition of the new blasphemous trend in ObRock lyrics, a song called "I Really Miss You, I Think," in which he managed to rhyme "Wiener," and "Mary Magdalener." A song which came to a thankful close when Fluffy the poodle and Hardy the cocker spaniel delicately steered him away.

For Chrissie, the point was... what was the point? The point was, before she never would have had the option to like or dislike the song, because no one would have sung to her. The point was, when you decided you would no longer be looked down upon, life really did change. Holding tight to the feeling of intelligence, just believing it, really did seem to make everything different.

"Chris-sie..." Hands on hips, she mimicked her mother under her breath, the exact same maternal tone of exasperation and disdain, in case there be some last little humiliating detail, some error of taste or judgment her good spirits might have caused her to overlook. The food? The drink? The music? The furniture? The way Celestina had gracefully taken over the hostess duties? Or perhaps the attendance of the Japanese Ambassador? No, she couldn't find fault with anything, nor see a single sight that made her stomach knot, her heart fibrillate, her throat freeze up, her mind go blank or her good spirits dissipate. Not a single indication that the guests, one and all, hadn't succumbed to the influence of her mood, her new way of looking at things. Everyone was on the same wavelength, everything just flowed. Whether it was O'Brien taking care of her mother, keeping her out of the game, off her back, or the funny little man from Swaziland, bouncing, with a wave of his comical little sausage fingers from conversation in the kitchen, to conversation with O'Brien, then to an impromptu game of hide and seek. Whether it was Yuichi remaining over by the balcony, playing with the dogs, graciously allowing her to hog the limelight, (which, in spite of her inability to forgive him yet for the hand washing and the failure to come, she had to admit was a nice gesture) or even the Japanese ambassador, lending an aura of dignity to the proceedings, and with the occasional friendly smile in her direction, placing her, by association, on a pedestal so high she felt dizzy, everyone seemed to be lending a helping hand.

For the first time in her life, Chrissie Luna realized she actually was the center of the party, her own party. She held up her glass and spun around full circle, toasting each and every one of them. "I forgive you, one and all."

"We forgive you," the answer came back to her in a deafening chorus, or so she imagined.

It occurred to her that she should celebrate Christmas all over again, right now, without telling anyone, and this time, do it right. "Happy Birthday to me," she sang sweetly to herself, "Happy Birthday to me." After all she had worried in the last six months, about being alone, about how little she had accomplished in this life, how little of the world she had seen, about finding a man and making a family before her ovaries turned brittle and cracked, she could all-of-a-sudden stop worrying. Why hadn't anyone told her it was this easy? It wasn't going to be that bad being forty, not that bad at all. She promised herself she would never get depressed again.

In fact, overall, at this precise, slightly tipsy moment in her life, she could see only one problem, a very small problem which actually had very little to do with turning forty whatsoever: hand washing. When she had toasted the party, she should have said "I forgive you all, except for Yuichi." For his sake, she hoped the hand washing was just a Japanese thing. For his sake, his holier-than-thou attitude had better not be a less-than-subtle way of saying "Chrissie Luna is filth." There was one sure way to find out, and she intended to do just that.

26

Ever since his encounter with Yuichi on his run this morning, the Japanese ambassador could think of little else than the scroll. Even though, after a day's worth of research, the embassy staff could come up with no record that such a scroll as *Chi No Maki* even existed, (and there were even doubts about the authenticity of the *jindai moji* script, which some scholars apparently maintained was a fabrication) even though at times the whole thing, the meeting with Yuichi and his tale of woe, seemed like an elaborate masquerade, as the day progressed, Ambassador Motowori became more and more convinced of its authenticity, more and more excited about what such a scroll might mean in the right hands. Not that he was entirely immune to the hope that might be raised by a scroll with world-saving truths, but Motowori's interest was much less philanthropic, much less long-term. In fact, he was much more interested in the public relations angle, the political ramifications, the possibility that this scroll, whatever its contents, would by its very existence say out loud what he, as a diplomat from a country that had lost World War II could not say himself: that the sun did indeed rise in the East, that civilization had started in Hinomoto Kuni, the Japanese Holy Land, that Dai Nippon, the nation with the sun on its flag was indeed both the Origin *and* the Salvation, and that His Honor the Iraqi ambassador, with his Euphrates River valley, and his "Mesopotamia-cradle-of-civilization" crap, could just go fuck himself. And all that, put together, was certainly worth canceling a few appointments and a dinner.

From what little Yuichi had managed to tell him about Chrissie, and from what he knew about Americans in general, Motowori, who fancied himself a master manipulator, didn't expect it would really take more than a minute or two to get Chrissie fully to swallow that she alone of the six billion souls on this planet was preventing the salvation of the world. All he would have to do was to get her to acknowledge just how bad things were, and let her come to her own conclusions about whose whimsical behavior might be responsible for perpetuating the situation. In the unlikely event this failed to bring instant results, in the event she turned out to be more willful, more armored, or less sensitive than average, in the event she might need to have her sense of culpability stoked, Motowori had prepared a mental list of subjects to spring on her, including pollution, war, starvation, child abuse, the increasingly terrible quality of movies, and, if she didn't crack before then, even testing of cosmetics on animals. Once her guilt was at its zenith, it would be child's play to bring the full weight of his authority to bear on her so as to virtually oblige her to relinquish the scroll as soon as the bank opened again. As far as Motowori was concerned, the only real challenge, given the unexpectedly-large social situation at 226 Lafayette, was to find a means to isolate Chrissie long enough to make his point.

A challenge complicated slightly, silly and trivial as it might seem given the stakes, by Motowori's determination, once he had actually seen Chrissie face-to-face, (simple psychology, nothing more), to have the obviously-fragile woman make the first move and approach him rather than the other way around. An initiative which, an hour into the party, maybe more, in spite of any number of smiles shot her way between the unavoidable encounters with nearly all of her degenerate friends, in spite even of a few brief efforts to cut the peach nearly in two and meet her just a fraction less than half way along the ten feet or so separating them, she had still failed to take.

Having made the mistake with one Japanese man, the last thing Chrissie Luna intended to do was make the same mistake with a second one. She hadn't forgotten that old story Yuichi had told her, and this time, no matter what happened, Izanami didn't intend to go first. On the other hand, in a story that old, old enough to be a myth, she was certain there must be literally dozens of loopholes. For example, just off the top of her head, what was to prevent Izanami from using an intermediary to initiate contact? Celestina was over by the kitchen, why not? "Celestina..." she called out, waving her over.

"Be right there..." Celestina answered, turning off the faucet and walking over. "Everything OK?"

"Yeah, thank you so much for the help..."

"Ah, it's nothing, I actually prefer it. Parties make me nervous, it gives me something to do..."

"I know what you mean," Chrissie laughed sympathetically, taking Celestina by the hand. "Listen, I just wanted to introduce you to someone..." In a flash she had closed the distance between them and the Japanese ambassador. "Have you met my friend Celestina?" she asked Motowori. "She's an astrologer."

"Very interesting," Motowori said, thinking exactly the opposite but giving them the interested face anyway to put the two of them at ease. "What kind of astrology?"

"Celestina works at the Grand Union, giving people advice on what to buy..." Chrissie answered for her.

"Just a way to keep the wolves from the door," Celestina answered with a warm, self-deprecating smile so genuine that it took the starch out of Motowori's smile, loosened his spine, unblocked his ears and got the attention of Jack Bravo, jealous and clumsy millenarian novelist, who charged out of the kitchen area and slammed into Chrissie, knocking her into the Japanese ambassador. Not hard enough to do any damage, but not so lightly that the ambassador got out of it without using his hands. Delicate, finely-manicured hands with perfect nails which, Chrissie duly noted, casting a triumphant sneer Yuichi's way, Motowori did not instantly have to rush off and wash.

"Jack! Please!" Celestina said, slightly irritated, as if this weren't the first time this had happened, and they had already discussed it.

"Sorry, sorry. My fault..."

"Please Jack."

"OK, OK, no problem," he said, retreating to the kitchen again. Celestina smiled and shook her head then focused back on Motowori. "You don't believe in astrology, do you?" she said. "You know what? I don't either. But... Some things you can't explain. Am I right?"

"No doubt," said Motowori, diplomatically.

"You can say that again!" said Chrissie.

"Do you mind if I tell you something about yourself?" Celestina resumed with Motowori. "No? Because some people mind. OK, you are eager to leave the job you have now, but you don't trust enough, and so you try too hard. You are very ambitious, but the ambition will get in the way. Your wife died five years ago, I'm sorry, perhaps I should stop?"

"No, go on," Motowori said, but in such a sleepy, almost drugged, fashion that Chrissie couldn't help but wonder if maybe she hadn't bumped into him either quite hard or long enough for him consciously to realize that he needed to wash his hands.

"Yes, and ever since you cannot bring yourself to trust. You spend much time wondering if you are in the right position. You wake up every day and wonder if today is the day somebody is going to discover that you are bluffing, that you are improvising, that you have no great master plan and that you are reacting to the events around you. Am I right?"

"You have a very great gift," Motowori said, bowing respectfully

"That's nothing." Celestina laughed. "What I just told you describes 99% of the human race."

"Not about my wife..." He bowed again, averting his attention from Chrissie just long enough to provide the opening she needed to crash into him again.

"Hey!" Chrissie said, turning around in a make-believe huff, as if someone else had bumped into her. This time she made sure that his hands were all over her, around her waist, on her breasts, around her shoulders, and even on the skin of her neck, before breaking the clinch. "I'm so sorry," she said, stepping back like a bullfighter, clearing a path to both kitchen and bathroom sinks so that there be no obstacle whatsoever in case hand washing was the ambassador's true nature after all. "Are you OK?"

"Yes, very fine..." The Japanese ambassador smiled and bowed reassuringly, having concluded by now, to his chagrin, that the only way to get Chrissie alone, in a comfortable situation, would be to stay to the very end of the party and figure out a way to be the last one to depart.

From wet-bar to balcony, Retter was almost trampled fully three times trying to get through the ring of sycophants and parasites surrounding Yuichi at a respectful distance. But he took it right in stride, responding to each aggression, making sure to give as good as he got, leaving a host of bruised shins and astonished looks behind him as he blasted through the legs keeping him from his man. "There is only one secret to leading the world," flush with yet another mini-victory, he turned around to address them, quoting Napoleon himself, not that they needed to know that, "And that is to be strong, because in force there is neither error nor illusion, it is the naked truth."

Only now that he and Yuichi were virtually face to face, did Retter realize with a sinking feeling that he had not prepared anything to say. Under any other circumstances, this would not be a problem. A simple, casual conversation about the art of suicide would be more than acceptable as an introduction to the subject of Yuichi's career in the motion picture business. But circumstances being what they were, he feared such an approach just might be misconstrued. For even while dispensing his Napoleonic wisdom to the leeches, it had occurred to Retter that the last time he and Yuichi had actually been physically together was on the street outside this very apartment, when the poor innocent had been carted off to jail subsequent to the fracas with the Mormon on that memorably cold and shitty day. And what if the monk harbored some resentment for Retter's refusal to take the rap with him, what if he bore some grudge for Retter's failure to bail him out? Or, even worse, even more delicate, what if the monk had somehow espied him with Chrissie during their post-meridian revenge-tryst? That, or, through some sneaky sixth sense or other, what if he had become aware of the betrayal without even having to see it? That would certainly explain the coldness with which the monk had treated him since the start of the party, his palpable refusal to leave the balcony even once to say hello. For a brief moment, retreat seemed like the best possible solution, until Retter remembered who he was, remembered that for some people, retreat is not an option. The jail-question? The heart-question? Clearly, it would be much safer to face the consequences of the former than the latter, but the real master-stroke would be to hit upon a subject which would obviate the need to worry about consequences altogether. A subject containing implicit praise for the monk's skill as an urban warrior, for example, a subject appealing to the Japanese man's martial side.

"There's a spot just below the patella, right?" Retter said, sidling up to Yuichi without so much as a how do you do, "When struck properly, you can drop a man in a second."

"Ho?"

"And there's another spot," Retter continued, talking without moving his lips, as if that would make them co-conspirators of some sort and re-establish the bond of respectful friendship which unfortunate, unplanned circumstances had temporarily rent asunder, "Another spot," Retter pivoted around to face the party, but more importantly, to be side-to-side with Yuichi like primeval hunters, shoulder-to-thigh like real soldiers, "*Ja!* Just where the calf muscle forms a sort of upside-down "V", where a precise toe kick produces the impression of a harmless little cramp on the moment, but sets in motion an insidious chain reaction which, over the years, results in circulation problems, lethargy, memory loss and even nerve damage."

"Ho..." Completely baffled, Yuichi looked down at the strange little man. A look and a lack of response which Agent First Class Retter understood, in spite of his brilliant martial opening, to mean that the monk had apparently not forgiven him after all for the afternoon dalliance with Chrissie. Chrissie, good old Chrissie, who had fallen into the Japanese ambassador a third time, so hard as to knock him over right onto the sofa, so hard as to trip herself up on the lovely Isfahan rug, and land herself full-length on top of him.

"Do you see what I see?" Retter said, "Scandalous!" By this point, he felt, there was only one way to make amends for his temporary lapse of good judgment, and that was, as an agent and a friend, to deliver Chrissie from the clutches of the lecherous ambassador, and return her back to Yuichi unsullied. "I'll take care of this," Retter said, waving his hand back to Yuichi, as if to say "wait here," then, with a "*Latoria, latoria, zwilli willi wick juhairassa,"* setting his jaw in the direction of the couch and proceeding to march marchingly across the wooden floor as four roving rovers fell in at his heel. It was time for the truth now, time to tell Chrissie that after much agonizing thought he had seen that he and she were simply not meant for each other, that they were like planets, destined to remain in the same sky but condemned to stay in their own orbits. Like Mars and Venus, for example, or like the stars and the moon.

Impulsive behavior? Perhaps, but that didn't dim Retter's resolve, he had worried enough about consequences for one evening. If the libertine ambassador decided that a social humiliation was grounds enough to deprive his Sharpeis of the best attention money could buy, then it would be his loss. The Chinese ambassador had three chows Retter was sure he could lay his hands on in the blink of an eye. Not that three Chinese chows was ideal, far from it, Retter would doubtless be obliged to kill one of them to attain the natural symmetry that two Sharpeis (a Chinese breed, incidentally) would give him right out of the box. Not to mention that as far as world hegemony was concerned, one would have to be a little more patient, since China was still not on the industrial or political level of Japan. But dogs representing the one billion people of a sleeping tiger versus dogs representing 125 million (or whatever) panty-sniffing comic book addicts? Where was the comparison? Besides, Retter could leave the chows alive and kill the Lhasa Apso, why not? Given the Chinese-Tibetan question, the Chinese ambassador would probably insist on it. Sure! If such a scenario were not in the cards, if destiny itself were not calling out, how did you explain that chow, in Japanese, was said *sayonara?* A small detail which, it just so happened, Karl-Heinz Retter already knew. *"Latoria, latoria,"* he hummed confidently as if the victory were already sealed, *"Zwilli willi wick boom boom."*

Delayed in his crossing of the planks by the need to teach a new set of manners to three reprobates, a French weakling (Talk about a nation of bad actors!), Chrissie's upstairs neighbor the model, a backslider, a coward, two parasites, and a man with a falcon on his shoulder who introduced himself as Marco Polo then followed him across the room with the biggest set of blow-job eyes Retter had ever seen, Karl-Heinz Retter did not finish covering the four-yard expanse from balcony to couch before a good half-dozen minutes had elapsed. Time enough for a couch-worth tangle of bodies to become untangled, time enough to conceal any *delicto flagrante* enough to justify the kind of forceful, testicles-in-the-ice-bucket irruption that Karl-Heinz Retter would normally be inclined to use in the event of crimes of simulated public fornication.

Time enough for the Japanese ambassador to give a nifty demonstration of the Tokyo Two-step, trying his best to keep someone between him and the madwoman at all times, for fear that the next time she tackled him he'd end up with a broken rib. Time enough indeed for the conversation about astrology between the strumpet, the bubble-head, her impotent sire (who had come charging back from the kitchen) and the Japanese ambassador to have gotten around to something more serious, notably Celestina's preposterous claim that her psychic gifts included the ability to consult the Akashic Records, the etheric sphere in which all that has happened in the history of the earth is recorded, and all that will happen too.

"So you can actually read the future?" Chrissie said. "Wow!"

"She can tell you anything you want to know," Jack Bravo, millenarian novelist, answered for her, "Believe me."

"Like what sorts of things?" Chrissie asked.

"Whatever you want," Celestina took over, smiling modestly, like it was no big thing. "I can even tell you the day of your death if you want..."

"Really!"

"But I recommend against it."

Heedless of the grumble of discontent mounting from the latest alliance of sore-shinned, cramped-calved, crushed-patella'd antagonists hovering just the other side of the dogs, Karl-Heinz Retter needed not a word more to inject himself into the conversation. "And why might that be? Pray tell?"

"Oh hello," Chrissie said, with a genuinely warm smile which completely failed to pierce Retter's determinedly-icy facade. "This is Karl-Heinz Retter," she introduced him, "A most impressive man. I believe you've met Celestina and Jack? And this is Mr. Motowori, the Japanese ambassador."

Clicking his heels in the Prussian manner, Retter nodded stiffly to each of them, making absolutely no distinctions, except perhaps for the Japanese ambassador, whose eyes he completely ignored, and Chrissie. Not that Karl-Heinz Retter intended to be distracted from the astrologer's blatant challenge. Neither by Chrissie's see-through blandishment nor by the proximity of the Japanese ambassador, for that matter. "*Ja,* und why exactly does the lady recommend against a man knowing the date of his death?"

"Well, for one reason, because it can drive you crazy. Think how you would feel if you knew."

"I should think I should feel quite fine. I should think that a man who knows the date of his death would increase his efficiency tenfold. He would know there would be no time to lose..." Retter felt confident that he could continue all night in the same vein, about how the mystery of death was no doubt necessary for lachrymose poets and other hand-wringing sentimentalists, etc, etc... but he decided to save his breath. An audience of cowards was doubtless not the best company in front of whom to air such pellucid thoughts. "How much do you charge to tell someone the day of their death?" Doubtless the bubble-head's fear-mongering was nothing more than a marketing tactic, a carnival charlatan's attempt to squeeze as much out of a mark as possible. "Go on, say a number, come on, come on, no thinking, out with it!"

"You really want to know what day you're going to die?" Celestina said.

"I really do want to know what day I'm going to die," Retter answered, mimicking her ever-so-slightly.

"All right, how 'bout this? I'll tell you for free."

"I'm waiting."

"All right. You are going to die on October 23, 2010."

"There, October 23, 2010," Retter said matter-of-factly, spinning slowly, 360 degrees, hand out to the vengeful posse behind him and the rest too, like what was the big deal? "Am I any different? Have I gone crazy? No." Was that a look of admiration he detected in Chrissie's eyes? No doubt, no doubt, but that look was nothing compared to the look she would have to learn once his master plan was complete. The time was just about ripe to herd the Japanese ambassador off to the side and have a man-to-man talk about dogs.

As far as Yuichi was concerned, the Japanese ambassador, in and of himself was nothing special. Compared to other human beings, perhaps his life-will was stronger, perhaps his spiritual sense was diluted by a few too many years on the golf-and-whiskey circuit, perhaps, like many Japanese born after the war, he suffered from excessive nostalgia about the glorious imperial past, and perhaps, as an adolescent, he had worked himself into paroxysms, reliving with his fellows the humiliation of that unimaginable day at the end of World War II when the Emperor announced that he was not divine after all, but merely human, when the Emperor stepped down from the throne. But beyond that Yuichi was not the sort to be overly impressed by a politician, by that lower form of consciousness, that lack of judgment and vision that had resulted in this world-divided, this planet on the brink of disaster. While it had certainly been a relief to speak Japanese again this morning, to feel the safety and comfort of similar references, land-origin and world-view, and while the enthusiastic Japanese ambassador to the UN would doubtless be a valuable ally once the scroll was finally recovered, Yuichi had no illusions about them being on the same wavelength. Still, as a man of breeding and authority, a man presumably with years of experience manipulating other people to give him what he wanted, Ambassador Kato Motowori was probably the best kind of champion Yuichi could hope for, a man of charm and impressive stature, stature intimidating enough, hopefully, to get and keep Chrissie's attention so as to bring this long, unfortunate scroll impasse to a merciful close.

As the day progressed, nothing had dampened Yuichi's good spirits, not Chrissie's potentially unfortunate announcement that she intended to throw a party, not even the fact that any decision on Chrissie's part to hand over the scroll would have to stand the test of time all the way to tomorrow morning, when the bank opened again. What could go wrong? As sure as the sun rises in the east, the unimaginably fortuitous nature of the morning's encounter, the improbable line leading from Chrissie's arms, through the vast dark city, and straight to the Japanese ambassador, hinted at ancestral intervention. Which could only mean that after 32 days of abandoning Yuichi in New York City confusion, after the jailings, the trials, the incomprehensible game of social Go he had had to endure with forgetful Chrissie Luna, apparently Yuichi had learned the lessons he was meant to learn, apparently his long ordeal could finally come to a close. Which in turn meant that inside of 48 hours, if all went smoothly, he could be back treading Japanese soil again. In 48 hours he would be back in Japan: he could think it, he could say it out loud, he could sing it from the rooftops, there was nothing anymore that could get in the way. Unless, for some reason, the sudden appearance of a second Japanese man in Chrissie's life awakened suspicions of plot, conspiracy or manipulative collusion which only reinforced her conscious and unconscious resistance to relinquishing the scroll.

Precisely to insure against this, Yuichi had greeted Motowori as perfunctorily as etiquette allowed, introduced him to Chrissie then promptly retreated to the far end of the apartment to let the diplomat get to work. Unfortunately, in spite of Yuichi's grateful prayers to the ancestors of the five races thanking them for their great wisdom and compassion, it was not long before he began to suspect that the ancestors might not be done toying with him after all. For not only did Motowori-san fail to take advantage of the opening Yuichi had given him, standing by the couch for over an hour like a blushing schoolgirl, but once he finally *did* bridge the gap, it was only to end up stretched out horizontal on the sofa with Chrissie on top of him. A questionable move which Motowori chose even-more-questionably to follow up by actually starting to dance with her, back and forth, back and forth like some kind of rutting organ-grinder baboon.

Now far be it from poor, cursed Yuichi to question tactics as far as either Chrissie or the scroll were concerned, still he couldn't help but wonder exactly what sort of aura of authority Motowori expected to project with behavior of the sort. Couldn't help but wonder whether Motowori's seemingly-clear morning vision had somehow become clouded in the space of a New York City day. Couldn't help but wonder, as the music changed but the monkey-dancing continued, if he and the diplomat really shared the same sense of urgency about either the state of the planet or the scroll.

Keeping his head down and his face half-hidden in an attempt to be as uncharismatic and invisible as possible, as soon as the dwarf departed, Yuichi crept over to the kitchen and poured himself a glass of water.

Desperate for guidance, he tried to summon the spirit of rat ass monkey O Sensei, or any ancestor who might happen to be in the neighborhood, who might care to explain the meaning of this latest joke. When no guidance was forthcoming other than a vague hint that the ancestors didn't look kindly on premature victory celebrations, Yuichi decided that he would only give Motowori a few minutes longer. A few more minutes, and to hell with strategy, to hell with what Chrissie might think. If Motowori had not made any progress, Yuichi would go over, grab him by the elbow and lead him to the side to find out just what exactly he thought he was trying to do.

Under the influence of mixed-liquor anesthesia, unfamiliar social euphoria, and Motowori's dizzying dance, Chrissie Luna decided that her hands-on test of the Japanese ambassador had not really proven anything after all. What if he were a hand washer, but too diplomatic or well-mannered to take advantage of the boulevards, the highways she had opened for him? What would happen, she wondered, if in all innocence she actually walked over to the kitchen to show him the way? What if she took it upon herself to lead him to the sink and even turned on the faucet? What would happen then in front of such clear temptation? Would he be able to resist? There was only one way to find out, and that was, coldly, immediately, to put him to the test. "Will you excuse me?" she said, smiling, as she took leave of the little circle of initiates and walked over to Yuichi in the kitchen.

"Will you excuse me?" The Japanese ambassador followed her right away, hoping this might be a chance after all to get her alone, to say the things he had to say.

"Will you excuse me?" Celestina said, seeing a chance to talk to Yuichi, in whose etheric future she could clearly see herself, just as she had on that first running-uptown day.

"Will you excuse me?" Retter said to Jack Bravo and the posse behind, finally, an opportunity to talk to the ambassador about dogs.

"Excuse us!" the Retter-haters chorused, crowding into the kitchen behind him, still kept at bay by the dogs, but determined to take action, because things had gone quite far enough.

One after the other after the other after the other, they followed Chrissie to the kitchen, domini-domino, bumping into each other as she came to a sudden halt in front of the sink. So shit-faced she could hardly talk without spitting, she turned on the faucet and stepped back, arms crossed. She looked the ambassador straight in the eye, pointed her hand at the faucet and drizzling a fine mist, said "OK Thlugger, go ahead. I dare you."

Motowori looked at her quizzically. "I'm afraid I don't understand..."

"What are you? Afraid of thomething?" she said, trying to keep from tottering back and forth. "Big puthy, are you? Don't want to wash your hands in public? Need some privacy? Well follow me," she said, marching off to the bathroom. Followed by the ambassador who just wanted to talk about a scroll, by Yuichi and Retter who wanted to talk to the ambassador about tactics and dogs, by Celestina and four dogs who wanted to talk to Yuichi about love, by a posse of political-korrektons who wanted to talk to Karl-Heinz Retter about revenge, by Chrissie's upstairs neighbor the model, who was curious to see what all the commotion was about, and almost by...

Jim O'Brien, who hadn't minded when Yuichi stayed by the balcony, and hadn't minded when Yuichi drifted over to the kitchen either, but who, when he saw Yuichi following Chrissie to the bathroom, his bathroom, to do god-knows-what with his Atlantic City tart, could not decently sit idly by. More than a little shit-faced himself, babbling about devious pindicks, unfair advantages and how he had entertained Chrissie's mother for free, which should be worth something, O'Brien failed to remember the presence of four small but spoiled-mean dogs. American dogs just old enough to feel someone owed them something, male dogs with boiling libidos who had been brought to a party expecting to party, egalitarian dogs who, after three hours of frustration, were ready to sink canines and more into just about anything that moved, regardless of race, creed or sexual preference. In other words into Jim O'Brien, who had all three. "Will you excuse us?" the dogs said to Chrissie's mother, still lying there on the ground where O'Brien had left her, and proceeded to do what dogs will do, tripping O'Brien up, then savaging shins, clothing and anything else they could reach through his flailing hands. A game which came to a close only because he finally stopped resisting, and because four other dogs, panting heavily, threatened to get more of Yuichi than would really be fair.

This time, when Chrissie turned on the faucet in the bathroom and offered Motowori the spot front and center, virtually dragging him by the lapels up to the sink, he rolled up his sleeves and bent down to wet his hands just to oblige her. "Chrissie, it would seem that you have a scroll in your possession," he began, stopping Yuichi in his tracks. Like a stewed eagle, Chrissie watched him, arms crossed even tighter, to see if he would actually take the soap. Celestina bumped into Yuichi, running her finger nails across his stomach through his robe, Fluffy the poodle grabbed Yuichi's right ankle, and Motowori, just trying to please her, grabbed the soap.

"I knew it!" Chrissie crowed, victory, she had been right all along. But right about what? What did it really prove? The Labrador seconded the poodle, latching on to Yuichi's left knee.

"Mr. Ambassador?" Retter chimed in, slipping through Celestina's legs just before the telescope-pervert reached out to collar him. Laurel, the smaller cocker spaniel and Werner the dachshund ricocheted off the toilet and grabbed Yuichi around the waist. "Honorable sir?" Retter said, a little more forcefully this time, wondering if the fact that Switzerland was only an observer at the United Nations and not actually a member, was playing any part in the Japaner's deaf-man act. What he ought to do was backhand the man right then and there. Except such a gesture was hardly worthy of Karl-Heinz Retter; if the President of Switzerland ever heard tell of such an astounding lack of subtlety, Retter knew he could kiss the mountain-side mausoleum goodbye for eternity.

"No! It doesn't prove anything!" Chrissie yelled out loud, angrily brushing Retter back. How dare he interrupt? Just because two out of two Japanese men washed their hands after touching her, didn't mean it was a cultural trait. "Shit!" Disgusted, she yanked Motowori by the collar and tossed him back into Yuichi. Staggering beneath the weight of six dogs, including two around his neck, Yuichi fell back into the rest trying to crowd into the too-small bathroom, and slowly went down. Frustrated, Chrissie grabbed Retter by the hand, rubbed him across her chest lengthwise and sideways, the sign of the carnal cross, then held him over the sink, head down, to see if he would wash his hands. In over his head, upside down, a rain of quarters pouring from his pockets, slightly dazzled by a world in a different perspective, Retter stared back at the door for help, straight at Melissa, Chrissie's gorgeous model neighbor. Melissa, so weary of the male gaze that she was ready to snap, marched forward and slapped him just once, a big old resounding movie slap which knocked him senseless, and brought a trickle of blood from his left ear.

Under the admiring eye of the Japanese ambassador, Yuichi, ever the healer, managed to break free from the dogs just long enough to crawl forward, remove Retter's shoe and bring him back to consciousness with a sharp whack to the sole of the left foot. But then the dogs got to him again. Fluffy the poodle grabbed him around the knees once more and the Labrador, standing on his hind legs, got him in a carotid-squeezing front paw vise grip so skilled that Yuichi had no time to react before blacking out. While the cocker spaniels stood guard in case any of the humans should try any funny stuff, the rest of the dogs, led by Adolf the Doberman, grabbed Yuichi by the collar and tugged him on his back all the way to the living room, where they proceeded to re-enact the more vigorously gymnastic, space-consuming parts of the canine lust cycle, moving the party out of the bathroom and back where it belonged.

As lightning crackled and thunder roared outside, the French artist put an ObRock 180 beats-per-minute version of "Ding Dong the Witch is Dead," on the stereo, and the posse danced a high-knee, high-five wish-we-

were-in-drag dance of victory, raiding Chrissie's crystal cabinet and breaking every last one of her glasses in sheer joy while singing along, none more loudly or out of key and rhythm than "God B. Rented," the French artist, rhyming "dead" with "pissed hon 'er fockeeng 'ead."

Inebriated though she might be, Chrissie dialed 911 and waited with Karl-Heinz Retter for the paramedics to arrive, holding his hand, trying to soothe him, to get him to stop babbling nonsense about the President of Switzerland, to stop saying (despite Celestina's prediction) he was no more than this far from death, the tiny space between two tiny misshapen fingers.

"Shh, it will be all right. Shh."

The two huge paramedics from West New York hospital prodded and poked Retter, shined a light into his eyes, then, before you could say Rumpelstiltskin, bundled him onto the stretcher. Quickly, all business, they rolled him to the elevator and pushed the button, provoking a surge forward and a menacing growl from the dachshund, two poodles and one Lhasa Apso.

Laying it on thick, ever closer to the gates of Hades, Retter licked his dry lips, then barely moving, crooked a finger at still-potted Chrissie, motioning for her to lean down. "Closer, closer, there's something I want to tell you," he said, with a rattle in his throat to reiterate how much he doubted he would be around to see morning light, and with a little dwarf cowboy smile to show how bravely he was taking it. "In the unlikely event that I am still around," he said, "And you, sweet you, decide to pursue this passion... that is stronger than both of us... there's something you probably ought to know..." he paused, panting, pointedly trying to muster his last bit of energy. "I'm not a nice man, Chrissie."

"Of course you are," she answered, squeezing his hand and brushing a tear out of her eye with the back of her sleeve. "Don't worry, I'm sure you'll be just fine."

"Tell the monk to take care of the dogs..." Retter croaked as the elevator doors opened, almost taking his keys out so that the President of Switzerland might say that even on the threshold of death Karl-Heinz Retter still had full clarity, but timing it perfectly, accidentally-on-purpose, so that the elevator doors closed before he could do so, *deus ex machina*, thus foiling both sycophantic President, and slanty-eyed viper in one fell swoop.

The snake would probably love nothing more than the opportunity to have the run of Retter's apartment. The chance to peruse, at his leisure, ten years of receipts and personal papers, looking for chinks in Retter's armor. Chinks, ha! No, there was no lack of clarity here, *meine Damen und Herren*. The only unfortunate thing, but it couldn't be helped, was that because of his decision to keep cherished keys in cherished pocket, Karl-Heinz Retter was the only one to know it.

Celestina and Jack Bravo left together, and the various freeloaders, fake aesthetes, TV sports fans and models took the cue and drifted away soon thereafter. After his initiation into the Dog-and-Japanese-Love-Boy Circle (highly detrimental to most of the red pinstripes on his $2000 tailored-to-impress flannel suit), Motowori left as well, deciding that given Chrissie's state of inebriated distraction, it would probably be best to talk to her another day.

Looking over the shambles of her apartment, Chrissie Luna had to admit that in spite of the moment of emotion with Retter and her shattered glassware, she felt strangely euphoric. If she had ever attended a better party she couldn't remember it, there had probably been not a collective minute of silence in three and a half hours. Karl-Heinz Retter, Celestina, the Japanese ambassador: you had to be special to belong to this group. Chrissie just dared her mother to say anything after witnessing her daughter at the center of a higher class of human being.

And then there was Yuichi, who apparently still just couldn't get enough of Retter's dogs. Yuichi, adorable woozy little teddy bear, with his cute little teddy bear head which Chrissie couldn't help but stroke as she tucked him in on the couch. Although Chrissie had still not forgiven Yuichi for his crimes of hygiene, and she planned to let Jim O'Brien occupy her bed tonight just to make that point crystal clear, let it not be said that Chrissie Luna was unable to give praise where praise was due. The list of the Japanese monk's flaws would probably be endless, but at least one thing was true: Yuichi had definitely improved her social life.

27

At the West New York hospital emergency room, they interrogated Karl-Heinz Retter about his insurance status under mercilessly bright lights, then tied him down, wired him up, gave him an MRI and a sound test and decided that despite the trickle of blood, the deafness he was experiencing in his left ear was due to calcification of the ossicles, a condition that had doubtless existed already for years.

Not much the doctors could do for his physical condition, but as a result of the deafness *they* were beginning to suffer after two hours of little-man ranting and raving, of Retter refusing to give anything other than name, rank and serial number, but giving it time and again, of Karl-Heinz Retter answering their nothing-wrong diagnosis by lalalaing Wagnerian death arias at the top of his lungs, it didn't seem unwise to recommend that he be detained for 24 hour psychiatric observation. Perhaps, on the New York City scale, Retter was neither crazy nor self-destructive enough to really warrant it, but these days medicine was no longer solely about the money, it was also about revenge.

"I can commit surgery better than any of you," Retter yelled, tongue thick with sedatives, a tiny bent figure in a frayed, stained straitjacket ten sizes too big rolling out of emergency on the gurney. Psychiatric lockdown didn't scare Karl-Heinz Retter, the small man would rise to this challenge like any other. "You think you know what crazy is? Ha!" He virtually rubbed his straitjacketed hands, he would show them: they didn't know anything yet.

28

Too weary to demand a walk, content to relieve themselves in the toilet as they had been trained, (but too tired to raise the seat), too tired even to fight the still-unconscious Yuichi for Chrissie's couch, eight angelic dogs spread out on the living room floor and slept through the stormy night. Slack-jowled, heads on paws, they were as oblivious to the relentless rain beating against the windows as to the deliberately-histrionic Celtic love-grunting coming through the open door from Chrissie's bedroom. It was not callous party-hound, end-of-century indifference which prevented them from losing sleep over the loss of their surrogate master so much as canine wisdom: tomorrow would bring what tomorrow would bring, no sense losing sleep over something you couldn't change.

Unfortunately, the next morning, suddenly sunny and warm though it might be, did not dawn nearly so rosy and wise. Neither for Yuichi, who, struggling to get his bearings, tried not to be overwhelmed by failure and a sinking sensation of dread, nor for the dogs, who woke feeling depleted, ornery, critical and ready to bite. Suddenly everything was wrong. The food was wrong, (hors d'oeuvres for breakfast? Please!) the water bowls were wrong, the emergence of Chrissie, Jim O'Brien and Chrissie's mother from Chrissie's bedroom, and all the unrequested, against-the-grain petting, all those fat, slobbery kisses reeking of licked human genitals, sour rubbing-alcohol and morning-mouth-fetid human lust was wrong, wrong, wrong.

But did irritatingly-slow Yuichi even recall that dogs in the morning needed to be walked? Did he grasp the urgency of the need to depart the gamy, glass-strewn apartment, not only on basic dog walking and scene-of-crime-fleeing principles, but because they were expected at Countess Effington's on 49th and 2nd to pick up two Yorkshire Terriers at eight ayem sharp? Did self-pity-man Yuichi, slumped on the edge of the couch, holding his head in his hands, suspect even a tenth of the disdain that eight dogs might have for the object of their lust the morning after? Did guileless Yuichi even begin to consider the potential consequences of canine post-coital depression, that self-indulgent mixture of emptiness, dependency, guilt, embarrassment, disgust and desire for flight which the need to regenerate produced? And did clumsy Yuichi manage to attach the leashes they brought him in time to prevent just such an event as Chrissie's downright humiliating attempt to apply mood-enhancing makeup to one of the cocker spaniels? No, no, no. Whose fault was it then that Laurel the cocker spaniel, quite naturally, sank his teeth deep into Chrissie Luna's cheek?

"Get out, get out right now, you and your dogs, out!" Chrissie said to Yuichi, in calm, cold furor, one finger applying pressure to her wound to prevent the fat red drops of blood from leaking onto the bathrobe (on which she had also silk screened the word Izanami), and a second finger pointing at the front door in such an authoritative manner that with the help of a bit of aggressive herding from the dogs, Yuichi, who up to this point had not even been informed of the dog-keeping duties he had inherited, could not help but comply.

With Chrissie's behind them, the sidewalk back underfoot, morning bladders emptied and lungs reinvigorated by the warm, spring-like air, Yuichi's breaches of morning protocol no longer seemed quite so serious, and the dogs were prepared to allow the canine-human relationship once again to assume its rightful hierarchy, dog on bottom, man on top. But did Yuichi take advantage of this generous concession? Did he line anyone at all into walking formation and set off briskly uptown as required? Did he demonstrate even the tiniest glimmer of leadership, or did he just remain there, dazed, defeated, directionless, practically obliging eight wanton dogs to take over after all?

Up Broadway they dragged him, right on 42nd street, up Fifth, then over, leaving a trail of devastation. They rolled around wantonly in the garbage and squatted anywhere they pleased, they joined in the tormenting of a gaggle of scarf-wearing, dog-fearing Afghani women by a bus stop just for the pleasure of hearing them cackle in horror, they chased invisible rats and cats, they bit taxi tires, they wrapped their leashes around policemen and homeless people on crutches, and they terrorized small children on their way to school. When the German dogs wanted to eat sausage, they went into a sausage shop. When the cocker spaniels wanted to hump blankets, they went into a blanket shop. When the Lhasa Apso had a craving for caviar, they knocked over an Iranian restaurant and pissed in the sour cream and chopped eggs. When the Peke, the relativist, the sex-fiend Mandarin, started itching, they climbed under the doors of the peep show cabins at Fun City, rolled in the mess for good measure and watched as the healer, smiling and bowing absurdly, tried his best to make amends. And...They arrived at Countess Effington's apartment building fully fifteen minutes late.

As if he didn't already know what time it was, the doorman, raising his eyebrows and putting on his instant-winter face, took out his pocket watch and shook his head as eight smelly, slime-covered, matted-fur dogs led Yuichi to the elevator, but this was as nothing compared to the cold reception awaiting Yuichi from the tardiness-loathing 75 year-old British Countess herself.

"And you are?" she said icily, squinting at the frazzled, leash-burned, glassy-eyed healer from behind her reading spectacles and the door chain. Pretending not to recognize him or the other dogs, even though she had seen Yuichi with Retter once before. On the spur of the moment, even aside from the tardiness, she could think of a hundred reasons not to hand over her precious little treasures to this guru. Reasons including the other dogs' appearance, their seeming complete loss of discipline and Retter's thoughtless failure to warn about the substitute walker. Not to mention Toyotas, Nissans, ubiquitous Sony video cameras cheapening world culture and the continuing decline of the Yen.

There was only one proper response here really: a huff and a puff, and a slam-the-proper-British-oak-door-in-Yuichi's-face which set eight post-coitally-depressed dogs howling with such canine glee that the Countess of Effington and Vulgargrad locked three of her ten locks. Wondering how much lower he could possibly sink, Yuichi just stood there, immobile, stunned. Ostensibly to console him, but in actuality to torture the Yorkshire terriers, whose taste for sexual deviance, he was sure, rivaled his own, Monsieur the Peke started by licking Yuichi's toes. Taking his cue, the poodles and cocker spaniels blocked his knees, and Duffer the Labrador, with a small running jump, applying his patented double-paw sleeper-lock to each side of Yuichi's neck, pulled him to the ground, flat on his back. There, while the poor excluded Yorkies howled miserably behind their solid oak door, eight dogs took one Japanese missionary in the missionary position, breathing mocking love sonnets into his ears and staring deep into his glassy, nobody-home eyes.

Stretched out on the Stain No MoreTM wool carpet, licking this and that while waiting for the healer to awaken, the dogs felt a great and unfamiliar sense of understanding, well-being and peace wash over them. This was a watershed, an epiphany, a harbinger of things to come, of twilight descending, of a long night ahead when the rules would be different. Was the missionary position responsible? No. Despite the quality of the latest orgasm, the missionary position, the sacred human idol, could still not be regarded as anything but geometrically impractical, an impediment to proper ejaculation (compensated for, in humans, by a host of other insanities like cuddling and drag racing), a patently pathetic innovation by a pathetic species to reduce an animal act to something vile and impure.

But just to be sure, solemnly, religiously, in testament to their new understanding, eight canines, like articulated metal toys, lifted their stiff, fucked-out bodies off the carpet, and proceeded to have their missionary way with Yuichi one last time. "I love you," "I can't live without you,"

"Where have you been all my life?" they snorted, snuffled and breathed hot, humid lupine passion straight into Yuichi's Eustachian tubes, competing with each other to come up with such words as would make the others go limp with laughter. "We were meant for each other," "You like that, don't you pumpkin?" Whatever else you could say about the millennium, one thing for sure: it was a great time to be a dog.

29

Pressing two fingers to the puncture wound in her cheek, declining all assistance, refusing to go to the hospital herself, Chrissie Luna ushered her mother and Jim O'Brien to the front door, then fetched her First Aid kit from under the sink, cleaned the wound, patted it dry with special organic, earth-friendly no-bleach Samsara cotton and applied a butterfly stitch so that she could get right to work. No regrets, the accident with the cocker spaniel had actually given her the idea for an entirely new line of products: makeup for animals. Horses, guinea pigs, cats, fish, dogs. Not only were the possibilities endless but, always a good sign, the advertising gimmick came right to mind: "No human testing." She imagined Raj Mikkelson putting an end to Nigel Forsythe and Hope! once and for all, not through sinking of ships and assassination, but through pure economics: peaceful means.

She could see herself set up already, a modern princess, and Raj Mikkelson hiding 24 carat gold peas under her mattress just to tease her, but knowing she would feel them even before he tried. She imagined a social life improving exponentially, and three secretaries working 24 hours a day in eight hour shifts to answer the mail from people whose sullen canaries the makeup had made sing, whose surly pet turtles now paddled around all day long, whose doleful cats had turned civilized and actually ate what was put before them, whose previously-gloomy race horses finished first, no photo, cuz you don't need a photo when you know you're looking good.

In fact, in this beautiful dream there was only one cloud, and a very small cloud at that. Last night, for a moment there in bed, was it just her imagination? Or did Jim O'Brien actually seem to prefer making love to her mother than to her? Was it just her imagination, or had she heard Jim O'Brien say "No offense Chrissie, but I guess I just prefer old-school?"

Only one teensie-weensie wispy cloud in a vast blue cloudless sky, but given this new crazy social life, it occurred to her it might be a good idea to draw up a list. "People who are not welcome in this apartment ever again," she wrote at the top of a yellow legal pad whose lines she numbered from one to twenty for starters. Number One was definitely Jim O'Brien for reasons too obvious to waste time writing down. Two was definitely her mother, for being a slut. Three was Yuichi, at least until he got rid of his dogs. Four was Celestina, who probably assumed Chrissie was just too plain daft to notice the astrologer giving Yuichi the eye. Five was just about anyone else at the party last night, excluding poor Karl-Heinz Retter and the Japanese ambassador. That was one, she had to admit, she still couldn't quite figure out.

In fact, now that she thought about it, with Nigel Forsythe assassins lurking in every doorway, and death waiting around every corner, it occurred to her that she must have been completely crazy to throw a party in the first place. Crazy to leave the door open like that. She wouldn't make that mistake again. Six and seven, she added Karl-Heinz Retter and the Japanese ambassador to her list just to be safe. "You never know," she told herself as she started the search for her vanishing pocketbook, a search she abandoned midway when she located the missing TV remote control.

Starved for TV, delighted to be alone for the first time in God-knows-when, before Chrissie knew it, she was completely engrossed in a documentary about the testing by Reaper Pharmaceuticals of the new prion drug. Apparently the drug was so prohibitively expensive that, regretfully, blabla blabla they had to limit the program to 20 people. The Reaper spokesman explained the importance of the drug, statistical projections extrapolated an American infection rate on the order of 500 per 100,000 people, but so far, bla bla bla, because of the extended incubation period of the disease, that was only a guess. Chrissie thought that if the drug weren't so expensive, she wouldn't mind trying it herself, just in case, but then she noticed her purse next to the couch and her attention returned to Karl-Heinz Retter.

Poor Karl-Heinz Retter, stuck there in the hospital, she really ought to go see him and cheer him up. It would be wrong not to, thank you very much, she preferred to live without the guilt. As soon as she was done at Samsara, presenting her animal makeup program to Raj Mikkelson, to the hospital is exactly where she would go.

30

Alone in his little cell, Karl-Heinz Retter slept heroically, a rest of historical quality, and woke up thanking Chrissie's swacked model neighbor for slapping him back to focus. In his dreams he was a paratrooper floating into the Swiss Congo on a custom parachute. A pill-bearing missionary dressed all in white, carrying, at great personal risk, needed medical supplies to the savages below. Blood clotters for the excisions, tetanus shots for the odd scrape on a rusted soup cauldron, juju-Gingko enemas to combat the encephalitis, and synthetic kudzu pills a thousand times more potent for cough than anything they could possibly concoct themselves with just kudzu root alone.

As tempted as Karl-Heinz Retter had been at first to make the doctors rewrite their textbooks, to show them craziness heretofore unseen, off the charts, this morning, since that was obviously what they were expecting in their observation room, he had decided to play it quite the other way: Karl-Heinz Retter, sanest man in the universe. It was never a good idea to let the masks fall too far, but this time something made him want to show the real man. A man who, in addition to all his other sane qualities, now, alone among mortals, had the added so-fantastic gift of knowing the day of his death.

As he lay there sanely in his bed, in that used-to-be-white room, their every provocation was like water off a Thunersee teal's back. The woman came with an injection and a tray of food, prepared for the worst? He showed her politeness like she had probably only read about in books, (assuming she knew how to read) and eating manners, in spite of the straitjacket, that were the very distillation of centuries of European royal refinement. The man came to change the straitjacket? Retter didn't talk even once about himself, like a crazy man, but spent the whole time discussing stitches and sail-cloth, even putting on a light Yiddish accent to make the tailor-fellow feel more at home. As if by accident an hour later, they let a little rabbit into the room? Not only did Retter not roll off the bed and smother it then bite its ears off or suck out its eyeballs, as a crazy man no doubt would, but within minutes he had the rabbit turning cartwheels on top of him, licking the salt off Retter's nose and, as a finale, in response to commands from Retter's eyelids, even bowing to the doctors behind the two-way mirror, because Retter himself could not. Was this the behavior of a crazy man, of a man who was a threat to himself or mankind? No, this was the behavior of a focused man, a dignified man serene in the most fundamental knowledge concerning the duration of his mortal term, a man who could write a book on rabbit training if he chose.

Twenty four hours they wanted to keep him? Let them keep him for forty eight, seventy two or as high as they could manage to multiply without bursting their brains. Let them imagine he was their pawn, their humble slave for life, he would go with the flow. Truth be told? It felt gloriously good to have a little spell away from the dogs and that whole obsessive, no-time-for-anything-else routine. A little bit of glorious, structured idleness, finally, for Karl-Heinz Retter, feeling for the first time in ages like a Germanically-precise idea factory, to devote some mentation to the long-neglected question of the nameless monk's acting career. What about a film starring Yuichi as a paratrooper distributing pills in the heart of darkness? Or better, a film called "Showdown in Chinaman Square," where Yuichi stopped a whole column of tanks, then proceeded to, proceeded to... Well, it didn't matter, he could come up with that later. A cast of thousands, Chinaman Square awash in blood, a ship sinking, the lead actress with some terrible Oscar-winning handicap or speech impediment: that's what mattered, that's what would bring people into the theaters. Three Oscars, maybe four, guaranteed. Plus... Ten percent of the body count, that's what Karl-Heinz Retter would insist on, or else no deal. Ten percent, ha-ha, ha-ha... The President of Switzerland could go fuck himself. The week before his death, Karl-Heinz Retter would buy his own mausoleum, a mini-pyramid he would set down in some country like Liechtenstein. Or some offshore haven, where banking was still banking, and anonymity was still respected.

But then, thinking about the monk caused him to think about the party, and thinking about the party caused him to think about the Japanese ambassador and his snobbish Sharpeis. And thinking about the Sharpeis caused Retter to remember the monk's theory on the potentially deleterious effect of the dogs' excessive sex play. What if this patently inane notion were something shared by all Japanese people? What if last night's humping frenzy, which anyone else would recognize as the epitome of doggie good health, had struck the undersexed ambassador as offensive and injurious? The thought made Retter's stomach sink. How could he not have considered something so obvious? Oh darkness, oh sloth, what sort of mausoleum did such a heedless little troll deserve? Nothing even close to Switzerland, that was for sure. More like a tar-paper cremation hut on the coldest-possible slope of Mount Ararat, a little two-hole hut where the Turkish president himself came to void his bowels on vacation. That's what Retter deserved, no more, a full, front-and-center view for eternity of the Turkish president wiping his ass with bare hand and water.

Unless... The situation was critical, Karl-Heinz Retter could not possibly wait for the 24 hour observation to come to an end. He scanned the room anxiously, the oxygen canisters, the handcarts, the bars on the windows, the video camera and two-way mirror. One way or another, he had to escape. Immediately! Strapped tight to the bed, Karl-Heinz Retter struggled briefly against the ties that bound him, then gave up and whistled through his teeth. A high-pitched sound inaudible to human ears, but which foolishly, subconsciously, he guessed he hoped the dogs could hear. As if they not only could hear, but could then jump up off the street, up to the second story, through the barred windows of the room and save him. That is how low he had sunk.

31

Some ten thousand years ago the wise men of this world assembled at the Koso Kotai Jingu, the Imperial Ancestors' Grand Shrine in Toyama Prefecture, to set in motion an intricate plot. Heirs of the Great Knowledge, missionaries, prophets, men and women of enormous capacity and deep judgment, they had reason to be concerned. Where once the Knowledge infused everyone with an understanding of the true order of things, so that peace and harmony reigned and the very notion of crime was quite impossible (the period symbolically referred to in the Bible as the Garden of Eden), a new current had begun to gain ground. The current symbolized by Susano-wo, covetous, destructive, aggressive, a current cast adrift from its mother, its heart, its foundation. A current which had already cost the lives of a number of missionaries, and which, over the next 50 to 100,000 years threatened not only to destroy the Garden of Eden, but the planet entire.

Rather than resign themselves to this as inevitable, rather than throw their hands up in surrender, the younger missionaries had a bold plan. What if, instead of allowing this progression to follow its course, they actually facilitated the spread of the new current by hiding the True Knowledge, by putting Amaterasu in a cave, and leaving the coast clear? Let Adam eat the apple, let humanity fully experience mortality and shame, let it indulge its curiosity about the material realm to its fullest. Then, if all went well, during one brief 10,000 year spasm, the new current, the current called Kanagi, the current symbolized by the star god, would rise, but more importantly, would also fall. At which point the way would be clear once again for Amaterasu, the sun goddess, to return, to light up the Garden of Eden and reveal the way back to the Tree of Life. Ten thousand years of darkness: just as in the aboriginal mythologies. What the Hindus call *Kaliyuga,* the Age of Iron, a time of illusion, ignorance and strife, of *Tendo-Muso,* the world upside down.

It is in the first scroll, the one called *Ten no Maki,* The Book of the Sky, that we find not only this most-esoteric account of history going back 300,000 years, but the details of the final occultation of the Knowledge three to four thousand years ago, (historically around the time of the Tower of Babel), and a list of names of the missionaries destined to guide society towards the scientific civilization. Men and women, demiurges, from near and far who journeyed to Hinomoto Kuni, the holy land, the world center, to study at the Koso Kotai Jingu, to learn about the True Knowledge and the magic inherent in it, and to assist in the monumental task of burying the old way and imposing the new. Names like Lao-Tzu, Confucius, Fu-Hi, Buddha, Mohammed, Moses, and Jesus, whose name is recorded on the list as Kirisuto...

In the Bible, Exodus 6:3, does it not say that the Lord came to Moses and said, "I appeared to Abraham, Isaac and Jacob, but by my name Jehovah was I not known to them?" Does the Lord not tell Moses to say to Pharaoh, Exodus 9:16, "I have raised you up for this very purpose, that I might show you my power and that my name might be proclaimed in all the earth?" Did the Lord not harden Pharaoh's heart so that the Hebrews themselves would follow the new god, Exodus 10:1, "I may perform these miraculous signs of mine among them that you may tell your children and grandchildren how I dealt harshly with the Egyptians and how I performed my signs among them, and that you may know that I am the LORD." After Pharaoh finally relented and let the Chosen People go, did his mind not cloud? Did he not pursue the Hebrews to the Red Sea at Pihahiroth, so that the Hebrews began already to doubt their mission? And did not Moses then demonstrate for them the power of the new god, Jehovah, YHWH, by holding up his rod and stretching his hand over the sea, so that the East wind came up, and the waters were divided? Did Moses not stretch his hand out over the water again once the Chosen People had reached the other side, so that the Egyptians would be drowned to a man, and Israel might, with these proofs of the power of the greater God, gain faith for the mission ahead?

All of that it had taken for the children of Israel to put their trust in this new monotheist God, this Jehovah. This God of Kanagi, also known as Susano-wo, the impetuous male, who chased Amaterasu the sun goddess into her cave, and ruled by the light of the stars. Jehovah, sacred god of science and cars, who had seen the Japanese Emperor step down from his throne, who had even converted the Chinese. Jehovah, the necessary one, who had demonstrated, with the help of his many gods, atom bombs, advertising, heart transplants and human blindness posing as progress, that nothing could resist him nor stand in his way.

Certainly, Yuichi was no Moses, for what modern man, even O Sensei, could pretend to even approach such dimension? Still there was solace in Moses' example, solace in the fact that Moses too had felt too small, too unworthy for the task he had been given, solace that he managed anyway, gaining power with every trial, rising to every occasion.

Now, the wheel was turning, and Amaterasu, the sun goddess, (maybe the exact same deity that Pharaoh worshipped as Ra), was attempting to come out of the cave again, to demonstrate that she was more powerful than Jehovah after all. She would have to show many miracles, and the democratic heart, like Pharaoh's, would doubtless be hardened a dozen times before it believed, before Amaterasu would be able to demonstrate her glory in a way convincing enough to take root. Staffs that had been turned into snakes would have to be turned back again, rivers that had been turned to blood would have to be cleansed, plague and pestilence would have to be purged from the land, blindness and deafness would have to be healed, and fear and evil purged from human hearts.

Heir to the tradition, abandoned missionary, canine lust-object, tragically unschooled victim of moon and star just returning to consciousness on Countess Effington's plush hallway carpet, Yuichi couldn't help but wonder exactly what his own role in this might be, or even if he would survive this Susano-wo City long enough to actually *have* a role. But whatever the case, catalyst or martyr, he knew he would have to play this out to the end, just like Moses, Jesus, Mohammed and Kung Fu Tzu.

It was raining by the time Yuichi and the dogs finally stepped outside again, a warm Groundhog Day Spring downpour which instantly left all and sundry soaked, but at least helped rinse off the more noticeable bits of slime and residue still clinging to the dogs' fur after the anything-goes walk uptown. Full of purpose and direction, Yuichi countered the first sign of renewed leash-pulling anarchy outside the door of Countess Effington's building by just freezing on the spot, sinking such solid roots into the ground that Fluffy and Light, now in the lead, flipped flat on their backs, much to the amusement of the bird dogs. No need to say anything, no need to kick or spank, or wave rolled-up newspapers, Yuichi waited motionless like that, face set, one minute, two minutes, three minutes, four, until the dogs, of their own accord, expecting much worse to come, bowed their heads, and looking out of the corner of their eyes, lined up meekly in two straight four-dog low-to-high lines, lap dogs, poodles, cocker spaniels, Labrador and Doberman, the way it was supposed to be, the way it had always been with Karl-Heinz Retter. When all was in order, Yuichi loosened the reins just a bit and they headed off, all nine of them, no less soaked but as orderly as orderly could be, in the direction of a familiar vibration, in the general direction of the West New York City Hospital. Face set, arms unwavering, Yuichi steered the pack across town in a flash, (no pipi breaks, no random sniffing), not thinking twice about the crisscross symphony of police sirens filling the air in the distance or the ominous black riot trucks rumbling by in the same direction, shields over windows. There were even blue police cars parked sideways across 12th street, blocking off traffic access to Eighth Avenue, but Yuichi didn't even slow down, and with eight dogs in front of him like that, a fine disguise, the police didn't think to ask questions.

Only once he heard the sound of megaphones, the noise of the crowd, and, crossing Eighth Avenue, actually got a sense of its size, (approximately) 799 people massed across the street from the hospital, did Yuichi's certainty begin to waver, did he begin to wonder if maybe, once again, he might not be in the wrong place. On the left: riot trucks. In front of the hospital entrance: a forest of police planted shoulder to shoulder, smacking unsheathed batons in black-gloved palms. In the middle: a speaker in surgical greens standing on a soapbox haranguing the crowd, a still-neat patchwork of groups distinguished by uniform, a hundred rainbow-colored T-shirts here, forty blue T-shirts in a tight circle there, a pack of red windbreakers, a pack of green ski jackets, etc... 799 people giving off a most familiar smell, that same dangerous, vengeful human perfume Yuichi had smelled on New Year's Day.

"Ho..." By now, Yuichi's intuition, his every sense, screamed "about-face," "retreat," "run." But, bolstered by the renewed sense of mission, he told himself it was simply his fear of crowds getting the better of him, so instead of fleeing, he pulled the dogs into a doorway to regroup, a safe haven from which to watch the scene evolve.

"...They want you to believe that this is eternal, that it has always been this way, and will always be so," a self-righteous scarecrow on a soapbox pointed an accusing finger at the crowd as he poured vitriol through a battery-powered megaphone, proceeding to denounce the whole of modern medicine, starting with the battle against malaria, and tuberculosis, before moving on to the spread of AIDS in Africa, and the consequences of birth control pills, the women with blood clots and fibromas, and the men become feminized thanks to synthetic female hormones seeping into the water table.

"Fuck you!" The first outraged voices of dissent sounded from the middle of the AIDS lobby, which, after much practice over the last decade, was well-trained to react at the drop of an insinuation.

But the scarecrow was oblivious, gaining momentum with each word. "You go into a hospital, and you have a one in ten chance of coming down with something you never had before. They tell us about laser surgery and organ transplants, they tell us about the switching mechanisms that produce cancer and all the rest of the miraculous mythology, and they wonder why we feel that modern medicine doesn't work..."

"Fuck you!" The wave of dissent set in motion by the AIDS lobby began to spread through the crowd, through the prion lobby to the Lassaites, and from there to the Ebolites, Hantavirusites and Marburgians, the Diptherians, the Parkinsonians and Alzheimerians. Water bottles, stones and paper cups flew through the air, little missiles now aimed at the speaker, but from group to group as well so that the previously neat patchwork of homogeneous colors began to break into a pointillist blend of people either running for cover, or seeking revenge. The scarecrow dropped his megaphone and ran for his life.

A man with a blue-green T-shirt with two hands clasped together in prayer and the caption "Prions" underneath it, grabbed the megaphone and took the stage. "Reaper Pharmaceuticals..." That's what they were here for, this was their demonstration originally, no matter what all the others who had appeared rather spontaneously might claim. "Reaper Pharmaceuticals tells us they have a new drug. Reaper Pharmaceuticals tells us it is too expensive to go around to more than the twenty people it chose, not entirely at random. Reaper is telling you that you don't have a right to live..."

"Heresy!" "Blasphemy!" The rest of the prion lobby, one hundred-odd people clad in identical clasped-hand, blue-green "Prions" T-shirts, put its weight behind its guy. Nobody knew what the side-effects of the drug were, nobody could predict its long-term effectiveness, but that Reaper was telling these people convinced that they were afflicted, that they didn't have the right to be guinea pigs, or at the very least, to be given the placebo! This was completely unacceptable.

That doctors were fallible and could be sued was all right. That drug companies made mistakes, that too was all right, because to err is human. But that the medical system itself should have come to the point where treatment was so expensive that only those with money or connections enough to be in the right place could survive? That was a fundamental corruption of democratic principles, egalitarian mythology and Constitutional privilege. And yet there it was: no matter how much economists and politicians put their faith in market forces to eventually straighten everything out, the time had clearly come when a human life, even an American life, was apparently no longer worth the money it took for the technology-intensive medicine to save it. Not a question of sentiment or Hippocratic morality, but purely of social cost.

"Self servers!" "Hypocrites!" "Shut the fuck up!" The same voices from the AIDS lobby tried to stifle the prion people. Ever since the press had latched onto the story about the possibility that indestructible prion molecules might jump from the animal kingdom to the vegetable kingdom, a possibility which presaged a spare-nobody epidemic which not only kept handwringers, vegetarian doomsayers and delighted millenarian Christians working overtime, but had effectively relegated the still-fearsome AIDS epidemic to the nostalgia pages of the newspaper, the marketing-savvy AIDS people had understood the signs. In a climate where there was no longer enough pie to go around, there could no longer be any such thing as solidarity of the afflicted.

"Fuck us? Wrong. More like fuck you," said the prion speaker, the AIDS lobby had occupied the moral high-ground way too long. "Go make your own demonstration."

"Oh yeah?" the head of the AIDS lobby charged, head into the prion speaker's gut, knocking him to the ground, and punching him in the face, once, twice, three times in rapid succession. Outraged, a prion woman pulled a brick from her purse and smashed the AIDS guy on the head. A second AIDS guy came to his defense with a can of mace, and then there was no holding the two camps back. Released from the burden of civility, the others also joined in the fray, looking for adversaries of their own. While the riot police stood on the periphery, arms crossed, not at all eager to mix it up with the sickos, the insect and rodent vector diseases attacked the respiratory-transmission diseases, before splitting and attacking each other. The Legionnaires, in a pincer movement, cut across the street targeting anything even remotely related to cardinal sin: the fornicators, the Salmonelites and the Botulites, the gluttony cancers of intestine and stomach, the hemophiliacs, etc... The tuberculars made peace and joined forces with the AIDS group (parallel pandemics think alike) and wiped out a half-dozen shakers, three hackers, a gimpette with an artificial hip, a transsexual with faulty breast implants, a sailor with scurvy and a banker with Lyme's disease. Then, all at once, the alliances shifted again, so that the "of-its," or "ovitz" or however they spelled it, those with diseases with short enough incubation times so that if you got it, you were likely to die "of it", faced off against the "with-its," those whose incubation rates were long enough so that the chances were you might die *with* it, but not *of* it.

The measles activists had only enough time to tell the TV cameras that not enough was being done to develop new vaccines before their woman was muscled aside by a small toxic shock troop, who in turn were blocked off by a photogenic out-of-breath white Rastafarian wearing a soaked-through "HIV Positive!" rainbow T-shirt on his back and carrying three blue-green prion T-shirt trophies on his shoulder. Last to go, before the TV crews decided they were ready to wrap, a coalition of malaria activists and onchocerciasis fanatics, who planted themselves in front of the Rastafarian and shouted slogans in English nobody could understand. A news item the networks would show that night with subtitles to demonstrate once again how badly the Third World was getting out of hand nowadays.

32

Figuring that Karl-Heinz Retter probably wasn't going to do himself any bodily harm after all, the doctors let him out of the straitjacket at about 11 a.m. and brought him his clothes. Retter thanked them, every bit as polite as you could wish, escorted them to the door of the room, telling them to come back any time, be my guest. Then, leaving his clothes on the bed as a diversion, just grabbing his keys, he made a dash for the garbage can, lifted the lid and disappeared inside.

Just for the experiment of it, or so he convinced himself, he spent most of the next hour hiding inside with the flaps of the garbage bag covering his head. He would be free inside of ten hours anyway, but if some underpaid janitor happened by and unwittingly helped him escape ten hours early, where was the harm?

At first when the riot started outside, Retter simply ignored it, as if it were nothing more than a silly siren song, designed by the hospital staff to lure him out of the can without getting their hands dirty. A Potemkin disturbance which men of lesser fortitude, men of weaker spine, men more congenitally prone to boredom might be seduced by, but certainly not Karl-Heinz Retter.

As the minute hand rounded the dial though, Retter began to re-evaluate. The idea of the garbage can was just an experiment, who could say it wasn't? And if the janitors of the West New York City Hospital were not capable even of such a simple task as emptying one garbage bag in one little mental ward hospital room, that didn't mean that Karl-Heinz Retter, in the name of pride, in the name of outlasting some *Lumpenproletariat* broom pusher, excuse me, sanitation engineer, ha-ha, ha-ha, should risk coming down with a terminal case of phlebitis. Besides, what was so wrong with curiosity in the first place? Karl-Heinz Retter would sure like to see a world without curiosity. Sure, it was easy to say 'stay in the garbage can, show us what you're made of little man.' But what would a world without curiosity look like? Would there be a Bulgarian humor festival? Would there be a Shirley Temple? No. And that was just for starters, that's what it would look like. Oh no, Karl-Heinz Retter had already stayed long enough in the garbage can, stayed until the sweat ran down his brow, until the can had turned into a veritable Orgone Box and he felt like he was almost going to explode. What other man would last as long, even without a full-scale riot brewing outside? What other man wouldn't just jump out of the can the second he heard someone yelling "peanuts," outside? You would have to be a complete, total pacifist, a deaf-mute onanist, a skin-and-bones diaper-and-beard yogi, to stay inside the garbage can any longer than Karl-Heinz Retter already had. You'd have to be like one of those patchy-fur dogs so old he doesn't even prick up his ears anymore when a truck goes by. And at least to his knowledge, in all humility, Karl-Heinz Retter was none of these.

From the second story window Karl-Heinz Retter could see the whole rabble-choked street, could see the police trucks and the television vans with their long antennae extended transmitting the orgy of self-pity to TV viewers around the world. It looked like one of those Holy Ghost rallies they used to show on TV, where the afflicted, the water heads, the elephant ankles, and the paralytics came rolling in, hoping for a miracle from the preacher in the toupee. Briefly Retter felt the old Nuremberg reflex rising, the obligation to harangue the crowd with some doxology, some miracle prescriptions of his own, except, except... Was it not? Did he not make out? Could it not be, there, of all places in this vast city, on the other side of the mob, one gloating monk hiding in a doorway with eight shivering dogs? Eight noble shivering dogs who had obviously, finally, heroically, doggedly, managed to steer the monkfish over here in response to Retter's whistle.

A sight so disturbing that Karl-Heinz Retter didn't even take the time to get dressed. So heinous that Karl-Heinz Retter, oblivious to either consequences or physical impossibilities, simply tossed his clothes into a spare garbage bag, opened the window, climbed up on the window sill and (ha-ha, ha-ha, advantage #3872 of being a dwarf) slipped through the too-wide psychiatric-observation-window bars. A short, angry, triumphant slide down the drain pipe, and he was free. Free to zip through the crowd, free to slalom between the legs of the most despicable specimens this city, this country had to offer, but zip, zip, zip, faster than anyone else on the entire planet.

Still crouching in the safety of the doorway, not quite ready to risk it out in the open, Yuichi watched the proceedings with eyes wide in wonder, heart filling once again with that familiar sense of glorious possibility. It was the medicine they prided themselves on most, the medicine that provided the foundation of their belief in progress, their belief in themselves as evolutionary beings in spite of all the evidence to the contrary. It was modern medicine that confirmed their view of history as an inexorable arrow leading from "tool-less" darkness to present light. Even if these protestors were just a vanguard, if this were just the start, they were confirmation that the god of medicine had begun to crack, that the time for the new gods and the new incarnation was nigh. A sign.

Perhaps, given Chrissie's foul morning mood, and the puncture wound on her face, it was still premature to press the issue of the scroll. But, just to prepare the terrain while giving Chrissie Luna the time to be affected by the apparent change in current, a quick, little detour to the United Nations did not seem to Yuichi like the worst idea. A scouting expedition which, in the interest of discretion, it seemed wisest to embark on alone, without eight unpredictable dogs. Eight dogs whose backside-exposed leader had, most fortuitously, at that very second, climbed on to the drainpipe high above the crowd and slid to the ground. With a deep breath, a little whip of the leashes and a last look over the shoulder to check his back, Yuichi forsook the safety of the doorway and marched into the fray to intercept the little man before he might run off.

Quite a picture, a less-than-fresh Asian with eight whining, howling, soaking dogs, a caricature (unfortunately for Yuichi), suggesting one thing and one thing alone to various anti-vivisectionists: the destitute opium fiend rounding up specimens for delivery straight to the hospital animal research lab. Not that they needed an excuse, but the anti-vivisectionists, whose imaginations, as a rule, were rarely that good to begin with, swarmed Yuichi without further ado, pummeling him with their most-virtuous fists. And this despite the valiant efforts of Walkiria, the gingham-skirted sprite Yuichi had helped save on New Year's Day, who tore at them yelling "Stop! For God's sake, stop!"

Concealing his card, keeping a lid on the volcano until the proper time should present itself, Karl-Heinz Retter hacked his way through the bipedal jungle, strode up just in time to watch one-upping Yuichi, with the unwitting help of the pulling dogs, a tangle of leashes and the rain and oil slippery sidewalk and street, dispatch the last of the anti-vivisectionists. All but Walkiria, who stood motionless in the storm, her soul weary with betrayal, her eyes brimming with tears, looking deep into Yuichi's eyes searching for explanation as to how a man who only one month ago seemed like a white-clad angel, could have turned into a such dog-delivering cad. She wanted to believe there was some explanation, but what explanation could there be? Did he not know the difference between Mormons and anti-vivisectionists? And what hypocrisy was this, that after knocking the last of her friends down, he kneeled to try and put them back on their feet again. "No, don't bother," she said, timidly, unfocused at first, then more loudly, outraged, "Don't touch them I said!"

"Thank you! I'll just take those off your hands," said Retter, snatching the leashes away from the monk and wrapping them around his fist. Jumping up and down on their hind legs, tails wagging, the dogs were so beside themselves with happiness, that their bladders let go, but Karl-Heinz Retter forgave them, because even he could not help but squirt out a drop or two in pure joy. Only hours ago Retter had been thinking how good it felt to be without the dogs, but now he had to admit how much better it felt to be with them, to have that fine old smell of wet dog fur in the nostrils again.

"They're looking a tad peakèd," Retter said with the most disdainful tone he could muster, giving the dogs the once over to estimate how many manikin-hours he was now facing to get them back into tonsorial trim, and shuddering at the reputation-damaging prospect of having to walk them all the way back to Park and 45th in such shape. Unless, of course, he could trick the monk into doing the dirty work for him...

Except did the monk expect Retter to get down on his knees in gratitude for this potential favor? Did the monk expect Retter to kiss his hand and thank him? Was delivering the dogs in a such a state what the monk called taking care of another man's treasure? Was this how the monk rewarded Retter's unequivocal trust? To hell with getting his help to walk the dogs back home, instantly wouldn't be soon enough to get the stench of fish out of his nostrils, a stench which only the mercifully pungent odor of wet dog fur made tolerable enough to prevent Retter from vacating his premises right on the spot. And another thing: how come there were only eight dogs, and not ten? That was more to the point. "Can we help you?" Retter said to the gingham-clad woman with the admiring eyes, a bit of magic flimflam to help him slide in closer to the monk to check his breath for the unmistakably distinctive odor of grilled Yorkie. Even if, by some miracle, the monk turned into a mega-galactic Hollywood star, even if ten percent of what he earned allowed Retter to buy the whole top floor of the Trump Tower, cash, it was a matter of ethics: you just didn't eat another man's dogs.

"Better we go now," Yuichi said, pointing to the riot police who had finally begun a cleanup sweep behind the gingham-clad woman's back.

"Is there nothing you'd care to tell me?" The dwarf crossed his arms and stomped his feet, one, two. Let the monk bow his head and cry great fishy tears, let him beg to walk the dogs home now, if 20% of the dogs in Retter's care ended up on skewers, Retter certainly didn't intend to take the rap. He stared Yuichi down with a custom *Oberland* stare so piercing that Yuichi finally just wilted, backed away and slithered off. All but signing a notarized confession right then and there.

Two lines of four, tight at the front and wide at the back, the bare-assed dwarf formed the dogs into a little "V" for victory which he thought he deserved after not only escaping so brilliantly from the hospital, but doing so in time to see right through the transparent monk's transparently devious tactic. And if the President of Switzerland happened to see satellite pictures of the hospital riot and demanded why the dogs had not been formed into an "S" for *Sieg*? If the President accused him of having succumbed to baleful Anglophonic influences after too long in this mongrel country? All Retter would have to tell him was that "V" also stood for "*Victoire*," ha-ha, ha-ha, and that Retter would erect his mausoleum in the French part of Switzerland if *Herr Präsident* gave him any more lip. Let the president try and form eight dogs into a calligraphically convincing "S" without getting his ankles wet. With twelve dogs, *Ja*, this was of course another story, but with eight dogs? Not a chance.

"What's your name baby?" Orgone-topped-up Retter said, giving the worshipful gingham-clad woman the look, and spitting on the ground, in spite of his Swiss self, because no woman on earth can resist a dwarf spitting. Perhaps she might like to walk the dogs home?

"My name? Walkiria," she said.

"Valkyria! Rea-lly," Retter said drawing it out to five syllables, and wasn't this a so-fantastic surprise? The name of the mythological Norse figure, the Wagnerian fury, who decided which warriors lived, and which died! "Retter, Karl-Heinz," he said, snapping his heels together and saluting with one hand, while placing the other hand over the little wet circles on the hospital gown where he noticed his excitement at seeing the dogs was showing through. "Walkiria," he tasted the name again. "Probably not many people know where that comes from, do they? If I were to have a daughter, I think I should like to name her Walkiria. Is that a good name to have?"

"I guess," Walkiria said, but suddenly without full enthusiasm, an attitude which only made Retter redouble his efforts.

"You don't, by any chance, drink coffee, do you? Mocha Java, or Brazilian, or no, Marogogype. Marogogype, that's it, tell me if I'm right. You seem like a woman of excellent taste. A woman with a phone number, perhaps?" Karl-Heinz Retter wondered if at last, finally, he might not have found a woman with a smell worthy of his own. Even if she offered to help with the dogs, Retter would have to decline. He would walk the dogs home on his own, and face the consequences like a man. Walkiria, he intended to save for something more long-term.

33

Yuichi stopped at a pay phone to see if Chrissie was home. No answer. He debated about going back to 226 Lafayette anyway on the off chance that she might return, but decided that the possibility of her actually appearing in time for them to get to the bank was quite small. And even if she *did* come home, and he asked her to go right out again, well, he didn't even want to imagine what sort of crisis and further delay that might cause.

And so, rather than risk it, now that old gods had begun to crumble, now that, clearly, the worm had finally begun to turn and the new current had started to flow, his intuition, his certainty, directed him to hop into a cab and try Plan B. This time, the head-high metal gate in front of the United Nations North Plaza was open, and in spite of the rain earlier in the day, 185 flags were flying on 185 flag poles, but Yuichi didn't even make it to the granite steps before the sharp, blue-clad guard on duty, a powerfully built black man, Yoruba most likely, Roger Smith by his name tag, very calm, very dignified, very assured, just shook his head. "You are not welcome, Sir, sorry to say," he said in a mellifluous accent more Caribbean than African. "You must turn around at this moment, otherwise I shall be obliged to take care of you."

"You don't understand..."

"I do understand, perfectly well, Sir, we know who you are, and you must turn around." A handful of visitors lined up behind Yuichi, but the guard motioned for them to wait.

"You know who I am?" Yuichi tried again.

"Sir, we are not stupid here."

"Perhaps you mistake me for someone else."

"I'm sorry, Sir."

"But I have a scroll that I must get to the UN."

"I am sure you must, Sir. But you also must turn around now and leave."

"This scroll will save the world."

"I hope it will, Sir."

"I am a citizen of the world."

"I expect so, Sir."

"Is there no way to get in then?"

"Not for you, Sir."

"Ho..."

"Yes Sir."

"This is a matter of destiny."

"In that case, Sir, when destiny calls, I hope to see your royalty. Sincerely, Sir. But now forgive me, Sir, you must please leave."

A police car cruised by and stopped just a few feet down the road, a handful of other guards appeared at the top of the steps behind the guard, two more police cars glided to a halt across the street, next to the police kiosk in front of the US Mission. All very subtle and low key, but impressive enough to convince Yuichi that retreat probably was in his best interest just now. A resigned bow to the guard, and a "Thank you, Sir," back, and Yuichi was on his way.

Intuition and certainty suddenly clouded by doubt, Yuichi crossed 1st Ave. and headed uptown for no real reason, trying not to read too much into the obstacle at the UN, trying to tell himself that it didn't really matter since he didn't have the scroll anyway, and that once he had the scroll in hand, no force in heaven or hell would stay him from his goal. Again he stopped at a pay phone to see if Chrissie was home. Again no answer, so he just hung up and continued to drift.

By 47th St. Yuichi began to suspect that one of the police cars was following him. Just to make sure, he let it tail him for a full block, then with a snap of the fingers as if he had forgotten something, he doubled back on 1st Ave. against the traffic, to see if he was just being paranoid, to see if the police would turn around, to see if another cop car would appear. All the way to 41st street he walked before deciding it was just his imagination.

This morning everything had seemed so promising, but now, ever since he had appeared at the UN, it was as if, yet again, the wind had changed. And he had the unsettling impression that for the rest of the day the meetings and events would only get more strange. A sense that the smell of fear and revenge that had permeated the street in front of the hospital had now drifted over the entire city, and that it had begun, quite specifically, to look for him.

On the sidewalk a Nez Perce on a skateboard smashed right into him, and instead of excusing himself, said "Fuck you."

"Fuck you?" Yuichi couldn't believe his ears.

"Fuck you, fuck your mothuh, fuck your mothuh's mothuh," he added, disappearing around the corner, leaving the stage free for a second lunatic, who looked at Yuichi and said, "Your mother sucks dick real good. Real good." Inside the police car, the cops were laughing again, pointing at him, and laughing again.

Suddenly deeply concerned, worried not for his own safety, but for the mission that depended on him staying alive, Yuichi buried his head in his collar and, trying to remain invisible, to keep his gait slow and steady, his heart and breathing even, headed downtown, roughly in the direction of 226 Lafayette.

Something told him it would be best not to take a cab or a bus, and to stay out of the subway as well. Something told him it would be best even if he didn't take the most direct route back, but drifted west a bit, or even back uptown to confuse the evil spirits hunting him. Suddenly everyone looked like an ear-plugged policeman. That or a cheap-suit Mormon. Suddenly every fat-ass with half-a-chance seemed determined to get in his way, to slow him down. Had he never noticed this before? They all had earplugs. Policemen everywhere. A woman across the street, five kids on roller blades, a UPS delivery guy, all talking into thin air, yelling slogans at each other "Take it to the people!" "Girls in space, yeah!" "Coffee in the machine!" A homeless guy held his hand out, "Come on brother, I'm hungry, god damn it!" But even he had an earplug, not connected to anything, but an earplug nonetheless, a no-frills, cold-night special, hope-is-on-the-way, direct line to God. A shiver ran down Yuichi's spine, and he had to stop, to say his sounds quickly, to reconnect to gratitude, to eternity, so as not to fall over, not to be completely overcome by the sense of futility, the sense of doom.

A police car stopped at a light across the way. Yuichi, all-too-obviously, tried to ignore it. No, the best thing would be to disappear for a few hours, a Karaoke bar maybe, just until the paranoia and the powerful sense of foreboding dissipated or the city calmed down.

"Hey buddy!" a barker in front of a church hissed at him, causing him to jump. "Got something I think you might like to see. Come on, come inside, have a look. Free, no obligation, put a rise in your Levi's. Come on buddy, twenty bucks if you stay. You don't like it, you leave, money back. Hey what's twenty bucks nowadays?" Yuichi studied the man's face, looked over the dilapidated church with the frayed banners, and looked around him 360 degrees to check for signs of a possible trap, then, finally nodded and headed into the church. "You won't regret it."

Inside, the church had been turned into a movie theater, concession stand in the front and inside, sticky, slippery floors smelling of spilled semen, spilled Thunderbird and Coke, and ratty, squeaky, torn red velvet seats. No more than a double handful of men sat there in the dark, spread out over the entire theater, making the seats squeak as they played with themselves. No more than eight or nine men, mouths open, staring up at the screen, where a terrible quality, scratched and burned but double-ultra-violent, corpse-a-minute Hong Kong karate movie, dubbed and subtitled in English as well as Mandarin, Cantonese and Greek, kept them transfixed.

"Hey Fatskin, your eggs about to feel power of my scramble," said a fellow with a Babyfoot T-shirt on, jumping out of the shadows in a dilapidated Hong Kong warehouse.

"You want kick me nuts?" His adversary, an ugly pug-faced bastard wearing a Fatskin T-shirt pulled out an Uzi, glowering as much as his face would let him.

"I kick you crazy nuts."

"You kick me crazy nuts?" Babyfoot pulled a gun of his own out of his boot, then circled carefully, kicking a crate out of the way. "I make you wish salt in you peter, then kill you dead very funny so you disgrace."

"How you kill me dead very funny? Only for dreaming," Fatskin said, with a burst from his Uzi which cut through a rope and loosened a sandbag which would have flattened Babyfoot if he had not rolled out of the way in the nick of time. "I kill you dead back to you ancestor first, you don't watch out now..."

Far from being able to relax in the darkness, as soon as his eyes managed to adjust to the darkness, Yuichi was, if anything, more nervous. He thought about standing up and getting his money back, but slumped down in his seat instead, squeaking along with all the others. That's all he needed now, to start the Bruce Lee, Jackie Chan delirium up again and add a half-dozen slime-palm autograph seekers to his troubles.

"Look! Reptile Mug try muscle in both us." Babyfoot tried what sounded like a distraction, but the aptly named Reptile Mug, gun drawn, had indeed appeared at the warehouse entrance, blinking stupidly as his eyes got used to the dark.

"Kill him with your bullets, make him intestine cry tears hotly. He kill you and me cousin Babyfoot, you forget. Now you make him feel offal."

"Don't forget, you first!" Fatskin snarled, jerking his gun back and forth between Reptile Face and Babyfoot. "Do I look like dog-slicer for other man?"

And so saying, Fatskin let Reptile Face have it, a burst from the Uzi that made the screen man dance and started the church-theater chairs squeaking in earnest.

Babyfoot laughed. "You bullet don't scare me."

"Maybe not," said Fatskin victoriously, "but these not my bullet. These my grandfather bullet."

A look of surprise creased Babyfoot's face. He clutched his hand to his gut, the blood seeped through his fingers. "I feeling cold where I should feeling warm."

"Take again then."

"I dead now maybe, but you ever die you smarter be careful, I waiting." And so saying, with his last energy, the nearly late, so-called Babyfoot, pulled the trigger of his own automatic so that both Fatskin and a dozen heretofore hidden cronies died as well, more than filling the film's corpse-a-minute quota. Not to mention, simultaneously, giving the green light to some fifty real-time New York City vice cops who burst through the theater door tossing stun grenades and promptly placed everybody under arrest. Mayor Morales had made a speech calling Hong Kong violence the pornography of the millennium, and the orders from City Hall were to stomp it out, pronto.

They read Yuichi his rights, charging him with promoting second-hand violence and assaulting an officer, an accident to be expected in his case on the sometimes sticky, sometimes slick church-theater floor. Resigned to his fate once he had gotten his footing, a marked contrast to the rest who, still under the influence of the cinema, had to be clubbed within an inch of their lives before they could be removed from the theater, he walked peacefully to the bomb-proof van for the ride to the local precinct house.

A brief ride during which they passed a riot between supporters of rival projects for a statue that was supposed to be commissioned, they plowed through a riot between Cubans, Peruvians and Brazilians on musical themes, they detoured around an enormous altercation between gays who wanted to remain in the closet, and those who wanted to out them. Watching it all through the steel mesh of the van window, Yuichi just shook his head. So he had a revelation this morning about changing gods? So he had been a bit wiser and actually anticipated the trouble that resulted in his third arrest in little over a month? The reality was that once again he was on his way to jail, no closer to delivering the scroll, no closer really to piercing the mystery of why such a simple task continued to elude him. In America, Groundhog Day, in Japan, a day short of *Setsubun,* when the tradition was to celebrate the last day of the old year and the first day of spring by scattering beans about your home to ward off evil spirits. No beans in hand, not enough beans in the world apparently to ward off all the evil spirits in New York City, wondering if the end of the year was a positive omen, Yuichi closed his eyes and sighed, missing a riot between cat lovers and dog lovers and a second one between pedophiles advocating lowering the age of consent to eight, and others prepared to accept ten, for now. As for Yuichi, he no longer hoped, he no longer expected. Bouncing along in the van, hands cuffed behind him, he took his pulses and just prayed that Amaterasu-o-mi-Kami hadn't been rendered feeble-minded by too long in the dark, prayed that the sun goddess knew what she was doing.

34

Karl-Heinz Retter pulled on a pair of Snow Leopard *Lederhosen*, made a slight detour downtown to purchase a huge bouquet of flowers from his usual flower shop (which the prison van with Yuichi in it actually passed), then set off for Countess Effington's with eight freshly laundered dogs, and a sharply rolled *Neue Zürcher Zeitung*. With any luck at all, she would not yet have heard of her dogs' demise, and if indeed she had not, he would explain their absence by telling her about the hospital, the Japanese man who had suddenly flipped, and how her adorable Yorkies were probably just missing, a little fugue, and would certainly turn up sooner or later. If she did know something, if the monk had done his Yorkitori worst right in the basement, it should be immediately obvious. Retter would hand her the flowers, offer his most sincere condolences and suggest a small bribe on the understanding that she remain mum about the matter of the barbecued loved-ones. And if she got emotional and threatened to call the police? If she thought such a small favor was worth more than a sum equivalent to the refund of February's bill? He would rip the bouquet out of her arms and beat her over the head with it while reminding her, in no uncertain terms, that she should feel blessed in the first place to have had her dogs walked by Karl-Heinz Retter for even the little while she did. He would tell her what he really thought about Yorkshire Terriers, about their ribbons and coconut oil baths, about their silly, shrill bark, their rat-like walk and their pathetic fear of absolutely everything. No surprise, given that owners resemble their dogs, that she had chosen such a breed, no surprise whatsoever that she insisted on having them home nights, and so what if that cost Karl-Heinz Retter an extra hour out of each precious remaining day?

Thus prepared, Karl-Heinz Retter rang the doorbell at Countess Effington's at five on the nose. What should he hear? What silly, shrill sound should greet his ears from the other side of the door, but the barking of two Yorkshire Terriers! *Jawohl*... This was going to be very interesting. Perhaps she had thought to kill the dogs for the insurance? Or perhaps she and the Japanese man were in collusion, and the fake-kidnapping plot was the best they could come up with to bring New York City's best dog walker to his knees.

Countess Effington herself opened the door with a wicked stuck-with-the-dogs-all-day-and-it's-all-your-fault look on her face. "Ha!" Retter said, which stopped her right in her tracks. "Ha!" He stared her down, looking right at her until she was obliged to avert her gaze, because she knew he knew of what cruel perfidy she was capable. And still she looked proud! Unbelievable.

He flipped the flowers in her face, and turned on his heel with a "Come," to the other eight dogs. Such presumption, the softened royal with the rotting intestines and superior look trying to match wits with the master! Not that he cared, but Retter hoped this would teach the revolting woman a lesson. A lesson she could pass on for free to the rest of the degenerates in her genealogical tree.

As soon as they left Countess Effington and Vulgargrad's, Retter took the dogs to the park, where they played with the children until well after dark. He thought about the decline of royalty everywhere, and didn't feel the least bit sorry about having jettisoned the Countess. He had taken her on to give old-European respectability to his operation, but, he now saw, that had been an error of vanity. Karl-Heinz Retter had learned his lesson: you didn't achieve world hegemony with depravity like that in your plus-column. But neither did you achieve world hegemony with a dumb-like-afox Japaner sticking swords in your spokes around every corner. He would deal with Fishworthy, all in due time, all in due time. But for now, sitting on the park bench, watching the dogs terrorize the mongrel children, he just laced his tiny fingers behind his increasingly-misshapen head and let out a contented sigh. He thought about coffee and calling the woman from the riot, but then thought better of it. Escaping a mental asylum, teaching a lesson to a monk, seducing a woman named Val, regrooming eight dogs, and putting English royalty in its well-deserved place was accomplishment enough for one day.

<h1 style="text-align:center">35</h1>

If outside in the city, something had changed, inside the walls of the City floating prison, they were not immune either. Thanks to Yuichi's healing hand, to his treatment of Nat Gold's groaning, Reverend Y had enjoyed two full nights of excellent sleep which had brought clarity to his mind and at least a modicum of peace to his soul. But on the third night, Nat Gold had begun to talk in his sleep, revealing, in a strange southern accent, the existence of his second persona, one Billy Joe Dupre, a pack-running, provoke-and-run two-hole-outhouse peckerwood. And hearing Billy Joe like that, picking fights and strutting in his dreams, had begun to cost Reverend Y all new kinds of sleep, keeping him tossing and turning trying to test all the new paranoia scenarios that his restless mind could not help but concoct. To wit: either Nat had summoned this Billy Joe Dupre character to let off some of the pressure accumulated in the cell with the fearsome Reverend Hate. Or he was actually crazy, completely schizophrenic, in which case there was nothing to be done other than remain vigilant in case "Nat Gold" and "Billy Joe Dupre," the two harmless lunatics revealed so far, hid a more dangerous third or fourth lunatic. Or, third possibility... Billy Joe Dupre was the original, and Nat Gold the fake, in which case: he was not Reverend Y, the man with the answers, but Reverend Chump, stone fool, unable to see the core of "Nat Gold," so obsessed was he with the surface. In which case: it was time to eat crow or humble pie.

It was at dinner, on Multiracial Night, the night when, to promote understanding between the races, the City floating jail served matzo ball soup, that Reverend Y made his first attempt to see if nocturnal revelations could be verified by waking confession. "Here, you have mine," Reverend Y said, pushing his bowl across the table to Nat Gold.

"Why's that?" First impulse: suspicion. Reverend Y had never shared his food before.

"Hunger strike."

"A hunger strike..." Nat Gold said, dubious.

"That's right."

"For any particular reason?"

"To protest the state of the world!"

"To protest the state of the world, right..." It wasn't hunger strikes in and of themselves that Nat Gold objected to, he thought, although, Lord knows, starving yourself to protest the state of the world was like starving yourself to protest the existence of the star Aldebaran, he couldn't really see the point. No, unaware as he was of his night talking, still in the grip of his initial fears, this is what it looked like from where Nat Gold was sitting: Reverend Y's refusal to eat his matzo ball soup almost required that Nat Gold, as a "Jew" trying to conceal his southern origins, eat the soup for him. Which Nat Gold, given his wife's culinary ineptness, simply could not force himself to do, the mere words "Matzo" and "ball" together being enough to cause total colonic occlusion. And although by now, thanks to Yuichi, Nat Gold figured that he and Reverend Y had been through enough that it really wouldn't matter if the ex-boxer man actually did figure out the truth of Nat's Southern origins, what concerned him now, were any of the other five thousand odd African-Americans behind bars in the floating jail, any one of whom he feared might interpret a Jew's refusal to eat matzo balls as the sign of something rotten in his woodpile. "OK, very well, count me in," Nat Gold said, pushing two bowls of matzo ball soup, the Reverend's and his, down the table. "A hunger strike to protest the state of the world, it is!"

When word got out Thursday morning that they had once again transported the crazy Jap molefockel back to his home-away-from-home, Reverend Y let it be known that he expected Yuichi to move into his cell within the hour, and no excuses.

"What happened? You miss us?" Reverend Y laughed and gave Yuichi a big hug, slapping him on the back.

"Yeah you miss us?" Nat Gold felt he should do the same.

The reunion was cordial enough, but Yuichi was a tad reserved. Nat Gold, he could see, was a ball of tension, pulses clearly sluggish, liver, stomach and kidney meridians all shut down. And Reverend Y? If the man's posture was any indication, both shoulders were sore now, not just the left. "I've been doing some thinking," said Reverend Y, "From now on, no more pretending, no more illusion. Cards on the table, no more hiding, the time has come for me to accept what I truly am."

"Which is?" said Nat Gold.

"Armenian."

"Don't mind him," Nat Gold snorted, "He hasn't eaten in two days." (With a slightly safer menu now, Nat Gold himself had continued to strike, but selectively, striking against boiled peas and carrots, runny scrambled eggs and soggy toast, but not against any of the other major food groups: hot dogs, potato chips or chocolate.)

"Ho?"

"And why can't I be Armenian?" Reverend Y repeated.

Nat Gold shook his head, and pronounced each word carefully, as if speaking to a three year-old. "Because... there... are... no... black... Armenians."

"Do you, Nat Gold, know that for sure? Have you, as a Jewish man, met every Armenian there is? Besides, you don't have to be pure Armenian to be Armenian, do you? My great, great granddaddy was an Armenian, and that makes me one."

"What was his name?"

"How the hell should I know? Did I say I was born back then?"

"OK..." Nat Gold shook his head.

"Damn right it's OK."

"A black Armenian..."

"That's right."

"If you don't mind my asking? What exactly does that get you?"

"Nah, no no no no no, my Jewish man isn't understanding me here. This isn't about 'Get you.' I didn't say I wanted to be Armenian, I said I am Armenian."

"Right."

"1.2 million," Reverend Y said, starting a game of Who Suffered More, pulling out the number of Armenians killed by the Turks in 1915.

"1.2 million," Nat Gold answered right back. What was Reverend Y getting at here?

"What do you mean '1.2 million?' I got you there, didn't I? Did you forget you're Jewish? Unless you aren't really Jewish? If you were you would say six!"

"A: a Jew never forgets he's Jewish. People won't let him. B: 1.2 million doesn't beat 6 million. C: if you want to play who-suffered-more, you're better off being African -- Rwandan, Angolan, take your pick. And D, last but not least: if you can be Armenian, so can I."

"And why's that?"

"Because we Armenians are about the most racist people on earth, and I say there are no black Armenians."

"We are not racist."

"If you say that, you just don't know Armenian-kind, that's all, simple as that."

"I don't know us? I don't know us? I spent my whole life being fucked over by white men."

"So?"

"So if we are racist as you say, then as a black Armenian, I've taken my destiny in my own hands, haven't I?"

"How's that?"

"Half Black, half Armenian racist: now I fuck myself."

"Nope, wrong again. You can't fuck yourself."

"And why's that?"

"Cause if you fucked yourself, and you were really Armenian, you'd have to kill yourself to avenge the affront."

"Hmm, yeah, that's bad. Didn't think about that."

"So you're not Armenian after all."

"OK... in that case, I'm Swedish."

"Swedish?"

"African-Swedish."

"No such thing."

"Used to call it 'Black,' that's probably why you're confused. Now it's African-Swedish."

"If you say so..."

"Is the Swedish man racist?"

"Does a moose shit in the woods?"

"Will a Swede man kill you if you say fuck you to him?"

"No, probably not."

"Then I'm Swedish, that's all there is to it. African-Swedish. I get to fuck myself, but I get to live, see what I'm saying?" At that, Reverend Y's tough guy facade blew apart, and he exploded with laughter, holding his hand out so that Nat Gold could give him five. "Got you there for a second, didn't I?"

Half incensed, half uncertain, good old Nat Gold didn't show a trace of humor on his face. And he certainly didn't give him five. He just shook his head until Reverend Y had stopped laughing. "Nope, sorry, don't buy it. You're not Swedish either."

"And why's that, Nat the Rat?"

"Because I am, Brother Y, I am..." And so saying, he burst out laughing, such a crazy laugh that the other two could not help but join in as well

Reverend Y wanted Yuichi to look at his shoulders right away, but he felt like he should let a decent interval pass before asking. The way Yuichi had fixed it last time was great, but it hadn't really stayed fixed. And while this did not in any way make Reverend Y doubt Yuichi's powers, he couldn't help but feel that the temporary relief owed more to hypnosis or suggestion than to actual healing. Not to mention that the pain was now in both shoulders. "Must be the weather, but you know that problem I had? Well now..."

"Maybe *is* weather, yes. Please," Yuichi said, smiling, gesturing for Reverend Y to lie down on the middle bunk. When an imbalance has become chronic, it is the imbalance which rules, the sickness which, by fighting for its life, causes the patient consistently to reproduce the old patterns which reinforce the sickness. Like a patient you ask to stop eating fruit, and whose body and organs, screaming for fructose, lets him think of little else for the next days. Reverend Y had turned his conflict with Nat Gold into a little joke, but Yuichi wasn't fooled: it was the same pattern, just disguised a different way. "Pulses say you have this condition long time." The shoulder pain came from problems in the Triple Heater meridian, the heart and small intestine meridians, and the stomach which had not taken kindly to being deprived of food.

"Yeah, 'bout three, four year now."

"No. Much longer than that, since child."

"No, really, only three or four years."

"Only three years you become aware of pain. Condition exist long before. Stagnation of ki from disappointment, emotional shock, maybe racism as you say. You get angry, unreleased anger damage liver, then diseased liver make easy anger. Racism bad, up to you to see if you let kill you. Everything connected..." No doubt the doctors who had treated him before had given him cortisone and painkillers, but that only masked the symptoms, and didn't address the condition from which they stemmed. "One thing, please: hunger strike in winter, very bad idea," Yuichi said, pressing on the blockage at the groin between the leg and pelvis.

"Ah, ah, OK!" Reverend Y exhaled like a walrus, like a boxer in training, trying to work through the pain.

"Like anger, do body harm, understand?"

"Yeah, understand," Reverend Y answered through gritted teeth.

"It's good. All done," Yuichi said, standing back after taking the pulses one last time. "How do you feel?"

"How do I feel?" The juice was coursing through his body, the legs, the head, everywhere. He sat up on the bed and rotated his shoulders, no pain. "How do I feel? I feel great!"

"Good. Body responded very well, remember instantly last treatment. Good, very good."

"What do you think it was?"

"What it was?" Yuichi smiled. "Always many things. Japanese medicine very complex. Inside body, liver deal with tendon and ligament, angry liver make everything tight. But outside body, many thing too. Could be weather, could be time of year, could be climate in city, could be cosmic energy, which you see everywhere, people going crazy, could be end of long dark era."

"Hmm."

155

"And one more thing for you, Mr. Reverend Why. Western religion say sin is the bad thing you do against God and Ten Commandments. Japanese medicine say only meaning of sin is when a body goes against itself."

It was at lunch the next day that something inside Reverend Y shifted for good. The loose shoulders, the freedom, once again, from pain, even if it was hypnosis: Reverend Y couldn't help but feel humbled by Yuichi's skill, by such impressively vast knowledge, even by this different notion of sin which had had the Reverend thinking overtime ever since. Not to mention the way Yuichi moved through the crowd on the way to the mess hall, gracefully, without conflict, you could just see the power. Quite a contrast to the "What are you looking at? Damn!" way he had felt inclined to react when the other brothers, especially the Ramadan-proud Muslims, started giving him the traitor-to-the-race look just because he was eating again. Eating with the Southern Jew, and the Japanese man.

There was no show to the man, no putting on airs, if you saw Yuichi in the street you would probably never even suspect the mastery inside, but the man definitely had power. It made Reverend Y feel hopelessly inadequate, as if he had wasted no end of time pontificating, provoking right and left like some punk teenage fool. As if, when it came right down to it, he had no right to be up there in the pulpit delivering the word to anybody at all.

Instead of filling Reverend Y with remorse though, this filled him with determination. How could he explain it? It was as if all of a sudden, play time was over now, and the moment had come to get serious. "So really, Luigi, what did happen out there, man?" Reverend Y asked Yuichi a question about himself for the first time. "Tell me you're not back inside because you missed us?"

"Long story," Yuichi smiled sadly.

"Most good ones are."

"Well," Yuichi started slowly then told him everything. About the endless waves of lunatics he had endured since his arrival, about the scroll, with its world-saving truth, about Chrissie Luna who had bailed him out twice and locked the scroll up in the bank, about Sumela Mikoto, the one who understood the truth and was able to guide society in the right direction, about Susano-wo, whose symbol was a star, Tsuki-Yomi, whose symbol was the moon and Amaterasu-o-mi-Kami, whose symbol was the sun.

Reverend Y looked at Yuichi carefully, his eyes darting back and forth across his face. When he spoke, it was not in the voice he usually reserved for his recitation of scripture, but a voice of awe. "Revelations 12:1: And there appeared a great wonder in heaven, a woman clothed with the sun, and the moon under her feet, and on her head a crown of twelve stars..."

That night before going to sleep, Reverend Y shadow-boxed for a while, marveling at how sweet and loose his shoulders still felt. What made them different? What was Yuichi's secret, where did he get his power? "Anger weakens you..." he had said. What if a life-time of frustration had caused Reverend Y to lose focus? What if all the rhetoric about the War Of All Against All was the device of a tired man lacking vitality? What had he once hoped for? A world where a man would not be judged by the color of his skin, just like Yuichi hinted at. Where was he now? Advocating that brothers kill their brothers. Maybe it was time to get back to his dreams, to try and regain that focus, to a woman clothed with the sun, that's what the Reverend thought that night before slipping into blessed sleep.

That night, before going to sleep, Yuichi closed his eyes and focused on the condition of a man in a cell down the way whose tubercular cough echoed through the vast metal shell of the prison. And when his cellmates had fallen asleep, without moving, just lying there on the bunk, sandwiched between them, Yuichi focused his attention on their vibrations, to see how the treatment was holding. With Reverend Y, it was the gall bladder meridian, which the anger, out of habit, had squeezed once again. With Nat Gold it was also the same old chronic story. A weak heart system resulting in anxiety, resulting in buildup of tension which the liver-gallbladder system could no longer purge, resulting in kidneys weakened by the constant burden of attempting to remove the heat in the blood, resulting in passive-aggressive behavior and fear, resulting in burden on the stomach as well, whose imbalance produces insomnia, nightmares, and an inability to think clearly.

36

When Chrissie Luna, woman on the moon, woke up to the fact that she hadn't seen Yuichi in twenty four hours, her first call was to the jail. "Hi, this is Chrissie Luna?" she said in her most charming, button-nose, question-at-the-end-of-a-statement, please-don't-hate-me voice.

"$35,000." A woman answered, a metallic, very bored woman.

"I'm sorry?"

"$35,000 bail. For the Jap?"

"Oh... 35,000 dollars!" Even if Chrissie had gotten the previous bail money back, which she hadn't, $20,000 dollars was not exactly thirty five. "Well, thank-you..."

"Whatever..." click.

Somehow, Chrissie knew this was all her fault. Who knows what trouble he had gotten into this time? If she hadn't kicked him out probably none of this ever would have happened, but that was quite beside the point. The only question now was where on earth she could come up with $35,000. Raj Mikkelson had absolutely adored her idea about the pet makeup, but he was in such a catatonic state, so distracted, that she couldn't be sure he would even remember the idea six minutes later, let alone long enough to consider giving her an advance on future profits. Who else, who else? Her mother the slut? You must be joking. Her clients? She riffled through her agenda briefly hoping a name would jump out at her. When none did, she discounted that idea too. The lottery? No, you had to be Puerto Rican, or have a huge, greedy family to win the lottery, and she, at least for now, fit neither case. No, there was only one solution that she could see, only one possible solution to this latest mess. She hit the speed-dial number she had vowed never to hit again. "Hello Jim?"

"Fucking hell!"

"Hi, it's Chrissie..."

"Jim's not here."

"Chrissie Luna..."

"Jim went back to Ireland, can I take a message?"

"I have a little business proposition for you..."

"Yeah? Well make it quick, I'm in the middle of something."

"What would you say if I told you Atlantic City?"

Little suspecting that Chrissie was only working with what remained of the $1000 she had lent Jim O'Brien after the Keno win, and thinking that maybe she'd like to lose back the 20 she'd walked off with the last time, the casino management comped Chrissie in a suite, complete with a dozen free $5 electronic keno cards to get her rolling, a bottle of Champagne on ice and a bouquet of flowers on the dresser. A little gesture which brought one tear then another to Chrissie's eye. Which in turn sent a trickle of warmth back into Jimmy's frozen groin.

He found the tears sexy, the way they made her mascara run, and how she tried to hide it, then swiped the back of her hand over her eyes, leaving even longer mascara-tracks. The way she wasn't trying to be pretty anymore, it made him feel like she was wide-open, vulnerable and that too was exciting. It was a fact, when a bird was emotional like that you could pierce through to her very core, give her satisfaction like she's never had before. You could make her think you're a god, which was OK from time to time, no matter what anyone said. At that point, when you had her all open like that, all you had to do was treat her a little mean, and she'd just about start begging you to take her to the hurling matches on Riker's Island. And lugging your pint of Black Bush for you to boot.

"C'mere," O'Brien said taking his shirt off, not even bothering to hold in his gut before flopping back on the bed hands behind his head. "Is this the fucking life?" he grabbed the remote control and tuned the TV to the greyhounds. "Bring that bottle with you, be a love? It's on the way." Holding the bottle in his fist and hitting on it every so often, he had her a dozen different ways before she had filled out the last of the free $5 electronic keno slips. It was like a dream! A Jesus-Mary-and-Joseph fucking dream. Treat 'em like dogs, Jim O'Brien thought. "Did you know that "dog" is "god" spelled backwards?" he said. It weren't for nothing that he came from a nation of poets.

While Jim O'Brien bonked her, Chrissie Luna kept an eye on the TV, enough of an eye to grasp that she had lost all her free Keno games outright. When O'Brien was done and had passed out in the bathtub, she quickly fixed her face, went downstairs and promptly another dozen too. Just to give it a break, she played craps for a while and lost $40, and, while drinking a glass of free Cabernet which turned her teeth black, switched to blackjack and dropped $30 more before deciding that cards probably weren't right either today.

Before, Atlantic City had felt like a lark, not exactly a fairy tale, but close. Today, on the other hand, she *needed* to win, to come up with $35,000 to pay Yuichi's bail, plus $3,500 as the ten percent cut she would feel morally obligated to give Jim O'Brien for lending her back $950 of the money she had lent him in the first place, plus bus fare back to town. And the need to win, even if in a good cause, made her feel ugly, desperate, dirty. It was as if they had designed the entire casino environment to be depressing: the mirrored ceilings, the bells and sirens, the red carpet, the barmaids in their short hardbody dresses and tight little butts, the Japanese tourists and Chinatown gambling addicts moving in packs, the terminally fat women bulging out of their pastel polyester pantsuits while drinking Tequila Sunrises and pulling on the slots, the cloud of cheap "Hope," perfume filling the air like bug spray, making Chrissie's nose itch, her eyes water and her mascara run all over again.

It was on her way out to get a breath of fresh air that she saw, was it possible, could it be? Neil Armstrong, wearing a space suit with "Trump" stenciled in red, white and blue, front and back, greeting people by the front door. "One small step for man, one giant leap for mankind, welcome to Trump's, enjoy your stay." Of all the astronauts, Neil Armstrong was by far her favorite, but Neil as a casino greeter? This was too good to be true!

"Neil?" she said, but behind his back and not very loudly, just in case it wasn't him, so that neither of them would be embarrassed. On the one hand it didn't seem possible that the first man to walk on the moon could possibly have become a casino greeter, on the other hand, she had once seen a documentary about Joe Louis, and that's the way *he* had finished, so why not? Not that Joe Louis was anything at all compared to Neil Armstrong, and anyone who said that was either jealous, a born cynic or had some other agenda.

159

"Neil Armstrong?" she said a bit louder, passing behind him again, with similar results. Maybe the space capsules weren't that well sound-proofed back then, and he had slowly gone deaf. Or maybe he was an astronaut-impersonator; she wouldn't be the least bit surprised, nowadays.

Trying not to look conspicuous, but keeping an eagle eye on him anyway, Chrissie sidled up to a nearby slot machine and tossed in a silver dollar. There were a dozen ways to find out if it really was him, you could ask him where he was born, (Wapokeneta, Ohio, 1930) you could ask him about Gemini 8, or all the little details about Apollo 11 that only he and Chrissie Luna might know, you could ask him what the risk of an asteroid hitting the earth really was, you could see how he reacted when she finally worked up the courage to introduce herself properly. The real Neil Armstrong couldn't help but chuckle then say "Hmm," "10-4!" or "Great," when he heard the name Luna. He would understand what his larger-than-life figure would have meant to an eight year-old girl, watching TV on July 20, 1969. Neil Armstrong, the man whose noble purity, courage, and calm heraldic grace, had made a little girl first believe in Prince Charming. Neil Arms-strong, Neil Arms-safe, Neil Arms-Understanding, the man to whom no flesh-and-blood man could possibly compare. In short, Neil Armstrong: the man who, by setting the bar so high, had basically wrecked her entire life.

"A giant leap for mankind, cut the bullshit, Neil," she said, trying to pull on the handle of the one-armed bandit, only to discover that the new Fly Me To The Moon slot machine she guessed he was there to promote actually required $31 dollars before you could pull the handle. Thirty one dollars! For a slot machine! Well she'd just have to add that on to Neil Armstrong's debt to her, wouldn't she? Thirty one dollars!

"Lady!" They were lining up behind her, but she didn't care.

I'm playing this machine," she screamed, her voice cracking so that the others backed away, and even Kneel, the man whose very first name suggested a lifetime of giving blow jobs to his higher ups, was forced to turn around, exposing his fake hearing-impaired act for what it was. Slowly, methodically, she pumped the big silver dollars into the machine, one by one, each coin like a dagger thrust into his tiny tin-foil astronaut heart. When she finally pulled the handle, the noise was overwhelming, deafening, bells and whistles and sirens, and an avalanche of coins hitting her in the small of the back. As cameras flashed in her face, dazzling her, immortalizing her, cheek Band-Aid, black teeth and all, she saw Neil Armstrong kangaroo-jumping over from the front door, Neil Armstrong bounding her way in slow motion, like in a dream, to the tune of "Fly Me To The Moon." It took a sweet-dream-eternity for him to reach her, and when he did it was with open arms ready to sweep her up and away in a beautiful Prince Charming hug. The new millionairess wet her lips, tossed her hair back in sexy windswept slow motion of her own and leaned forward ever so slightly, lips parted, until he was near enough to touch.... then shot a knee straight to his balls which took the jump right out of the kangaroo and sent his halo flying.

37

Just as Karl-Heinz Retter had suspected she might, Walkiria the anti-vivisectionist turned out to have excellent taste. Except for her choice of venue, a pretentiously unpretentious Eurotrash, sandal-crowd health food place called Zen-tropa, off Union Square, where even if she had good taste in coffee, you couldn't get any, because they didn't *believe in coffee*. The strongest thing they had was something called Mu Tea, which offered her an opportunity to make her second blunder of the afternoon, by failing either to understand his pun or laugh convincingly, when he told the waitress, "I'm a little too old for *Mutti*, don't you think?"

"No you're not, mu tea is great, try it I'm sure you'll like it," Walkiria said right under the half-dead eyes of the waitress, a muffin-head almost arrogantly wearing a shapeless hemp dress.

"Actually, *Mutti* in Cherman, means mother. It vas a choke." Retter smiled at the waitress and said "Moo tea will be fine," anything to get her to go away.

"It means Muzzer?" Walkiria couldn't let well enough alone. "Oh! Mother. Oh come on, you don't mean that, we're never too old for mother. I don't think that's funny at all."

If missing a joke, then finding it not funny again after having it explained, wasn't one of the seventy-seven mortal sins, it ought to be. Twenty years ago, he would have demolished her for that, snap of the fingers. But with the advancing years, Karl-Heinz had become more tolerant, Karl-Heinz Retter had mellowed to the point where he could almost ignore first impressions. For truly, what was the point of that sort of guard-dog posturing, that sort of Rottweiler constant aggression? What was the point of being closed to the world in that way? How many things did you end up missing out on when you looked at the world through vindictive spectacles, when you always expected the worst?

Out of the grandeur of his heart, Karl-Heinz Retter managed not only to forgive Walkiria for forcing him to mingle with these kinds of people, not only for bringing him to some place where there was no coffee, even though coffee was what was initially discussed, but even for not getting his joke as well. After all, it's not as if people in everyday life were used to intellect of his magnitude. No, with human beings, you had to make allowances. You had to give them time to settle in, to get comfortable, to get up to speed gradually. And then, only then, demolish them...

Of all people in this world, probably the last person Karl-Heinz Retter expected to see pass by the window of Zen-tropa right then was Chrissie Luna. Fearing the cat fight that might ensue if Chrissie saw him with Walkiria, if Chrissie smelled the unmistakable odor of rutting female in the air, Retter instantly, with superb instinct, pulled the phone book from under his buttocks and buried his nose in it. But no good, Chrissie had a nose like a bloodhound: next thing Karl-Heinz Retter knew, she was right on top of him.

"Hi!" she squealed.

"Oh hi," he tried to act surprised.

"I saw the dogs outside..."

"Oh yes, the dogs ha-ha, ha-ha..."

"Were you aware that one of them bit me?"

"And I'm sure with good reason, ha-ha," Retter tried to make a joke out of it, the poor woman was so jealous she was hallucinating. "This is Val," Retter said, pretending to have forgotten Chrissie's name, then plunging his nose back into the phone book, behavior which any normally constituted being would understand as the height of lowness, as an open invitation for instant departure.

"Hi, I'm Chrissie." Quite oblivious to the innuendo, aggressively oblivious, she shook hands with Walkiria and even looked like she wanted to sit down with them. And probably would have, if Karl-Heinz Retter, with supreme foresight, as ever, had not chosen a two-chair table right next to the passageway, where the addition of a third chair would be quite impossible, would block the aisle, and prevent the waitress from working. Not that the self-righteous hemp-slave deserved any better, mind you.

"Did you know Yuichi is in jail?" Even though forced to stand, Chrissie seemed determined to make small talk. A roundabout, absolutely transparent way of seeing just how she, a woman with the commonest name in the commonest, most culturally barren country in the world, if you didn't count Australia, compared to a woman with the name Walkiria.

"Who?"

"Yuichi, Japanese guy, you remember..." Veritably steaming with jealousy, she added a little ironic, insulting Yankee upturn to the end of her sentence, as if Karl-Heinz Retter were the one with the deficient memory!

"Yuichi, of course I remember. In jail? Small wonder." So that was the banana snake's name! "Ha!" The little snake should have known he couldn't conceal the information forever, Retter was surprised he had even tried. Pointedly ignoring Chrissie, Retter locked his gaze on Walkiria and gave her the smile. Her eyes not only shone with the you-saved-the-dogs-from-vivisection look, but now with an admiring, have-you-ever-seen-such-a-babe-magnet look as well.

"I just got back from Atlantic City?" Chrissie just couldn't stop.

"I'm sure you did."

"I won six million dollars playing the slots."

"Of course." It was pathetic sometimes how obtuse people could be.

"Can you believe it? I was thinking of having a party."

"That's nice."

"As soon as I get Yuichi out of jail."

"Can't wait." What must he do to get her to take the hint? Retter wondered. Should he say they were talking business? No, he didn't like the idea of being caught in a lie by his Walkiria so early in the relationship, and doubted somehow that even real business would get the chatterbox Chrissie Luna to leave.

"Would you like to come too?" Chrissie said, turning to Walkiria.

Retter laughed out loud, great idea, why have the cat fight now when we can postpone for a day or two? He watched Chrissie smile and very deliberately take out her agenda.

"I've got to run now, but give me your number and I'll call you, OK?"

Miracle of miracles, five minutes after saying "I've got to run now," five minutes of excruciating pleasantries about all manner of most incredibly trivial matters, Chrissie finally decamped, leaving the way clear for Karl-Heinz Retter to turn the mini-man charm-ray back on again, full blast. But then the waitress brought the "moo" tea, and it turned out to be absolutely ghastly, a barely-believable decoction full of twigs, foul-smelling herbs, mouse lips, marsupial bile, squirrel claws and what have you, a witch's brew which no cow in his right mind would ever drink. "*Ja*, so why do they call this moo tea?" he snorted.

"Mu tea? I don't know?"

"No, of course." So vile was the smell, that on olfactory grounds alone, Retter couldn't help but remember all over how Walkiria had failed to grasp his joke, and the almost desperately indelicate way she had combined with her muffin-head hemp-sister to badger him into ordering a potion that not only he, but anyone sane enough to remember his own name, couldn't possibly swallow. An imposition which, were Karl-Heinz Retter younger, he would have quickly tallied up as Walkiria's fourth major blunder inside of five minutes, but which thanks to experience, patience and maturity, Retter merely took care of without comment, by "accidentally" spilling his "tea" into a nearby fern. "Everyone has bad days," he laughed it off, fully expecting that with a name like Walkiria, she would comprehend that the "everyone" he was talking about was her, not himself. "Do you think the plant will survive? Ha-ha, ha-ha," he added, thinking that she probably didn't grasp it after all, thinking that coffee with a woman named Walkiria was turning into an unexpectedly difficult ordeal. That's what he got for denying his responsibility and letting someone else lead! There must be ten thousand more interesting things he could be wasting time on at this very moment, including shaving his ears or clipping his nose hairs, for instance, or taking the dogs to the park. Or even... beginning seriously to look into the financing for whatever film project he ended up doing with the monk. With Yuichi.

Thankfully, before he actually had to climb down off the remaining phone book and bid her adieu, patience and charitable impulse did finally begin to bear fruit, as the discussion about whether the fern would survive evolved into a passionate and far-ranging discussion on all matters horticultural, a subject, *Ja*, a discipline, about which, already for some time now, Karl-Heinz Retter had been seriously considering writing a monograph or two.

A proud little secret that he was millimeters from sharing, when so-called Walkiria suddenly decided it was time to begin sharing her opinions. Opinions such as what a strange coincidence it was that Karl-Heinz Retter was from Switzerland, since her favorite flower just happened to be the Giant Swiss Pansy.

"The pansy! Really!" Retter smiled, full charm ahead, not letting on at all, but wondering just exactly what she was trying to tell him with this floral preference that seemed just slightly too convenient, this choice whose insulting innuendo Karl-Heinz Retter did not instantly, of course, fail to grasp. "Tell me Val, that name of yours, if you don't mind my asking. Did your parents give that to you, or did you choose it yourself?" She had a lesson or three to learn about dealing with a man who knows the date of his death.

"My name?"

"Yes. Did you or did you not wrongly expropriate it all on your own, because you liked the sound of it? For it would not be possible for you to have been named that from birth, would it? I mean, just look at you!"

"I'm sorry?"

"You know something sweetheart? When you've lived as long as I have, there's not much that surprises you anymore. Little diseased Valhalla hags like you are a dime a dozen. Siri, Freyja, Fjorgynn, dig a little deeper and you're all the same: foes to war and progress, sticky little spiders overflowing with populist poison. Walkiria! The gall! I think we've wasted enough time, don't you? You will pick up the bill, I think, yes. Gingham, ha-ha, ha-ha, obviously no one told you this is the year 2000, poor thing."

38

The morning after Yuichi's return to the cell, Reverend Y woke up and quietly tested his shoulders, rotating them one way then the next, then snapping off a few punches just to make sure the healing magic hadn't dissipated overnight.

"How does it feel?" Yuichi laughed.

"Fine, just fine, better than fine. Amazing!" Still astonished by Yuichi's healing abilities, still humbled by his capacity, Reverend Y wanted nothing more than to pay him back. As if, on the cosmic scale, that might begin to make amends for the many bruised souls he and his anger had left in their wake. The only question was with what coin he might conceivably even his debt, what a sinner like himself could offer that a man like Yuichi could possibly use. That was the problem...

A problem which turned urgent just before lunch, while Yuichi was giving Reverend Y another treatment, when Chuckles the orderly opened the door of the cell and with a "Sorry to interrupt you, fellas," announced that one Chrissie Luna was downstairs, with $35,000 cash in hand, and that Yuichi was once again free to leave.

"Wait, just hold on a second here, not so fast," said Reverend Y. "There's something I gotta say."

"Ho?"

"Long time ago, I almost became heavyweight champion of the world, right?" Reverend Y fished around, the preacher talking an automatic blue stream in the hope of finding inspiration. "And you know what I found out? They don't like it. They don't like it when you got power, they don't like a man being a man because they're scared, they're scared of the black man. They're scared of any man, black, white, zebra, or yellow who shows them what it is to be a man. And you know why? Because most of them gave up on that before they even started. You understand what I'm saying?"

"Sure."

That was it, Reverend Y had figured it out! He pushed Yuichi's hands off him and sat up straight. "They had to put me in jail, I realize that. Just like they gotta put you in jail, molefockel. Yeah, man, I don't just talk, I also keep my eyes open. And I tell you what you're going to do. I'm going to become Heavyweight Champion of the world, and you're going to help me. And you know why? Because they will think you will have resurrected me. And I will let them think that, you have my word. You don't believe me, do you? You're thinking, who is this crazy big black man? Why should I help this War-Of-All-Against-All guy?"

"Yes."

"Last night I had this dream. Yeah. It was a field full of statues. Nighttime... you could barely see. There were the statues of the gods, with this kind of weird light around them, and there were a whole shitload of people, so many that the Parks folks couldn't even count 'em. And the people started coming at the statues, raising clouds of dust and making noise. Some began to spit on the statues, some pulled out ropes which they cast around the statues to topple them off their pedestals. And then the sky began to turn light, and you know what I saw? I saw you! You molefockel, in my dream, and you've got a rope too, only yours is attached to the sun which you're pulling across the sky. You know what I mean? Yeah, I see you know. So man, if you can do that, you can damn sure be in my corner, and I'll let the world know. And I'll tell you something else. You're a strong little mo'fucker, and you got you some real power. But one thing I know, you ain't never going to make it here on your own, 'cause you don't know dick about how the game runs here. If you don't know where to find the strings, you ain't never gonna make the puppets dance. Tell the crazy woman to go away, what you gonna do out there with her again, how you going to get her to give up your scroll? You got a plan? Stay with me for a while, make her sweat. You get me back in shape, six weeks, and we take it from there." Reverend Y put his hands up in front of his face, bouncing and moving the gloves back and forth. "See what I'm saying? We both get what we want. Like a cat watching a mouse hole, you got to be patient. You watch, you watch, then, pow, you pounce."

39

Willi Roth, head of Nigel Forsythe Cosmetics began experimenting with a new drug call Crystal Glass Cream that his six year old brought home one weekend when daddy had custody. Raj Mikkelson, head of Samsara Cosmetics, stuck with the old familiar, the good old opiates and the occasional coca pick-me-up in times of need.

Willi Roth, head of Nigel Forsythe Cosmetics, went down to the Amazon and personally started fires in the rainforest, hoping to wipe out the ecosystem from which Samsara harvested 90% of its raw materials. Raj Mikkelson retaliated by buying a cut-rate handful of mothballed MiGs, and obliterating not only the petroleum refineries and coal mines around the coal-pot German city of Bochum from which Nigel Forsythe got its raw materials, but the chemistry labs where they put their foul potions together.

Willi Roth, head of Nigel Forsythe cosmetics, got his hands on some Ukrainian plutonium and set in motion a huge clandestine operation in Iraq, Libya and the former Soviet Union, to hire the talent with which to use that plutonium to make an atomic bomb. Raj Mikkelson, among whose clients was the wife of the President of Russia, eliminated the whole development stage entirely and got his hands on a Russian SS-22, some anthrax shells, and a little personal-size battlefield atom bomb small enough to keep under the chauffeur in the Samsara limousine, just in case.

Willi Roth's girlfriend, 6'4" and 200 pounds, stood by her man until she owned the deeds to three houses and two sports cars, both of which she found too small, then complained that he didn't love her anymore. Raj Mikkelson's girlfriend, 6'5" and 205, made the mistake of telling a confidant that Raj couldn't get it up anymore. The next day she went up in flames, a rare case of spontaneous combustion, which not only saved on the costs of cremation but provided the opportunity for an East Hamptons wake which the Clarion rated afterwards as the social event of the month. An event at which Raj Mikkelson was consoled by a 6'6" She-Gladiator named Velvet Underground whom some said had already shared his bed, tsk tsk, and what did that say about the times when the next woman hopped into bed with a man before the last love's ashes had even cooled? An event at which Chrissie Luna, drinking the Long Island Ice Tea of rejection and binging on crab dip with taro chips, probably gained three pounds easy, and almost met Elton John, by now a veteran of the funeral circuit at $100,000 a pop, who had retooled "Candle in the Wind" yet again, personalizing it for the occasion, causing everyone but Chrissie Luna to cry.

Sitting off by herself, far away from the house, at the edge of the vast lawn on a little wall overlooking the ocean, Chrissie wondered if Raj Mikkelson would ever get around to being serious about the pet makeup thing. Chrissie Luna wondered how, after all she had done for Yuichi, he could have possibly turned down her offer of bail money. Was someone else's bail money better? And if so, where was that other person the first two times out? Or was it simply that Yuichi really, truly, actually, preferred to stay in jail? If that was the case, then, that was it, she'd make a quick surgical end. If he wanted his silly little scroll back, then she'd just go down to the bank and get it for him. Wash her hands of him for once, give him a little bit of his own medicine, see how he liked that. With the $6 million she had put in the bank, she had imagined herself staking him to just about any crime spree he wanted, but once she had washed her hands of him, it would be too late. When a woman's heart breaks, it's broken and no amount of begging can sway her. With $6 million in the bank? She could afford to hire Elton John fully sixty times over, couldn't she? But on the spur of the moment, sitting at the edge of the lawn like that while the rest of the crows networked around the poor dead giantess's extra-large urn, she couldn't come up with anyone whose death she imagined she would really care enough about to hire Elton even so much as once.

40

With Nat Gold looking on, giving all manner of unwanted advice, Reverend Y began training for his comeback. Pushups, sit-ups and skipping rope in the tiny cell, running laps on the floating jail mezzanine while the other short-termers cheered, and under Yuichi's supervision stretching, stretching, stretching. Stretching his shoulders, stretching his hamstrings and back to strengthen the kidneys, twisting his torso where the gallbladder meridian runs down on the side.

"Loosen gallbladder, then gallbladder loosen liver. Loosen liver, take care of ligament and tendon all over."

"Hey Luigi, you know what? You don't have to talk in that fucky-wucky way, anymore. I do understand you, you know..."

"You do?"

"You're my brother."

"OK, good."

What part of Reverend Y's initial impulse to return to the ring was actually motivated by a sense of obligation to Yuichi, and what part was the attempt to recapture a dream of glory interrupted by shoulder pain ten years previously, no man could say, probably not even Reverend Y himself. Crazy as his comeback sometimes seemed, in those moments when he could not help but be aware of how long he had been out of the game, how soft his body had gotten, how much longer it took for him to recover from the workouts, the punishment, how unimaginably far he had to go to regain that ability to transform the burn, the pain, into something acceptable and not agonizing, Reverend Y did not for a second allow himself to doubt, nor try to back out of his commitment. The fight would come off no matter what obstacles were put in his way, he would push himself through every barrier. This was bigger than him, this was theater on a grand scale. This was not just Apocalyptic rhetoric and idle fomentation, this was the fate of the planet held in his gloved hands. And if it turned out that neither Yuichi, nor Jesus Christ, nor destiny could prevent him from getting a whuppin' then that's exactly what he would get. But not before escorting a woman clothed in the sun just a little closer to home.

In the meantime, as impresario and director, puppet and puppeteer, he was prepared to bluff them all the way to the top. "What we want," every night while Yuichi massaged him, (with particular attention to two points, Stomach 44 and Liver 3, for the sore muscles) he shared with Yuichi and Nat Gold, the evolution of his thinking. "What we want is to come up with a card like in the good old days... Louis-Schmeling, Liston-Clay, Ali-Frazier, right? When a fight was not just for money, but a fight was a morality play. Two men, good or evil, left or right, us or them and the destiny of the human race on the line, see what I'm saying?"

To that end, even though Reverend Y hadn't fought in ten years, the man he decided on as an opponent was one Nephi Samuels, the WBA Number 2 contender, a rock hard 24 year-old from Salt Lake City, the only Caucasian ranked in the top ten. Great White Hope vs. Crazy Nigger, Backwater Mormon Conservative vs. Chiliastic Avenger, Future vs. Past, no other potential opponent even came close.

"Nephi Samuels? He'll kill you!" Nat Gold, the expert, couldn't believe his ears.

"What's done is done. Madison Square Garden, Saturday April 1, 2000..."

"April Fool's day? Nice choice!" Nat Gold jumped down off his bunk to protest. A comeback was a slow, gradual thing, you didn't just jump in against the highest ranking man with a hole in his schedule in the not-too-distant future.

"Crazy nigger keepin' 'em guessing."

"April Fool's..."

"That's right." Reverend Y just smiled, because Nat Gold obviously had no idea what it was like to be infused with a holy mission, to wake up every morning with a purpose.

"How close is that to Palm Sunday this year, Reverend?" Nat Gold, said, added a whacking-the-lou-lou hand gesture, in case the irony wasn't clear on its own.

"Why don't you tell me..."

"He will kill you."

"Maybe yes, maybe no," answered Reverend Y, adding, like George Foreman before him: "All I need is one punch."

Just as expected, thanks to his notoriety and the usual "goodwill" of the Clarion, Reverend Y's decision to lace up the gloves again created a lot more excitement than the return to the ring of a journeyman heavyweight might otherwise have warranted. And just as hoped for, everyone began to take sides. No detail of Reverend Y's comeback regimen was too small or insignificant to end up in print and Clarion readers soaked it all up. The Reverend's special diet, no tomatoes, no potatoes, no eggplant, no pork, no coffee or other stimulants, (just like Nephi Samuels) his weight loss and endurance gain, the New York boxing commission guy who gave the shoulder a clean bill of health, the inch by inch progress as, after ten years off, Reverend Y tried to relax his anger-stiffened body enough to touch his toes, and even the scrappy, scroll-bearing, Mormon-slaying masseur who had inspired the comeback, who insisted on putting Reverend Y though all manner of unboxerly exercises to strengthen his ki. "You know what this fight is about?" Reverend Y said. "This fight is about predictable vs. unpredictable, man vs. machine..."

To which Nephi Samuels, who had been stung by various comments in the press chiding him for accepting a bout with such an ostensibly weak opponent, provided an answer the very next day: "A weathervane spins around whenever the wind blows, but that don't make it unpredictable, you always know right where it is." Reverend Y thought he was so smart, but Nephi Samuels wanted the press to know he had some opinions of his own. For instance about the Panama Canal, and how peeved he was that we had handed it back, or what a bad sign it was that February had 29 days, this year, a centesimal leap year for the first time since the year 1600. "1600" which just happened to be the address of the White House, proof again of humans messing with the divine plan. And the bout, Nephi? "That's what I'm talking about: the bout. I expect this boxing contest to be just one last three-round-max tune-up on my way to Number 1."

A prediction with which, Notorious MEDIUM, Reverend Y's clairvoyant ex-trainer, could not help but agree. "If Julius had a year to train? Under the proper conditions? Assuming the shoulder isn't a problem anymore? Which I doubt. Sure. But at the age of 36? After a ten year layoff like that? With only eight weeks of training? I mean, personally I like the cat, and I believe in miracles as much as the next guy, but..."

"I guess that makes it official," said Nat Gold, closing the paper and shaking his head with the usual hangdog look at Reverend Y.

"What?"

"You're the underdog."

"You know what?" Before, if he'd seen that kind of doubt around him prior to a match, Reverend Y would have lashed out, sent the guy to the hospital. Now, he just played with him.

"What?"

"Underdog is right where Reverend Y wants to be."

"Ho? Under dog?" Yuichi said, sincerely mystified, having recently been under a dog or two himself.

Two weeks after the start of the comeback, Reverend Y and Nat Gold, but not Yuichi, were released from prison along with a flood of other minor convicts statewide, double parkers, tax evaders, jaywalkers, petty dealers and graffiti addicts. A President's Day amnesty ordered by the governor, a move he tried to spin as a healing gesture, a demonstration of goodwill worthy of Abraham Lincoln, a move with the added benefit of opening up the jails for those more deserving.

"A sign! It's a sign," Reverend Y exulted, "Don't worry, Luigi, I'll raise your bail money myself, and we'll get you out in no time flat."

As it turned out though, that too proved unnecessary, another sign, as the little hiccup in the training, the brief separation, was remedied just two days later, even without bail. A most unexpected event courtesy of the ACLU, which, after reading the articles about the mystic masseur in the paper, had gone to bat for Yuichi, as part of a larger crusade against the Mayor's morality crackdown, and First Amendment rights generally. A campaign which the overburdened judge, the governor's man to begin with, not to mention a big fan of Reverend Y's from way back, rewarded inside of fifteen minutes of the opening gavel.

"If just being in a place where people are masturbating is a crime," he said, explaining why he was throwing Yuichi's case out of court on grounds of false arrest, then every judge and every politician in the land would have to be incarcerated. Including Mayor Morales, might I add, who will kindly stop trying to imitate Ayatollah Khomeini from now on, and kindly let the people live. Next..."

Of the millions of people across the country looking forward to the April Fool's Day bout, and more specifically, the 800 or so grouped outside the New York City Floating prison, probably none saw it quite like a certain Japheth Joseph Abram Brigham Smith, the Mormon with the twice-fractured jaw. No lover of pugilism, he had nonetheless become convinced, thanks to a series of dreams, that the bout between the Black man (who just happened to have the Shinto "monk" in his corner), and the boy from Salt Lake City (even if he wasn't exactly the most devout Mormon) was simply the Lord's doubly-mysterious way of demonstrating, once and for all, that the Church of Latter Day Saints was indeed the true church, the one religion where all the parts fit together snugly, perfectly. He had come to the prison to tell Yuichi, in person, that he had informed the court he was no longer pressing charges for the Lafayette St. assault, that he knew it was an accident, that, as a matter of fact, the Church of Latter Day Saints also had a number of highly secret scrolls, whose higher truths Yuichi might just consider adopting in lieu of his own.

From the beginning, from the very first slipper-to-teeth contact with Yuichi on the United Nations North Plaza, New Year's Day, Japheth Joseph Abram Brigham Smith had a sense of destinies crossing. On that day he had been a man adrift, a bitter man drawn blindly, inexplicably to the United Nations with Jack Daniels on his breath, fornication on his fingers and violence in his heart. But the broken jaw had given him time to think. What else could it be than divine warning, chastisement for his lack of purity, for moments of weakness in the last wandering years, for the coffee drinking, the sister-sleeping, the dancing with John Barleycorn, for desperation so desperate that Satan had pushed him verily to the brink of the door of the Church of Scientology?

What else could it be but Divine chastisement, a wakeup call for him to rise from sinful sloth and slumber and become the Lord's tool? Answer: it could also be condemnation of the present Church of Latter Day Saints entire, the less-than-ten commandments church whose flexible doctrine and loss of charisma he felt had caused him to drift in the first place. A church that, as he learned when he began to look into it, had signed a pact with the devil as long ago as 1874, 126 years ago, when the elders rejected Consecration and the United Order, abandoned the striving for the pure paradise of Zion in favor of becoming the State of Utah, disavowed revelation about polygamy as if it were some kind of idle doctrine and not divine fiat channeled through the Prophet Joseph Smith.

This is what he would like to tell the people: that there were two Mormon churches, the real one, the true one, the pure one and then the other one, the bastard LDS, the one everyone made jokes about, the one the Book of Mormon warned about, Book of Mormon 8:28. "Yea, it shall come in a day when the power of God shall be denied, and churches become defiled and be lifted up in the pride of their hearts; yea, even in a day when leaders of churches and teachers shall rise in the pride of their hearts, even to the envying of them who belong to their churches." Or even, "Book of Mormon, 8:32. Yea, it shall come in a day when there shall be churches built up that shall say: Come unto me, and for your money you shall be forgiven of your sins."

Verily he had seen that church, a Hollywood church where they played piano music at critical moments to heighten the emotional peaks. A church where ushers carried boxes of Kleenex up and down the aisles to encourage Sunday tears so that the people might forget righteousness the rest of the week. Verily he had tried his best to move away from that, only to discover that it was not enough to testify, to confront the devil, and seek out evil wherever it flowered, not enough simply to have a pure heart. Two fractured jaws later, Japheth Joseph Abram Brigham Smith, the unbending, the prideful, had finally been granted a vision. Though his message be sound, the presentation was defective. "One word for you , Japheth Joseph Abram Brigham Smith," spake the Lord in his dream: "Ventriloquism!" Of course! To trick the devil with the same virtuous bolts of righteous scriptural lightning as before, but delivered from a safe distance by throwing his voice.

Outside the prison for Yuichi's coming-out party, there were any number of targets. Reverend Y playing "Smack the Weasel" with a good-natured Nat Gold to demonstrate for a horde of greasy photographers, TV people and fans, just how soft and pathetic the white man was by his very nature; Karl-Heinz Retter struggling to rein in eight randy dogs; the Iraqi and Japanese ambassadors to the UN trying to settle once and for all whether Hinomoto Kuni or Mesopotamia was the cradle of civilization by calling each other "Camelfucker" back and forth; any number of the usual Christians, Santerians, mystics, messianists and millenarian revisionists, etc... bumping into each other in an attempt to ignite a new battle, to set it off once again; and even an emaciated Ethiopian busker playing guitar and singing Chubby Checkers' "Twist Again," a special, enervated, batteries-low, no-enthusiasm version, "Come... on... let's... twist... again..."

In fact, the only person the Mormon noticed in whom a brief spurt of shining truth might not produce an instant violent reaction was contrite Chrissie Luna. And so, surrounded by four bodyguards just-in-case, lurking by the edge of the prison parking lot, ready to flee, it was into her ear that Japheth Joseph Abram Brigham Smith tossed the first long-distance scripture, her ear alone, and not the rest of the roughly 794 others waiting for Yuichi to appear. "Ever try a Mormon?"

Shivering deliciously, Chrissie Luna was instantly drawn right to him, causing the bodyguards to tighten ranks. "You look better than you did on TV," she said, trying to slide the words through the cracks between the bodyguards' shoulders, careful not to let on about how much better he would look still with just a tiny makeover and a little attention to style. Polygamy didn't seem like such a bad idea really. What if you didn't have to be so perfect for each other, what if you could get what you needed from a third party? Yuichi for massage and foreplay, Jim O'Brien for abuse, Neil Armstrong, (who had forgiven her for the knee to the groin in Atlantic City) for his seed, Karl-Heinz Retter for those sicko days, and who knows, maybe this multi-womb More-man to fill in the gaps. Right here, right now, the picture looked just fine to Chrissie Luna. "We're having a party in Yuichi's honor?" She nodded at the prison just in case the Mormon didn't understand to whom she was referring.

"Yes..." Japheth Joseph Abram Brigham Smith answered warily.

"Well, would you like to co-ome?"

"Don't rightly know. Tonight's my ventriloquism class."

"Ventriloquism class!" Chrissie said with a big testosterone laugh, she thought she had heard them all. "Sorry, would love to, but I have to go bathe my giraffe," she said.

"I'm sorry?"

"Ventriloquism, eh? You're funny." Confident as she was, she decided to act as if he weren't just telling her some fib to get out of seeing her. "Come on, don't be silly. You'll see, he's not such a bad guy. I'm sure you two will get along just fine if you just get to know each other. 8:00, 226 Lafayette, fifth floor. The name is Luna, Chrissie Luna," she added sticking a $6 million confident hand out to shake. "See you there."

And how could Chrissie Luna be so sure that Yuichi would even accept an invitation to yet another party? Very simple: she had something he wanted, something cylindrical and ancient to be a tad more precise. (No, not her vag, shame on you!) Casually, confidently, perfectly posted in the mouth of the antechamber when Yuichi finally appeared around six p.m., that is exactly what Chrissie told him. That and, loud enough for everyone else to hear, "Party at my place tonight, 8 o'clock, bring anyone you like." An approach just as sassy, dry and smooth as she had planned it, and time enough to boot, before the rest of them had completely surrounded Yuichi and cut off his sight lines, to turn her back on him, march over to her waiting limo, get in, and know that he was watching. The ice dolphin was waiting in the new extra-large freezer, the hors d'oeuvres chef had been working since 11:30 a.m., the flowers were already in place. If traffic wasn't too bad, she would have an hour and a half to get ready, an hour and a half just for herself.

Reverend Y, the Mormon, the Japanese ambassador, Walkiria, Karl-Heinz Retter, Celestina and Jack Bravo, Raj Mikkelson, Neil Armstrong and Buzz Aldrin, to say nothing of the regulars, Jim O'Brien, etc... If everyone she expected actually did come, and the photographers showed up outside, it would be the party of the year, they might even make a documentary. Then she'd like to hear what her mother would have to say the morning after. It would be worth it just for that.

41

The biggest little man in the world, Karl-Heinz Retter, arrived at 226 Lafayette at 8:30 sharp, fashionably late, wearing his box-fresh Greeley's outfit with the blinding pearl snaps, crisp-creased riding pants and so-new-they-mooed little knee boots. To which he had added sunglasses and a bushy, fake mustache with which he hoped to pass unnoticed, in spite of the eight dogs sprouting from his gnarled little fists. And who should he run into right off the bat? Not formal-gingham Walkiria-the-insidious off cackling away with Chrissie's Mormon, not the Japanese ambassador who had brought his silly Sharpeis to the party and was so ashamed of them that he didn't dare leave the wet-bar where they could almost remain out of sight, not Yuichi, who probably didn't intend to show at all, which was making Chrissie Luna, wife of the seven dragons, go all kinds of nuts. Who should he run into but Jack Bravo, Millenarian novelist? Jack Bravo, who had apparently just sold his first novel and had decided this entitled him to commandeer the entire hors d'oeuvre high-ground and offer, like a blessing, some sort of abject lexiphanic rodomontade on the subject of his magnificent, exemplary life. The secret of a life so splendid and pure, that after 20 years of willful parasitism, freeloading and generally keeping from freezing thanks only to the heating system of the New York City public library, it could lead to such glorious, overnight success. "You know how I finally got published?"

"Coffee?" Retter asked with a mild yawn, hoping the "writer" would take the hint. The hors d'oeuvre chef smiled and try to squeeze by Jack Bravo to put some of the delicacies on a platter, but no luck, the oblivious beanstalk just kept talking, gesticulating and smiling as if his tired story, his demonstration of the-obvious-parading-as-wisdom were compensation for keeping 12 famished people from their God-given snacks and just desserts.

With a big sigh, weary from being called, yet again, to do what was right, to give the example, to lead, Retter just elbowed his way past the writer, made it to the hors d'oeuvres after all and picked up an oyster.

"Oyster Shanghai," said the proud caterer.

"Yes..." Retter answered, trying to change the course of things, to start a stampede, slurping on the oyster from between the novelist's legs, smacking his lips greedily and letting a little fish roe and scallion stick on the tip of his nose before cleaning it off with a quick amphibian flick of the tongue. And still the cowards waited at a safe distance, didn't dare advance on the food their greedy hands lusted for, didn't dare stick up for themselves, (or for common decency), and put a rapid, merciful end to the fable-monger's time in the limelight.

When you write, there's something strange you notice," Jack Bravo just couldn't get enough of himself. "Say you write about the future, well if you write with full intensity, things you write about tend to come true. You write about falling in love with a woman? Boom, it comes true. You write about people going nuts? Boom, they go nuts. You write about disaster? Next thing you know it's in the papers. It's like alchemy, magic, and you know what I had to do? After writing about all sorts of other things happening to all sorts of other people? I never took the trouble to write about a novelist selling his own book. So I did, and then *I did*, simple as that..."

"Is anyone listening to this guy?" Retter canvassed the crowd, but apart from the caterer, who stood there rolling his eyes, the anesthetic effect of the novelist's words had apparently so diminished their mental acuity that they couldn't respond. Retter grabbed a second oyster, slurped it down, wiped his chin, and said a little louder, "Hey Jack Bravo, maybe people are hungry?"

"Shh..." Celestina hushed him with a finger to her lips as if he were some kind of Kindergarten flunk-out, and not Karl-Heinz Retter to whom she had confided what no man must know, the date of his death.

"I'm szorry?" He could feel the oysters coming back up. Karl-Heinz Retter took the sunglasses off his nose and stuck them on his forehead, perhaps she just hadn't recognized him? Then, just as quickly, he jerked his head forward to make the sunglasses slide off his forehead and back over his eyes, chance over. Standing on tiptoes, he scanned the hors d'oeuvre selection, and finally picked out a lobster *taquito* with the idea that by eating something higher on the food chain, he might convince the oysters to stay down. Except who did the lobster think it was claiming to be higher on the food chain than an oyster? Where did the lobster get off... "Sssstt!" Retter rebuked himself, reminding himself to focus on the business at hand. This was no time to become wrapped up in questions of shellfish hierarchy and unwarranted crustacean arrogance. A subject, of course, which no man on earth was better qualified to discuss, sure, but which might well demand a ranking of the entire animal kingdom before he had done it justice. A risk which, in light of the enemy all around, Karl-Heinz Retter could not reasonably, chronometrically, afford to take just now.

Oh yes, the little astrologer-tramp had thrown quite a wrench in Karl-Heinz Retter's delicate Swiss works by insisting on telling him the day of his death. That he had to confess. But did Karl-Heinz Retter share his inner turmoil, and burden poor innocent people whose only wish was to get to the hors d'oeuvres? Did he feel obliged to impress on these poor people, these sheep, the depth of trauma one experienced as the only man in the world to know the date of his death? Did he strut back and forth and bleat out what it was like to be marooned among time-wasters, idlers and weather-talkers? Did he shear them within an inch of their trivial lives with stories of what it was like to try to invite death openly, to look for a marriage in death for time and all eternity, just to prove one astrology-slattern wrong?

Sure he could tell them how it felt, when in the throes of an only-eight-dogs depression, to find the very walls of the city suddenly covered with mocking graffiti, teleological taunts directed at him and only him, "Repenting of time squandered," "It's too late baby now," "Don't you wish you'd thought about this earlier?" But could he even begin to attempt to explain what it was like for a Swiss man to catch a policeman's eye, then suddenly run the other way madly, through a forest of legs, zoom, zoom, zip, zip, just inviting retribution? Or did he seek their sympathy by recounting how difficult it was, when you were high on heroin from a dirty needle, to suck off a transvestite inside the Disney store without a rubber, and still keep eight dogs in line? No, he kept it to himself, kept it behind the sunglasses and the mustache.

In fact, Karl-Heinz Retter would not even have honored the party with his presence tonight, didn't see what there was possibly to be gained, except that outside the prison, seeing Yuichi with the boxer like that and putting two and two together, he had had a so-fantastic idea. What if he called his dog-walking clients and informed them that plans had changed, that the yearly dog visitation had been moved up to tonight, nine o'clock, 226 Lafayette? Told them that, although he couldn't guarantee it, the chances were excellent that an appearance would be put in by none other than so-called Minister Y? A name that a man who knew the date of his death would only mention in the first place to conceal his real motive, which was to inquire whether any of those wealthy people might care to invest in a certain film starring a certain Shinto monk.

Even if they had no desire whatsoever to visit with their dogs, Retter was sure at least a good half of his clients would be completely powerless to decline a potential meeting with the boxer, ha-ha, ha-ha. In America, you could be a triple rapist, an arsonist, a billion dollar embezzler, a hack actor with a drug problem or a lying politician, but if you had been out of circulation long enough, if you managed to demonstrate a modicum of remorse, a hint of having learned your lesson, you could attain the kind of celebrity and fortune which solid hard work alone would *never* get you. Then absolutely everyone wanted to shake your hand, as if by just brushing up against you, they could magically come away with your charisma, your good luck. Disgraceful, true, but that's just the way it was, and how was one Swiss man with only one pair of small shoulders to alter the tides of history? Maybe in the future, yes, but not yet, sadly, not yet.

Yuichi arrived in an elevator with Reverend Y, Nat and Sarah Gold, Marakchi, the Iraqi ambassador, Wella Balsam, the actress, Max Gilmore, the publisher of the Clarion, with his four year old son, Max Jr., Raj Mikkelson with his 6'7" girlfriend who stood 6'11" in her platform shoes, not to mention Neil Armstrong and Buzz Aldrin, wearing actual space suits in case anyone had forgotten who they were. A grouping which, thanks to the Law of Higher Celebrity, pretty much obliged Jack Bravo, finally, thankfully, to shut up.

In spite of the fact that Reverend Y had drilled Yuichi for three hours before the party on the need for patience, for letting Chrissie come to him, as soon as they had stepped in the door Yuichi made a beeline for the window, within easy striking distance of Chrissie's court. There, coiled like a spring, completely deaf to any words of caution, Yuichi waited for an opening, determined to ascertain as soon as possible exactly what it was she had for him, so that they could just turn around and leave if yet again she proved to have nothing. "What can she possibly have?" he said for about the tenth time in the last hour, thinking that even if she had finally gone to the bank, without his signature, she wouldn't be able to get the scroll out either.

"Patience Luigi, patience. We enjoy the party, we take our time."

"Yes, enjoy the party," Yuichi parroted back, trying to concentrate his energy into the minds of those around her, to them to go away. But there were just too many of them, and their brains didn't seem to be responding to suggestion on this night. There were the two astronauts, taking up more space than necessary in their suits, there was Karl-Heinz Retter with eight dogs circling around the little group trying to get away from Wella Balsam who couldn't stop saying, "But they're my dogs," there was Jim O'Brien with one possessive arm around Chrissie's shoulder and a bottle of Black Bush in his free hand, a bottle which, with seemingly-drunk abandon, he waved through the air, dangerously close to the nose of anyone coming too near.

"What's with the monkey suits, lads?" O'Brien said to Armstrong and Aldrin. Richer by $660,000 since the last trip to Atlantic City, Jim O'Brien had come around. Jim O'Brien had no choice but to think that he and Chrissie Luna actually made a pretty fair pair.

"The suits are because we're astronauts?" the Apollo-boys chorused, giving the old question-mark-at-the-end-of-the-sentence act.

"Astronauts, really?"

"We were the first men to step on the moon?" Ever since the start of construction of the Space Station, astronauts were hot, or cool, whatever word people were using these days. But you never knew how long that might last.

"Sure, and I'm the Pope."

"One small step for man?" Neil Armstrong said.

"One giant leap for mankind?" Buzz Aldrin added.

"You're not really the guys, are you?"

"You want to call Mission Control?"

"Go on." Jim O'Brien shook his head, took a swig from the bottle, then looked at Chrissie Luna for confirmation.

"It's true..." Chrissie said.

Jim O'Brien wanted to slap her on the back of the head, but instead took another swig from the bottle, then offered it to the astronauts, who both refused. "Tell you the truth?" O'Brien said, "I'd rather meet Tom Hanks."

"Jim, how could you?" Chrissie said, thinking she probably would too, at least Tom Hanks wouldn't need to come to a party in a spacesuit. But she tried to reassure the astronauts nonetheless. "Don't listen to him."

"Tom Hanks was Apollo 13. We were Apollo 11," Neil Armstrong said with a hint of exasperation betraying that this wasn't the first time he had had to make the clarification.

"Well if what you did was so fucking great, how come no one made a fill-em out of it?"

"No one made a what?"

"A moo-vee for fuck's sake..."

"What do you mean, how come nobody made a movie? It was a giant leap for mankind, who cares if they made a movie?"

"Well if you ask me, you can take a giant leap at a rolling donut. Anyway, you're just here to chat up my bird, aren't you?"

"I've got six million reasons to like her," Neil Armstrong said with a huge laugh, as if confessing out loud the actual, real, true reason for his presence at the party tonight would make Chrissie think that was absolutely the last thing on his mind.

"Well get in line then," Jim O'Brien said with an equally huge laugh of his own.

"I am," "We are," answered Neil Armstrong and Buzz Aldrin respectively, with an even larger huge laugh back, thinking how wonderful it would be to be able to get off the casino greeting circuit and back into something with a little dignity.

"*We* are?" Neil Armstrong looked at Buzz Aldrin, with the largest huge laugh yet. He thought they had talked this over, and Buzz Aldrin had agreed to be the wingman. Now Buzz Aldrin was gold-digging too?

"You are," Buzz Aldrin said with the hugest large laugh to date, thinking about just how much he really hated Neil Armstrong, and what a complete asshole he had turned into ever since the moon and all the "Giant leap for mankind" crap. Which he didn't come up with himself to begin with, little known fact, but which he stole from one of the Mission Control janitors, giving him a hundred dollar shopping voucher and a food basket so he'd keep mum until they got around to killing him in a car accident, true story.

"How many times a week do you think a dog should ejaculate?" Retter piped up out of left field when he had finally caught his breath, congratulating himself as the words came out, on his ability to interrupt a conversation properly, a most underrated social skill. It took pure imagination to come up with an incongruous-enough subject to stop a conversation cold. "The monk says dogs, and men, should only have sex once or twice a week," Retter added, jerking a thumb at Yuichi to show who he meant. Just the distraction he needed to slip between the astronauts, grab Chrissie's hand and move his fake mustache so close to her skin that only she and he knew he didn't actually touch, before clicking his heels and withdrawing, mission accomplished. Wella Balsam was spellbound, mesmerized, the Irisher around Chrissie's neck stopped waving his bottle through the air, and the space boys stopped laughing on the spot, which was a blessing because their dopey moonhead laughter had been hurting the dogs' ears. Only Chrissie herself didn't seem to be quite so charmed.

"You brought the dogs..." she said, her lips pursed, her brow furrowed.

"Yes I did!" Retter answered. On an impulse, with a sweet sweeping gesture refined over many, many years, Karl-Heinz Retter removed eight leashes, swung them like a lasso around his head, then snapped them back on the dog's collars with a quick flick of the wrist, not quite daring yet to set the dogs free. "Ha-ha, ha-ha," he laughed, not that it was funny, but in such a way that Neil Armstrong, Buzz Aldrin and even Jim O'Brien, couldn't help but join right in.

Still exuding nervousness, finding Chrissie's display of self-assurance highly suspect, Yuichi wandered through the party trying to remain loose and unattached, while waiting for Chrissie to become more available. A fifteen minute period during which he managed to offend Motowori, the Japanese ambassador, (by appearing to be a tad too friendly with the Iraqi ambassador), to offend Marakchi, the Iraqi ambassador, (by listening with only half-an-ear to the diplomat's comparison of the word "Yuichi" and the Arabic word, *"Ouidji,"* meaning a man looking for himself), to offend Japheth Joseph Abram Brigham Smith, the Mormon, (on basic principle), to offend the French artist by leaving in the middle of his explanation about why, after much reflection, he had changed his name to "God B. Sold," instead of God B. Rented. "Eez not a Fransh pon, but eez logical, non?" He even managed to offend the head freeloader, who cornered Yuichi by the kitchen with a "Can I tell you something?" new confession, something that had happened while he was off on vacation for a week in Puerto Vallarta. Something about his boyfriend Pedro, the serotonin junkie, who after threatening to do so forever, had finally gotten a sex change operation after all. "I loved him as a man, I'm just not sure I can love Pedro quite so much now that he's a woman," the freeloader said, remembering how supportive and interested Yuichi was the last time he was open for confession, and wondering if the lack of attention now was just his imagination, the result of emotional stress. "It just isn't the same. I mean what does that make me now? What would you do? Are you listening to me? Hello?"

"Will you excuse me?" Yuichi put his hand on the freeloader's shoulder, "Have something to eat, I'll be right back, OK?" Over by the window, where the publisher stood exchanging pleasantries with Reverend Y, the publisher's son had begun to cry. Already in the elevator, Yuichi had noticed there was something wrong with the boy: kidney, dark circles under the eyes and a chalky complexion that spoke of more than just fatigue.

"Come on, son, we'll just see your dog and then we'll go, OK?" The father tried to distract the boy, but a bit clumsily, lacking confidence, as if he weren't really that used to taking care of him.

"I don't want to see my dog," said Max Jr., crying even louder, loud enough to turn heads, rubbing his ear in obvious pain.

"Then you don't have to see your dog," Max Sr. tried again to console him, but with just as little confidence, so that for that reason or another Max Jr. began to cry even louder. "He has these ear aches, I couldn't get a baby-sitter..." Max Sr. explained with a "that's kids for you" nervous laugh for Reverend Y, just as Yuichi came up. Without hesitation he kneeled on the ground in front of the little boy and forgetting instantly all about Chrissie and whatever it was she did or didn't have for him, laid his warm hands over the boy's ears. "You're going to be OK..." he said, in such a reassuring way that the little boy's tears slowed.

"His name is Max Jr.," the publisher almost whispered so as not to disturb the mood. Irrational as it might be, a little swell of hope had risen in his heart, a little sob had stuck in his throat at the possibility that the healer might be able to do what no else had: take away his child's pain. "He gets these ear aches, been having them for months, we've tried everything," Max Sr. said, but a little louder this time, starting Max Jr.'s tears all over again. "Draining, antibiotics, you name it, so many things I can't remember. My poor little boy."

"Shh," Yuichi said to both father and son. Nothing but the boy and the energy existed anymore, the imbalance in the kidney meridian, the blockages keeping the body in Kanagi rhythm, when clearly it wanted to be in Sugaso. "Will you lie down for me Max? Right here on the floor? Can you do that for me? There's a good boy." Knowing that he had to work quickly before the boy's attention wandered and the little bit of trust or curiosity dissipated, Yuichi placed his fingers on the boy's pulses without preliminaries. "You like candy Max? Yes I can see that. And you like milk too? *Hai,*" he said with an imperious grunt that made the little boy laugh. *"Hai!"* he tried it again, making him laugh even harder. "Max I'm going to rub your legs a little bit, here on the inside, but you'll see, it will make the hurt in your ears go away. OK? Would you like that? *Hai!"*

"Yes..."

"No, not yes, little boy say *Hai!"*

"Hai..." Max Jr. squeaked gamely.

"No, no, like this: *Hai!!!"*

"Hai!"

"OK for now then, here we go."

To Max Gilmore's complete astonishment, within fifteen minutes, no more, Max Jr. was sound asleep right there in the middle of the party, so sound asleep that he didn't even wake up when Yuichi lifted him, carried him into Chrissie's bedroom and set him down on the bed. For thirty minutes he treated him, in the usual fashion, running hands over the spine, massaging the feet, breaking up the little knots in the abdomen, thirty minutes during which Max Gilmore, hoping against hope, stood back-to-wall, side-by-side with Reverend Y, watching quietly. When Yuichi was done, the little boy was breathing deeply, regularly, no creases of pain on his angelic face. Yuichi bowed to the boy, smiled and stood up.

"If you... If this could..." Max Gilmore couldn't find words to express his gratitude. "You don't know how many nights..." A very influential man had just seen a firsthand demonstration of the power of the new god. Reverend Y winked at Yuichi, as if to say "You see?"

"It's all right..." Yuichi disappeared into the bathroom to wash his hands, "If you could try to avoid milk products and sugar, candy?" he said over the sound of running water.

"OK..."

"Maybe a few more treatments, but he should be fine..."

"OK, thank you so much."

It was at this moment, with the sink water still running, that the bedroom door opened, letting in, first, the noise of the party, and second, the belle of the ball, Chrissie the Queen, fresh from a seduction of the two astronauts so thorough that she had actually begun to find them fatuous.

"What's everybody doing?" she said, over-loud, barging into the bedroom still on party volume, expecting something else. "Where's

181

Yuichi?" She had not failed to notice Yuichi treating the little boy in the living room, had not failed to see him carry the boy in the direction of her bedroom, it had just taken her thirty minutes to work the party, thirty minutes for her curiosity to get the better of her, thirty minutes until she just had to find out what she might be missing.

"Shh." Max Gilmore put his finger to his lips showing her the little boy stretched out on the bed.

"Oh," she whispered, scrunching up her face in apology, and closing the door softly behind her, "Sorry..." But then the sink tap went off, and Yuichi appeared in the doorway drying his hands on the hand towel, and she put two and two together. This time it wasn't even her, but a little boy. "Ah ha!" she said, forgetting to whisper all over again. There he was, caught wet handed, and with witnesses to boot. She couldn't wait to see him talk his way out of this one!

"It would be best for him to sleep a little bit right now. If you can spare the time?" Yuichi said quietly to Max Gilmore, virtually ignoring Chrissie Luna. "Maybe you enjoy the party a bit? There is something I must say now to our hostess..."

"Chrissie," Yuichi began as soon as Max Gilmore and Reverend Y had left the room, speaking in a soft, firm voice, "Do you remember when the French exploded an atom bomb on Mururoa?"

"Yes."

Yuichi sat Chrissie down on the edge of the bed, and with his hands on her shoulders, looked into her eyes. "Everyone found about it the next day in the newspapers, but I knew right away. You know why? Because every meridian had gone instantly out of balance. Do you understand? They said the ecology of Mururoa was not affected, so where was the problem? But what happened to me, happened to everyone else on the planet too. I was able to fix my energy, but what about all the others around the world who just woke up angry that day, and most of the following month? What about the earthquakes that followed, that always follow, around the earth? In Oriental medicine five element system they say water follows fire. Is it a coincidence that right after that, in China and America, there were floods? What does it take to convince people? In ancient times there was no such thing as democracy, men of judgment called Sumela Mikoto determined in which direction the society would go, and nobody objected because they could see the path they traced was true. What are the leaders now? How will history judge them, Chrissie? How will history judge the way they brought the dark ages to a close? The tremendous loss of life and untold suffering? Maybe it wasn't just to protect a few rich people and let everyone else get stupid. Do you understand, Chrissie? You didn't understand when I told you I am not a man. You can't feel why I wash my hands after touching you, how can I explain that it is just to remove the energy I have taken from you? Did you feel the atomic blast at Mururoa? Do you trust me? You want me to sleep with you? I will, it doesn't matter. But Chrissie," he paused and looked deep into her eyes, "There is no longer time for playing games. Do you understand? Think now, I'm begging you: how will history judge Chrissie Luna?"

Like a bucket of ice water, Yuichi's words poured over Chrissie's head, causing her party euphoria instantly to vanish, causing the last weeks to roll by in front of her like a horror movie. The attempts to seduce him, the forgetfulness, Atlantic City, the swings of mood, it made her face flush red with embarrassment and her heart cramp with horror. Six million dollars or no, the world Chrissie Luna inhabited had suddenly become a poor, sad place. "I'm sorry, I really am, I didn't realize, I feel so stupid," she said, struggling for words to express her contrition, hoping that he would understand how appalled she was by the person she had been, the being she had presented to him since the beginning, hoping that he could find it in his heart to forgive her. And then she moved to the head of the bed, gently lifted the pillow on which the little boy's sleeping head rested, and pulled out... the scroll. "Forgive me, please," she said, handing it to Yuichi.

Speechless, breathless, unable to believe his eyes, Yuichi could only wonder at the miracle, wonder how on earth she had managed to get the scroll from the bank.

"A girl's gotta do what a girl's gotta do, right?" she answered reading his mind. "Forgive me, I should be getting back to the party now, OK?"

42

In theory, Karl-Heinz Retter had nothing against letting owners see their dogs, although truth be told, it wasn't really all that good for the pooches themselves. Nothing against it at all, except that it made the dogs slothful and directionless, and sometimes it knocked their bowels out of whack for days on end. He had nothing against letting the owners, with careful supervision, in carefully-controlled environments of Retter's choosing, make brief physical contact with limited parts of their animals, even if the notion of being just one more person to submit to the wishes of these people who were used to getting everything they wanted was repellent to him. It was the bad side of the dog walker's life, the ugly, unavoidable public relations chore. But that didn't mean Karl-Heinz Retter had to like it. Nor did it mean that he treated all owners equally, especially not Wella Balsam who always seemed to go straight off her rocker on owners' day. To the innocent bystander, Wella Balsam might seem to be enthusiastic, getting down on all fours and following Retter under tables, through chairs and between people's legs. But in reality she wasn't the least bit interested in the reunion with Doberman and Dachshund. What she really wanted, Karl-Heinz Retter knew, was to get her hands on Karl-Heinz Retter, to resume the conversation about tranquilizers, cough medicines, sleeping pills and anti-depressants thanks to which, with blindingly luminous insight, he had gotten the custody of her dogs in the first place. Subjects which he alone among mortals supposedly understood. And that, Karl-Heinz Retter intended to avoid at all costs.

When the publisher and the boxer (wearing his insolent little smile) appeared back in the living room, it was the perfect excuse. A swift, accidental, kick to the bridge of Wella Balsam's nose and a quick move to within striking distance, dogs and all, zip, zip, zip. "There's this film, right?" Retter gave his pitch one more brief rehearsal, so as not to come off like just another insecure pan-handling dwarf. "We got the actor, right? All we need now is the money, which is where you come in, etc, etc... What do you mean who's the writer?" What arrogance! Retter hadn't even broached the subject to Gilmore and already the ingrate publisher was raising objections, as if the writer even mattered, *Gottinhimmel!* He mopped his brow, wiped off his sunglasses, then dabbed under the mustache, where the beads of perspiration were beginning to play havoc with the diligent but overmatched twin lines of mustache glue. "The writer? Right there. One of the hottest writers in the business, Jack Bravo, perhaps you haven't had the pleasure? What do you mean is there an actress?" Was the man blind? Couldn't he see Wella Balsam when she was right in front of him, eyes filled with tears? Did he know another actress with such a range of emotion? "So what's the story? There is a story, don't worry. It's called, it's called... *The Man Who Saved the World.*" Here Karl-Heinz Retter was giving him an opportunity to make a fortune with a major motion picture, and all Retter was "hearing" were objections.

In need of a quick social victory after this latest imaginary humiliation, Retter finally decided to take the dogs off their leashes after all. But when he did so, did they bolt towards the food like famished lions or drag the party down into instant anarchy? Did they throw themselves against the bedroom door and force themselves on the monk? Did they bare their fangs and trample women and children in the race to attack the Japanese ambassador's Sharpeis? No, not at all, they remained perfectly, placidly, in place on a telepathic Swiss leash, a leash even stronger than leather, a mental leash penetrating to the base of their little doggie skulls. Where was the danger, Chrissie Luna? Where was the danger unless someone provoked them?

Because of course then, *Ja,* in the event of provocation? It was a different matter, a different matter entirely. Even with the owners there, Karl-Heinz Retter could not be held responsible in the face of provocation. And what else was it other than a provocation that Walkiria had insisted on coming to this party? Fluffy! Light! he gave the mental order for the poodles to attack the Mormon, herding him away from Walkiria, and bringing the chess game to a close, check mate, before the poor fool even knew the pieces were on the board. Laurel! Hardy! The cocker spaniels raced in, grabbing Walkiria around the knees and humping away for dear life, provoked by the scent of gingham, whose aphrodisiac effect on cocker spaniels ranks behind only Japanese linen and certain Scottish wools.

And was it not a provocation that Motowori, by bringing his two pathetic Sharpeis to the party, had caused Chrissie to greet Retter and his dogs in such icy fashion? As if it were Retter who had encouraged Motowori to bring his wormy mutts to the ball! As if Karl-Heinz Retter needed help making bad impressions!

With only four dogs left in his gun belt, looking for suitable inspiration against the terrible sex-fearing Japanese adversary, trying, as yet unsuccessfully, to magnify the Sharpei provocation into something large enough to demand retaliation, Karl-Heinz Retter fixed his mustache like a gunslinger, and drifted towards Motowori the long way, via the kitchen. Via the kitchen where Jack Bravo appeared to be repeating his story, but at least didn't get in the way when Retter pushed through to the counter to grab a beer and six little pizza treats, four for his dogs, and two for the Sharpeis, you never knew.

Someone like Motowori, someone with that proud, Imperial heritage, you didn't just jump in and neutralize with a couple of poodles or cocker spaniels. No, you needed much more planning and subterfuge than that, much, much more. And Karl-Heinz Retter was on the point of coming up with just that, when from the other side of the room, over by the wet-bar, Motowori began gesturing at him, motioning him over, drawing the fire to the moth. "Little man! Come here! Something I want to say to you..."

A Japanese man calling him little, ha! With only four dogs by his side, Retter knew he would have to be supremely wary and cunning, lest through some sort of sneaky psychological *jiu jitsu*, he suddenly found himself flat on his back, with the roles of fire and moth suddenly reversed in Motowori's favor. Taking a big virile gunslinger-slug-of-beer from the bottle, a slug which foamed over and which, unbeknownst to Retter, made the whole right side of his mustache fall from three to six o'clock, Retter aligned the pearl snaps on his shirt so that the light bounced blindingly into the soup-slurper's reptile eyes and marched the ten baby steps over to his destiny, knowing one thing alone: when the dust cleared, there would be only one of them lying on the figurative ground. And that one man would most certainly not be the sort to warrant burial by the President of Switzerland. "*Ja*, is zere a problem, chief?" he said, laying on the *Oberland Chässchnitt* accent extra hard.

"You know what I'd like to do?" Motowori said.

"No, but I'm sure you von't fail to tell me."

And so he did, revealing to Retter how, despite the most thorough research, they still had found no reason to believe that any such scroll as Yuichi claimed to possess even existed, and sharing with Retter the elaborate plan he had come up with as a consequence, to put together a game show where contestants would come from Tokyo with tiny video cameras on their heads, to compete to see who could bring Yuichi the most misfortune. With the whole thing broadcast live.

Such an admirably cynical little plan, delivered in such minute detail, and with so many different little scenarios, some with tourists pretending to be Red Army terrorists convincing Yuichi to blow up the bank, some where they took Yuichi ice skating in Harlem, that Karl-Heinz Retter forgot all about the little game of social humiliation, forgot all about the publisher of the Clarion, forgot that beer was not Kirschwasser which a Swiss man could drink at will, with theoretical impunity, forgot that his head spun with even one beer, let alone six. Drunk from the alcohol, drunk from the meeting of minds, Karl-Heinz Retter tossed the pizza treats to the Sharpeis, climbed up on Motowori's lap, and kissed him on the mouth, transferring his mustache to the ambassador's upper lip. Kissed him and stroked his cheek like a brother, a long lost brother from the Bernese Oberland.

What Retter and Motowori missed: the rumor going around the party that Raj Mikkelson had spiked the punch, the hors d'oeuvres and even the bottled water with some sort of pharmaceutical compound which caused people not to be responsible for their actions. What they missed: Chrissie emerging from the bedroom followed by Yuichi carrying the scroll, the triumphant look Yuichi flashed at Reverend Y, and the thick-as-thieves look Reverend Y flashed back, a look that said, "See? What did I tell you, everything's gonna turn out just fine." What they missed: the Iraqi ambassador trying to stop Yuichi again until he was pushed out of the way by the head freeloader, the French artist, Marco Polo and a handful of others who planted themselves in front of Yuichi demanding to know exactly where Yuichi came off promulgating such a reactionary, two-shots-a-week take on promiscuity, such a patently Protestant, (some said Catholic) tight-sphincter notion. What they missed: the Iraqi ambassador fulminating about how people were always picking on the Arabs, and the freeloader working himself into such a frenzy on the sexual question, "Don't you understand how hard we fought for this?" that as an act of solidarity, "God B. Sold" felt compelled to spit straight into Yuichi's face. What they missed: Reverend Y rushing forward and knocking God B. Sold to the ground, which in turn tripped up the hors d'oeuvre chef and sent a fresh platter of Oysters Shanghai flying into the ice dolphin, causing kit and caboodle to end up on the hardwood floor. What they missed: Nat Gold's attempt to use the distraction to come up with something intelligent to say to Wella

Balsam ("Was it originally Balsamic? Yugoslav? Or Balsamico? Italian?) interrupted by a not-unexpected Scale 4 argument with his wife Botox Sarah, which flowed directly, naturally into a more strenuous, Scale 7 argument with the Iraqi ambassador for saying that everyone always picked on the Arabs, and not the Jews, which was a typical Arab thing to say, wasn't it? What they missed: two astronauts wrestling on the ground; Raj Mikkelson's face being cut to ribbons by the nails of a six foot eight inch tall woman who only two weeks earlier had said 'I love you' to Willi Roth; eight relentless dogs awakening such latent hatred for mammals as to convince Walkiria to forsake anti-vivisection and gingham forever in favor of Lycra and a vow to go on a white rhino poaching safari in East Africa; Jack Bravo falling into another jealous fit and Celestina telling him she never wanted to see him again, that in his future, if he must know, he was a loser, a screenwriter. What they missed: Yuichi confessing to the Mormon that he didn't actually know what was in the scroll called the Book of the Earth, and Yuichi, slipping and sliding on poor toppled oysters and shattered ice dolphin, dispatching the Mormon, Japheth Joseph Abram Brigham Smith yet again.

"Stop!" Chrissie turned off the music, and gently but firmly, no-nonsense, began to push people to the door. "Stop, I said. Party's over, I want to be alone."

With the help of Reverend Y, Chrissie Luna filled a first elevator with the French artist, (despite his insistence that it was his right to remain at the party as long as he wanted), with a woozy Mormon, with the head freeloader, with the telescope pervert, with the caterer, with Sarah Gold, with Chrissie's easy-on-the-eyes neighbor, who needed to go up, not down, with Jack Bravo without Celestina, and with Motowori and Marakchi, the two camelfucker diplomats, who on the way to the door, grabbed each other by the throat, trying to strangle each other or worse. "You leave Japanese citizen alone..." said So-Sorry Motowori, the scheming ambassador, still wearing Retter's mustache. "I kill you," answered Marakchi, who had had no ulterior motive with Yuichi, but was certain that Motowori's mustache was meant as some kind of deliberately mocking insult to the Arab people in general and Saddam Hussein in particular, and he'd been pushed around one time too many tonight. "Out, out, out."

With the help of Reverend Y, Chrissie Luna filled a second elevator with Raj Mikkelson and his two amazons, Wella Balsam, Celestina, Chrissie's mother, Jim O'Brien, very surprised, and Nat Gold, who got into a comfortable Scale 5 with Warren, the AAAAAAppliance guy, who had just stopped by on a whim to reprogram Chrissie's speed dial, "A Jew pretending to be a cracker?" Nat Gold instantly saw right through him, "Ha!" But a Scale 5 was not nearly loud enough to drown out the Scale 10 demonstration by two out-of-breath astronauts, who no human force could induce to let go of each others' space suits and who you could hear yelling at each other in the elevator all the way down to the first floor.

"I'd rather go to the moon with Hitler and Idi Amin than you," Buzz Aldrin yelled at Neil Armstrong.

"Yeah, well I'd rather go with... with..."

"Oh yeah?"

For one reason or another, it turned out that Karl-Heinz Retter and the dogs were in the last elevator down, along with Max and Max Jr., Reverend Y and a very grateful, scroll-cradling Yuichi. Yuichi, who had tried to give Chrissie back her keys before the elevator door closed. "No, better hold on to them," she said, "You never know when they might come in handy."

Karl-Heinz Retter couldn't believe that of all the dog owners, only Wella Balsam and Max Gilmore had deigned come to the party. Not obese Bunny Sella, the five-chin stockbroker with the poodles, who could probably afford to finance the film with the coinage he carried in the huge fat-man pockets of his mega-zipper pants, not Goldberg the dentist with the vault full of gold fillings, not the Austrian consul's wife, the meretrice, whom Retter couldn't help but suspect must have found a lover, not even spineless Winston Nelson, heir to the Colgate-Palmolive fortune, who could probably drop anything under eight figures without even blinking, assuming you could split him off from his henpecker wife.

Given the situation, between the third and second floors, Karl-Heinz Retter took a brief shot at pitching *The Man Who Saved the World* to the publisher, prepared to accept a nice fat check in exchange for the right to pet his dog, but the elevator ride was over before he knew it, and he found himself standing alone outside in the freezing night, trying unsuccessfully to button his coat, mentally retracing the elevator ride, wondering if the pitch had actually come off this time, or whether it was all, yet again, just in his mind. All alone but with one, two, three, four, five, six, seven... ten dogs. Miracle of miracles, just to show what happens when you expect nothing, Karl-Heinz Retter had walked away with Motowori's Sharpeis.

There was a graffito on the wall of 226 Lafayette, saying "Adios baby," but even if Karl-Heinz Retter's beer-swimming eyes could have focused on it, he wouldn't have cared. He had no idea how he would get home tonight, but he had come away with the Japanese ambassador's Sharpeis. He smacked a sloppy *Neue Zürcher Zeitung* on his thigh so that eight already-trained superdogs lifted their legs, four to the right and four to the left, and let fly with eight most-welcome, most precise streams. Standing at the back of the line, seeing them behave so, the Sharpeis got the urge too, and in perfect two-part unison... lowered their hindquarters and squatted, flooding the sidewalk with two amorphous puddles that wet both their paws and

Karl-Heinz Retter's disbelieving riding boots. What was this? What manner of infamy? What art of treason? Instantly, if only temporarily, sobered by rage, Karl-Heinz Retter raised his *Neue Zürcher Zeitung* high above his head, prepared to give the smirking Sharpeis their very first taste of how a true dog walker rewards impudence. And then he took a closer look, and noticed the unimaginable. They were females! The two Sharpeis were girls! "Vy me? Vy me?" Retter sobbed, raising a second arm to the sky, and sinking slowly to his knees, right in the obscene puddle of Sharpei piss. An excess of melodrama which would have greater consequences than he expected, Karl-Heinz Retter discovered, as a sudden, simultaneous attack of gout and sciatica made him quite unable to get back on his feet. "Help me, please help me," he called out to the few passersby still about on the chilly chilly night.

But did anybody stop to help a disheveled dwarf with ten dogs on his hands and six beers on his breath? No, the good citizens just buried their heads deeper in their collars, and rushed on by, pretending not to see. Waiting until they were a safe distance away to start clucking, "Don't you just hate it when the homeless have dogs?"

"I mean if he's that hungry, why doesn't he just get rid of the dogs?"

"You give 'em something, they just use it to buy more booze."

It was the paramedics from the station down Lafayette, alerted by the howling of ten cold, miserable dogs, who found Karl-Heinz Retter, riding-pant knees welded to the ground by an imprecise puddle of frozen bitch urine, body nearly stiff, a rolled up newspaper in one rigid hand and a check in the other. A check written out in the slightly shaky calligraphic strokes of Ambassador Kato Motowori, a check for $2135, with an inscription bottom left: "Dog walking: first two months."

43

Heart pounding, blood coursing with a mixture of elation and dread, Yuichi couldn't get to sleep all night long, couldn't even close his eyes for fear that if he relaxed even for one second, the demons of one o'clock, two o'clock, three o'clock and four might sneak in and wreak some heretofore unimagined mischief. For fear, now that he actually had the scroll, that he might neglect some trifling detail and once again mess the whole thing up.

The Book of the Earth must only be unveiled once human ears were at last ready to listen, when things couldn't get much worse, when the future of the planet lay clearly in the balance, when the human race, disgusted with itself, would choose either finally to wake up, or extinguish itself for good: that's what the ancestors had said. If the scroll had fallen so miraculously back into his hands, what else could it mean but that the time was ripe, that people had apparently begun to listen, to understand? What else could it mean but that things really could not get much worse?

But how to get the scroll where it had to go? That remained the question. The Japanese ambassador was the most logical solution, but the scheming way his eyes darted here and there when you talked to him, the way he had thrown himself into the brawl, didn't inspire Yuichi to believe that the ancestors might approve the choice. Not that the energy coming off the Iraqi ambassador, assuming that that's what he really was, was all that much better, nor his motives more pure or noble. Motowori-Marakchi, Marakchi-Motowori? Or perhaps even another solo effort? Maybe, now that everything else seemed to be going Yuichi's way, the UN guards too would be receptive to a man-to-man approach? But what if they weren't? None of the alternatives seemed foolproof or sure. Yuichi just had to pray the day would come when one would.

"Patience, right?" said Reverend Y, who couldn't sleep either for all Yuichi's tossing and turning. "We wait until after the fight."

"Patience, right..." Patience was fine, but what Reverend Y didn't seem to grasp was that even just holding onto the scroll felt like a risk.

"Is there something you're afraid of?"

"No..."

"Have I steered you wrong so far?"

"No..."

"Are you my brother?"

"Yes..."

"Damn straight, so just go to sleep now, all right?"

44

With five weeks to go before the April Fool's bout, the preparation of Reverend Y continued, picking up speed with the help of a fitness expert brought in from France, ex-trainer for the boxer, Oscar de la Hoya. Where at first, when he was still in jail, even a slow thirty minute jog would take Reverend Y three days to recover from, now, in no small part due to Yuichi, Reverend Y was putting in seven hours a day, with no soreness to speak of, and a daily, palpable, gain of strength. Eight miles of roadwork at the crack of dawn, then down to the gym for warm-up, six rounds of shadow-boxing, seven rounds of sparring with 18 ounce gloves, then the rest of the day split up into rope skipping, skill work, action-reaction, rhythm, sets, movement, relax, speed bag, heavy bag, medicine ball and sit-ups, sit-ups, sit-ups. Not enough to give him that racy, concave six-pack abdomen he used to be so proud of when he was younger, but enough to make a solid wall behind the layer of fat, and to look OK in a photo if the shorts were large enough and pulled high. So of course, when the press came to look at him, Reverend Y wore the smallest shorts he could find, the ones he could just barely wriggle up over his butt. "I'm in the best shape of my life," he fulminated, gut bulging over the elastic, "You tell that white boy he ain't got a chance."

More convinced than ever of Yuichi's vast skill, Max Gilmore brought Max Jr. to see Yuichi again. Not because the publisher thought he really needed it, but because Max Sr. himself wanted to spend a little more time with Yuichi, and the little boy provided the perfect excuse. The astonishing change in Max Jr., not a single ear ache since the night of the party, the boy cheery and energetic, and getting to sleep easily every night, had started the publisher thinking. Just last year he had watched his mother die of breast cancer, watched as the drugs they gave her, tamoxifen, raloxifene, stopped the disease in one place but sent it elsewhere. The breast cancer turned into bone cancer, then became a tumor in the brain which they removed successfully. Except that the anesthetic caused her kidneys to fail, so that they had to put her on dialysis, and then somehow the kidneys rallied, but then three weeks later, she came down with pleurisy... What if Yuichi had been there? the publisher wondered. Would it have made any difference? Didn't a medicine that got results without expensive machines make sense? A medicine that didn't depend on drugs that ended up killing people? The AMA would fight it to the bitter end, but what would it do to the problem with social security if a patient could be healed without being hospitalized, could be diagnosed simply with fingers on pulses."So how many more treatments do you think he will need," Max Gilmore asked.

"A few more, but it might be better to treat his father now."

"Really? Why's that?"

"A boy imitates his father's energy. Very simple, if the parent is not well, the child is not well. See the bags under your eyes? You too have kidney problems."

"No..."

"Problems with memory maybe?"

"Maybe."

"Lie down, please." Yuichi motioned to the massage table. "What do you think, Max, should Daddy get treated, or you?"

"Daddy..." said the four year-old.

"Daddy, right?" said Yuichi.

"Hai!"

"OK, Daddy it is..." So Max Gilmore too climbed up onto the massage table and felt the pain and the surge of energy, felt the incredible warmth surging through his gut from the hands held high above, felt as if he had never in his life been cared for by a physician with as much concern and time. Which of his friends, he wondered, or the people he knew, might benefit from similar treatment, by exposure to a man with such unfathomably vast knowledge that in order to treat the son, he asked to treat the father. What would happen, he wondered, if all the influential people he knew received treatment from Yuichi, starting with the President? What might that change in the world?

"I was talking to the health writer of the paper?"

"Yes."

"I asked her about acupuncture, about oriental medicine."

"Yes."

"She said they've done double-blind studies, that they think it helps with stopping smoking, and stress a little bit, and sometimes anesthesia, but otherwise the evidence is weak."

"Evidence, yes."

"Statistics."

"Is your Max better? How do you feel?"

"I know, I know, I'm not arguing. I'm just saying, for the AMA, for social security, they need proof. They need statistics."

"Until people regain judgment..." Yuichi shrugged as if to say there's nothing you can do.

"But my health editor said there is a new machine, invented by a Japanese man. Have you heard of it?"

"A machine?"

"A machine which measures the energy that comes off your fingers, or something like that. What they're trying to prove is that there is a quantitative difference in the electrical current. Instead of patients saying, 'I don't know, I just feel better,' they can actually measure a change."

"*Ho*..." It sounded like Chrissie's aurometer all over again.

"If I could arrange it, would you be interested in doing research with this machine?"

"It's a machine."

"I know, but it might make a difference. We talk to people with words they can understand, right? What do you say?"

"Maybe..."

"Max Gilmore!" Reverend Y came in just at that moment.

"Hey!" That was something else Max Gilmore had intended to take care of. Seduced by Reverend Y's little ironic smile, more and more fascinated by the phenomenon, by the unexpectedly wise, soft-spoken man at the center of the media storm, Max Gilmore thought an apology was in order for the image of insanity the paper continued to project. He promised to order the editors to put a stop to it post-haste. But Reverend Y, fast approaching the best shape of his life, knocking off sparring partners like flies, just laughed and shook his head. For one he didn't care what they said about him anymore, and for two, everything was going exactly according to the plan. T-shirt sales were running 5-1 in his favor. What other suit fit better than that of fool and rebel and clown? "I appreciate the thought, but hey, we got 'em right where we want 'em. Please, if you're my friend, don't change a thing. Not a single thing."

45

As soon as Karl-Heinz Retter thawed out from his night on the sidewalk, he began plotting again. At first, somewhat humbled by his body's betrayal, Karl-Heinz Retter almost managed to see the film through the publisher's eyes, excoriating himself. Even though he had never quite worked up the courage to actually talk to him, how could Karl-Heinz Retter possibly have expected the publisher to bite on such an inchoate project, a story whose necessarily intricate details he himself had not yet even bothered to work out? Thus aroused, Retter took pen to paper, wrote "The Man Who Saved The World" across the top of the page, tried to imagine a Japanese man saving the world in the first place and promptly gave up. If Max Gilmore, publisher of the Clarion were so obtuse, so absolutely impermeable to reason, to the once-in-a-lifetime chance to become rich beyond his wildest dreams, perhaps a more complex strategy needed to be implemented to force his hand.

But, no rest for the weary, before Karl-Heinz Retter could begin to calculate the logistics, before he could fetch the scissors with which to lop off part of Duffer the Labrador's anatomy to show he meant business, before he could even choose the proper font for the prospective ransom note in which he would suggest that Max Jr. would never forgive his father if he found out that Daddy's refusal to play along, to pay ransom, was what was responsible for Duffer's last walk to the taxidermist's, there were the dogs to take care of. Two females, and eight males upon whom the females were having a most distressing effect.

At breakfast, the Sharpeis finished their bowls in seconds as if they had never been given meat before, while the other dogs left their bowls untouched. On the street, even though Retter managed to train the Sharpeis rather quickly to lift their legs and pee like males, not perfect, but not bad, to Retter's horror, the other dogs suddenly began to squat. At the park, it was the Sharpeis who ran around biting the children, while the others just sat around the bench licking themselves, composing poetry and moaning. It was the early stage of love, no mistaking it, the stage of hope and wonderful expectation against which even a *Neue Zürcher Zeitung* beaten to a pulp served no purpose. The short days of heaven, which, as Retter had learned long ago, during a difficult imaginary relationship with that little tart Shirley Temple, are inevitably followed by long days of hell. Maybe "The Man Who Saved The World" should be about someone, OK, a man, who, knowing the day of his death, invents a device with which you can actually remove the blinders and see the perils of love. Or else, about a small Swiss man with slanted eyes and a sacred Helvetic scroll he needed to get to the UN before October 23, 2010, his destined death-day. A world-saving action that the gods and the furies and the times and tides themselves would try to prevent.

Absorbed in creation, Retter pretty much abandoned the attempt to guard the Sharpeis' virtue, and let the girls fend for themselves. Which they did quite well, he had to admit, growling ferociously when necessary, and giving out favors in the most admirably, instructively, Machiavellian fashion, wherever and whenever it would do the most harm. Tricks which the sex-slinging, Swiss-Japanese, world saving hero, when not working out the details of his glorious future burial, was not too proud to appropriate for himself. Flush with his hero's courage, Karl-Heinz Retter finally forgot himself just long enough to work up the courage to get back in imaginary touch with Hristo Boromirov and Dagmar Zwingli, just in case Max Gilmore did not work out after all.

46

On Valentine's Day, February 14, NASA announced that after a four year journey through the inner solar system, with a nudge from a small rocket, a spacecraft named NEAR had pulled into orbit around an asteroid named Eros, a potato shaped rock roughly twice the size of Manhattan. On February 21, the newspaper announced that the city had almost made good on its promise to close the dump at Fresh Kills, but that along Canal St. where the trucks passed on their way to the Holland Tunnel to transport the garbage elsewhere, air pollution had gone up 16%. On March 12, Pope John Paul II gave a sermon in Saint Peter's Basilica asking forgiveness, humbly repenting for the errors of the Roman Catholic Church over the last 2000 years, saying the new evangelization he was calling for in the third millennium could only occur after a church-wide purification of memory. On March 14, a ten year old boy in Toms River, N.J., had an argument with his father about a missing box of chocolate frosting. When the father handed the boy a 5-inch kitchen knife, telling him to stab him if he really hated him so much, the boy planted it in his father's chest, a fatal blow. A sign of the times, the people at Hallmark Cards tried to turn the Ides of March into a holiday, a reason to sell cards in the slack period before Passover, Secretaries' Day and Easter. Although some people got dressed up in black togas and thought deliberately-morbid thoughts all day, as far as card sales were concerned, Ides of March day wasn't exactly a success. But the people at Hallmark Cards didn't seem overly worried, even Mother's Day had taken time to get off the ground and now look at it!

With two weeks to go before the bout, Reverend Y brought the endurance part of his training to a close and began to concentrate on speed, speed, speed. Japheth Joseph Abram Brigham Smith became a regular at the gym, standing off to the side, glaring at Yuichi. While everyone patted everyone else on the back, champ this, and champ that, he seethed with quiet rage, sent silent curses over their heads and prayers to Heavenly Father for vast, righteous Mormon mercenary armies to descend on the city of Ur, and, with particular attention to the Japanese parts, smash it to dust.

On March 20th, Raj Mikkelson gave the green light for Chrissie's animal makeup project, and on March 21st he chased a limousine with Willi Roth in it all the way to Akron, Ohio, where he set off the atom bomb that finally ended Willi Roth's life, not to mention several others, including his own.

More thoughtful, less flighty, less forgetful, less tortured, Chrissie was greatly saddened by the death of Raj Mikkelson, but saw it as one last, very good sign to move on. There was no funeral, nothing left to bury, but saddened by the death nonetheless, saddened by the terrible carnage, and the great waste of time, Chrissie Luna decided she would get out of town. She bought a ticket to Rome, thinking to find some sympathetic, pure spirits at the Jubilee, but there were reports of an outbreak of a new, virulent strain of tuberculosis, so she decided to call the trip off, decided that just maybe Rome was not in her cards after all. Resigned, she hung around the 42nd St. gym and tried to make herself useful.

If occasionally, while on the massage table, she still indulged herself, imagining what it might be like to have Yuichi's child, she knew that she was not at all the same woman she was just two months ago, (was that all it was?) when she had first bailed him out of jail. The money had given her real, enduring, confidence, and not only because people's attitudes changed when you could buy them fifty times over. Ever since her party-night epiphany, she had felt there was a purpose to life, a direction, and a vast, heretofore-unsuspected world beginning to open up to her. Gone was the insecure testosterone laugh, the too-loud-talking and the neediness of a too-full heart. She was a different kind of Izanami now, an Izanami coming up to the light, and just waiting for Izanagi to roll the big boulder away so that she could get back together with him. And if that showed in her eyes, if she too was still orbiting Eros, so to speak, then too bad, some feelings the eyes just shouldn't hide.

Greatly encouraged by the atomic explosion in Ohio which confirmed the power of his prayers, even if slightly humbled by his relatively poor aim, Japheth Joseph Abram Brigham Smith finally felt both inspiration and fortitude enough to embark on the part of his mission upon which, in retrospect, he probably should have embarked from the start: the seduction of Nephi Samuels.

Given the odds, it wouldn't have seemed that Nephi Samuels would really need any help, but so snookered had he been by Reverend Y's posturing, that he found himself quite unable to keep himself motivated. Training sessions were so listless, so uninspired, that Nephi Samuels even began to sneak caffeine pills on the sly just to stay awake. Wracked by guilt, alarmed, for from there to Starbucks was a small step indeed, Nephi Samuels had moved his training camp from the Poconos back to Salt Lake City, where hopefully the sharp-eyed scrutiny of his Latter Day Saints brethren would keep him from further backsliding. Where hopefully, the holier climate of home would re-ignite his sense of mission enough to help keep him conscious, to keep his mind on something other than his ever-greater obsession with the Panama Canal, most particularly with the idea of stealing it back. An obsession which could almost have been called pathological, except that an increasing number of impressively-armed right-wing groups had sprung up around the country, organized around precisely that nostalgically jingoistic notion, so you couldn't really call it pathological any more, you had to call it a trend.

Nephi Samuels' "gym" was set up inside the visitor's center of the Mormon temple, a soft target which Japheth Joseph Abram Brigham Smith had no trouble whatsoever penetrating in his freshly bought John Q. Mormon, gray Mister Mack's disguise. Loudspeakers played an inspirational tape on a loop, a deep basso voice, as if coming straight from the mouth of the large marble statue of Christus: "Heavenly Father has a mansion for us when we die... The day will come when we will see God face-to-face. Nothing's going to startle us more than to realize how well we know our father, how familiar his face is to us..." Still lacking in motivation, still uninspired, immune to the voice of Christus, immune to the voice of his trainer whose face turned so angry red that his ears looked like they were going to explode, inside the ring Nephi Samuels sparred, but remained lethargic, distracted, still just going through the motions.

Japheth Joseph Abram Brigham Smith waited until the moment was right then took his best shot, throwing his voice with not-unimpressive ventriloquial skill so that it echoed and boomed, like the voice of God himself. "Book of Ether, 11:6. And there was great calamity in all the land, for they had testified that a great curse should come upon the land, and also upon the people, and that there should be a great destruction among them, such a one as never had been upon the face of the earth, and canals that belonged to the righteous were stolen away for the purpose of Satan..."

Suddenly infused with holiness, empowered by righteousness, Nephi Samuels threw an extra-hard left hook to his sparring partner's chin, a blow which not only knocked the man out, but sent him clear through the ropes.

"Who said that?" Alone in the ring, too stunned to take out his mouthpiece, Nephi Samuels pivoted this way and that, scanning the crowd.

"I did," Japheth Joseph Abram Brigham Smith said, unflinching, but bouncing his voice off a different part of the "gym" this time, still the voice of God-who-is-everywhere.

"I said, who's talking there now?" Nephi Samuels demanded, feeling the holy fire rise in his soul."

"'Tis I!" Once again Japheth Joseph Abram Brigham Smith bounced his voice off the opposite side of the "gym." By now, his body shook with divine inspiration, Heavenly Father himself took over his tongue, fire and brimstone.

"Bring the next guy on!" Invigorated, electrified, Nephi Samuels popped his mouth guard back in, and didn't even wait for the gong, before charging forward and dispatching the poor man as if he were King of Infidels and Killer of Christ rolled into one. "Next!"

It was then that Japheth Joseph Abram Brigham Smith dropped his cover and stepped forward, into the ring, tongue still wagging mighty scriptural inspirations in divine sounding bass. Infused with holy inspiration, with the punching power of the Lord, hearing the harps of angels, Nephi Samuels, rocket scientist, dropped him to the canvas with a right to the liver and a left to the temple. "Hire this man," he said as they carried   Japheth Joseph Abram Brigham Smith out of the ring on a stretcher, "I want him in my corner."

Thus, a mere nine days before the bout, did Japheth Joseph Abram Brigham Smith Punching Bag, insinuate himself into Nephi Samuels' corner. Signed on at a modest fee to follow the boxer around the clock, to reinforce his courage when he was pounding on the heavy bag and his arms began to feel like slabs of meat, to flush out the devil when the devil said quitting time before Nephi Samuels put in the hours, to remind Nephi Samuels, whenever he forgot, that this was not just the last warm-up before his shot at Number One, but preparation for the new, truer, hard-line Church and the future glory of the Mormon Jesus Christ.

Counting the days until the fight, Yuichi kept the scroll next to his body at all times, night and day, in a little pouch Chrissie had sewn into his robe. Thanks to Max Gilmore, when Reverend Y was resting, or otherwise employed, Yuichi began to make money by giving treatments to an increasing number of VIPs and celebrities at $60 to $100 a pop, depending on the case. Some got better and sent their friends, and some who doubted came away relieved, victorious, justified, saying "Nobody can cure what I have."

As for Reverend Y, he continued to take enormous pleasure in toying with the press, changing religions from moment to moment and engaging Nat Gold in public games of "Smashing Peckerwood" and "Soft White Devil," to swell the ranks of Samuels supporters, which Mr. Mormon Charisma clearly could still not do on his own. Nat Gold who, in private, converted pessimist that he was, continued to echo the Clarion party line, to tell Yuichi that the only way Reverend Y could possibly win against Nephi Samuels was with the help of a miracle.

"A miracle..." Yuichi thought about Moses at the Red Sea, and how even until the very last moment there were Hebrews who were prepared to turn around and go back with Pharaoh to Egypt, rather than venture out into the wilderness. And how it took the miracle of the parting of the waters to finally convince them of the power of Jehovah, the new God. Perhaps, Yuichi thought, in this day and age, Reverend Y's victory was precisely the kind of miracle the world needed. In any case, how could Yuichi doubt that the time for Amaterasu was nearing? Every day the conditions were more propitious for the scroll, more and more people flooding to him, some of them obviously getting the message, and everywhere else in the world, flood and famine, war and greed, things getting worse.

47

Everyone expected the weigh-in to turn into a circus and just in case it did Nephi Samuels had learned and rehearsed a number of lines to try and get through it without losing too many feathers. Except Reverend Y had weighed in at 235 pounds and not an ounce of fat on him. Except, for the first time since the bout had been announced, the clown was nowhere to be seen. Deadly serious, Reverend Y ignored Nephi Samuels altogether, ignored the reporters' questions and attempts to raise the pre-fight tension that final notch. Instead, he informed all and sundry that the only thing he intended to talk about today was Yuichi, about how the healer had opened his eyes, and about the deal they had struck, that if Yuichi would help him train for the fight, Reverend Y would tell the world who was responsible, would tell them about the scroll.

Wondering what it meant that the man he had gotten used to as a running-scared clown for the last two months had suddenly turned serious, wondering if he too had not been suckered, Nephi Samuels, who had never been good at improvisation anyway, could not think of a single thing to say. Japheth Joseph Abram Brigham Smith tried to boost his soldier's morale in a roundabout way, whispering into his ear, pointing out Nat Gold, and Chrissie Luna and the Japanese man, the Pharisees and bearers of devilishly malefic, secret-combination scrolls, but even that failed to awaken his pride and sense of mission, failed to wipe the scared little boy look off Nephi Samuel's face.

The day of the fight dawned sunny and warm, with Reverend Y feeling strong and optimistic and taking the weather as an omen. "This is the day little man. You keep that scroll of yours warm."

"OK. Please, lie down." Yuichi took Reverend Y's pulses, but Reverend Y was in too fine spirits to hold still very long.

"So how do I feel?" Reverend Y said, the little sly smile pulling at the left corner of his mouth.

"You feel fine."

"Remember when you told me that endurance runners get this condition that makes them able to endure pain?"

"Yes, spleen closing, makes you less aware of physical effort."

"Can you do that to me? Make the spleen close like that?"

"What for?"

"I don't know, you never know. Any little edge a man can get."

48

After nine weeks of training, after all the press and hoopla, all the hopes invested in the rise of the phoenix, and all the tales of tickets being scalped for thirty-times face value, the real story, the resuscitation of Reverend Y was finally ready to begin. Nephi Samuels was already in the ring by the time Reverend Y came out of the dressing room, caught by the ballet of spotlights darting this way and that over the darkened arena, carried by the roar of the crowd, a roar of hope that tonight would end with a victory for the common man's man, a victory for the world.

Strong and full of beans, carried by that roar, Reverend Y did not just slip through the ropes, but vaulted over them and into the ring. But even before he landed, grimacing in pain and clutching his left shoulder, everyone could see there was something wrong. Instantly Yuichi slipped into the ring, raced to his side and placed his hands on the shoulder, whispering into his ear, but when it was time for the referee to give the instructions, you could tell the shoulder still wasn't right. An impression only confirmed as Reverend Y slipped into the role of the clown again, eyes wide in fright, knees knocking together, gloved hands shaking as they tried to block out Nephi Samuels' fearsome stare. The crowd held its breath, horrified at the unexpected turn of events. Some prayed for the play to continue anyway, others prayed for it to be called off and cursed Reverend Y for his pride, the damn fool, when he pushed the ring doctor away, when it appeared he was determined to fight after all.

When the gong sounded for round one, Reverend Y came out gingerly, swiveling the shoulder slightly and dancing, fighting southpaw. Nephi Samuels walked right into it, a monstrous left hook from a suddenly-healed left shoulder, a punch that sent the Mormon reeling to the canvas, and Reverend Y dancing to his corner, swinging his perfectly-fine, it-was-all-a-joke left arm. The referee motioned Reverend Y to the neutral corner then moved in to begin the count, while the crowd, suckered in too by the charade, its breath temporarily taken away, suddenly found its voice and began to roar its approval, its delight, a noise fit to blast the Garden roof into orbit.

One, two, three, standing in the corner, Japheth Joseph Abram Brigham Smith struggled to find the proper scriptural inspiration with which to lift Nephi Samuels off the canvas, to put the starch back in his knees: "Get up you lazy cocksucker!" By the count of six, Nephi Samuels began to claw his way up and out of hell, by the count of seven he was on one knee then the other, and by the count of eight, he was back on his feet, wobbly, backpedaling, but gloves forward for the referee, a good enough imitation of lucidity to keep the bout from ending right then and there.

It was in the third round, by which time Japheth Joseph Abram Brigham Smith was already hoarse, that Nephi Samuels finally got his revenge. Backing Reverend Y into a corner with the left jab, he faked a left hook, then came in with a roundhouse right so hard that Reverend Y's mouthpiece went sailing into the second row, and Reverend Y just crumpled against the ropes, eyes rolled into the top of his head.

Yuichi was first into the ring, even before the referee had counted five, cutting open Reverend Y's gloves and feeling for the big black man's pulses, every one of which had flopped 180 degrees.

"How am I doing?" Reverend Y came to briefly, his usual little smile at the corner of his mouth.

"I think you got him in big trouble."

"Yeah..." Reverend Y laughed, "Mo'fucker's strong, tell you what. I think he got me this time. But don't worry I'll get him next time. Don't worry, OK? You just gotta be patient. Promise me."

"It's OK, I promise."

"Otherwise you'll tell them Reverend Y is a liar just like everyone else..."

"It's OK..."

"A woman clothed with the sun..." And that was it, those were Reverend Y's last words before his head dropped back on the canvas.

"No!" Yuichi's hand raced over the big black man's body, Yuichi cut away his friend's shoe and smacked him on the sole of the foot, trying to bring him back. Could this be the miracle required? Could it? "Nooo!" A trickle of blood came out of Reverend Y's mouth and dribbled down his cheek. Yuichi prayed to the ancestors, Yuichi prayed to the sky, Yuichi prayed to Amaterasu. But in the end all the humble healer's skill and all the humble healer's method could not save Reverend Y. And although the paramedics were inside the ring within seconds with oxygen which they strapped over his mouth, and paddles with which they tried to jump start Reverend Y's brave old heart, even though the ring doctor gave him a shot of adrenaline and they raced him to the hospital, neither could anyone else.

49

The funeral cortege wound its way through Harlem to the Church of Apocalypse, Profanity-Allowed. It was the biggest outpouring of grief since Louis Armstrong, representatives from every religion known, poor man, rich man, sinner and saint, hearts united by the loss of the man who brought back imagination and play, if only for a while. This modern passion play, this story of dream and fall, this Sisyphean tragedy, this striving and futile end somehow summarized why it was that you couldn't afford to hope anymore, because nowadays the end was never in doubt. Some people kept their grief to themselves, others wept or yelled out "Keep fightin' Champ!" And then of course, there were others, immune to the moment, like Chrissie's mother, for example, who criticized Chrissie's choice of dress, criticized her hair and choice of shoes, and then finally confessed what her real problem was: that Chrissie had been too cheap to hire Elton John. "I mean, you've got six million dollars in the bank, for Chrissakes!" she said, which ten dogs and Karl-Heinz Retter could not help but overhear. Just how long did Chrissie Luna expect to conceal her fortune from him, he wondered did she so underestimate him as to imagine he would never find out on his own?

Standing by himself in a corner of the church, Yuichi listened to the various people giving eulogies. Max Gilmore, and others Yuichi had never met. He thought about what he might possibly say about Reverend Y, say in such a situation. He would like to tell people that Reverend Y was not really dead, that if they could manage they must try to see Reverend Y as not just the man who had inhabited that mighty body from its first heartbeat to its last, but rather as a current, an accumulation of thousands of years of hopes, fears, and unfinished business from the ancestors. And that in spite of his sacrifice, he was still alive in every one of them. He would like to share with them the stories he had shared with Reverend Y in the last few weeks, the story of Indotyuulani, King of the Black Race, and Haulaimutai, Amatu Imuin and Abeluhaulame his noble descendents. He would like to tell them about how, at one time there was such a thing as Sumela Mikoto, the King of Kings, the one who understood the truth and was able to guide society in the right direction. He wanted to tell them about the man-god the Bible calls YHWH or Jehovah, whom O Sensei had calculated was Sumela Mikoto in the 69th Generation of Fuki Aizo Tyu, because that too was part of the current in Reverend Y, as it is in us all. But at this point, standing in his corner trying to hold back the tears and the great sorrow locked in his breast, Yuichi had no heart for eulogies. What was the point? The ancestors had left orders for the scroll to be revealed when things got so bad that people would finally listen. All Yuichi really wanted was the answer to one simple question: "How much worse does it have to get?"

50

In the aftermath of Reverend Y's passing, and the failure of his plan for the scroll, Yuichi moved back in with Chrissie and tried to start anew. The good news: he continued to look after the patients he had treated before, and Max Gilmore pulled a few strings to arrange for Yuichi to get a green card, in exchange for research on Max Gilmore's marvelous acupuncture machine which, miraculously, caused the AMA finally to acknowledge there was something to Oriental medicine after all. The bad news: the scroll.

Motowori, Marakchi, or even Max Gilmore? None of the possible options still available seemed to Yuichi like the proper way to get the scroll where it needed to go. What if the scroll never really was intended to go to the UN in the first place? What if the money he had earned from the treatments he had given had been provided by the ancestors solely to help him pay for a plane ticket back to Japan? What if his life were nothing more than a modern version of one of those Zen tales where the seeker goes on a long journey only to find the answers he needs right at home? And what if the inexplicable line he had drawn through Susano-wo City from the beginning on January 1st were nothing more than an arrow pointing him back to Tokyo or Isohara and the Koso Kotai Jingu? Anything was possible, there was no real reason not to just hop on a flight and find out. But the option of returning to Japan didn't sit any better in his gut than Motowori, Marakchi or Max.

Drifting, disconnected, desperate for signs, Yuichi scoured the bars on 2nd Ave. hoping to run into some diplomat, some drunken Scandinavian perhaps, whose ear he could bend and whose empathy he could awaken. Reckless, he even made a half-dozen more attempts to get by the guards at the UN, the first time with the charismatic approach, wearing a Reverend Y T-shirt, and the next five times, thanks to Chrissie, with makeup and disguise. But the guards were uncannily vigilant and the only time their sixth sense failed them, so that Yuichi actually managed to make it all the way into the General Assembly Building, the metal detectors picked up the slack, earning him a rough escort to the street for his efforts and a vague menacing warning from Campbell, the Australian special forces guy, "If we ever see you here again..."

Still apparently not done toying with him, the ancestors sent Yuichi a Japanese businessman from Kyoto, a seller of origami coffins who led him into Queens, where they barely escaped with their lives after being attacked by Italian mafia guys protecting the local funeral trade. A week later, the ancestors sent him a busload of Shinto nationalists and relatives of kamikaze pilots, a story which ended rather rapidly, and with maximum damage, on the slick marble floors of 30 Rock, when they tried to pin Yuichi to the wall and wrest the scroll away. As if that weren't trial enough, yet another week later, the ancestors even sent him a Japanese man who claimed to be the Director General of the World Health Organization and who invited Yuichi to come talk to him healer-to-healer, the very next day. But the next day there were Japanese guards posted in front of the UN, who barred his path just as effectively, showing him just as little sympathy as the guards from the other four races and even throwing in a bit of humiliation for good measure, searching him and planting things in his bag as they did so, the most perverted *manga* comics, and sealed baggies with used white cotton panties worn by actual Japanese school girls, whose signed pictures were on the packs.

After three full days of most gallant, well-mannered seduction on the part of one impeccably well-mannered dwarf, Chrissie Luna finally put $1.5 million in escrow and gave Karl-Heinz Retter a letter of intent with which he was not only able to bluff Jack Bravo to get to work on a screenplay for nothing other than a promise of future reward, but also to con a stupid someone-else-believes-so-I-might-as-well-too production company from Japan to come up with $1.5 million of its own to match, poor fools. Initially, Jack Bravo seemed to think that working for free entitled him to make changes to the story, but Karl-Heinz Retter let him know in no uncertain terms that the only person entitled to change the story was Retter himself. And just to insure that Jack Bravo understood this, Karl-Heinz Retter, Hollywood professional, made sure to change the story virtually every day.

He had reason to be confident. Thanks to the Japanese ambassador, from whom he learned that after only three episodes, *The Monk With the Golden Touch* had become the most watched show in Japanese television history, he no longer had any doubts as to whether Yuichi would actually be able to pull off the acting. Apparently the show was so successful that Kato Motowori could afford to quit his job as Japanese Ambassador to the United Nations and just focus on coming up with one crazy situation after another to inflict upon poor Yuichi. The origami coffin salesman, the Shinto nationalists, the director of WHO-UN guard idea had attracted the audience with its simple tried-and-true formula: monk walks to river, monk crosses bridge and falls off, monk climbs out of water, monk crosses bridge and falls off, hahahahaha. The difference now was that there was enough money to make catastrophe on a grand scale, higher bridges, lower rivers, jumbo jets exploding, ships sinking titanically one after another, after another.

The two Sharpeis played it tough as long as they could before finally falling in love with the two poodles. Distressed, the other six dogs licked themselves raw in jealous horny rage for a week or three, until the Sharpeis began to lose it. Imbalanced, for no real reason, (a wayward look misinterpreted, a momentary lapse of poodle attention, an inbred fear that dogs would turn out to be dogs?) from one day to the next the Sharpeis stopped eating altogether, and spent inordinate amounts of time in front of the mirror, wallowing in self-hatred and insecurity, finding themselves wrinkled and ugly, and generally, in spite of themselves, doing their best to make their worst fears come true. Married to their pain as the Sharpeis were, suddenly no proof of poodle love could ever be good enough, no amount of nuzzling served to brighten black Sharpei horizons, no smooth poodle-words were heard the way they were spoken, and even the most innocent sniffs and gentle tonguings were instantly misinterpreted and cut short by Sharpei tears and accusations of sinister intent and false love.

Karl-Heinz Retter was no help at all. Aside from distributing anti-depressants, all he could think to do was call up Jack Bravo, and let him know he expected the script of *The Man Who Saved the World* to reflect somehow this fundamental love situation, or else Karl-Heinz Retter would be obliged to hire himself another writer.

On Monday, October 23, six months and change after Reverend Y's death, and exactly ten years before Karl-Heinz Retter's death, as predicted by an astrologer named Celestina, shooting finally began on "The Man Who Saved the World," a $60 million budget picture with Yuichi, not Jackie Chan, playing the karate expert with the scroll who knew the date of his death, Wella Balsam playing the love interest, Chuck Heston playing the Mormon, and Leo di Caprio playing the dog walker. Script by Jack Bravo. Dagmar Zwingli directing. A creative choice which Karl-Heinz Retter managed to impose by telling the Japanese producer it was a matter of political correctness. Two scoundrelly words he had never requested his tongue to combine before, but which he certainly intended to use together again, given the result.

From the beginning, Karl-Heinz Retter had been determined that the film should be a drama, a tragedy, and the very precise script was written precisely that way, with a glorious death and burial at the end. But on the first day of shooting, in the very first scene, when Yuichi stepped out of the airplane at JFK, he slipped on some mineral oil dribbling from one of the smoke machines and from that moment on the Japanese producer, wise from the success of The Monk With The Golden Touch, threatened that if "The Man Who Saved The World" was not turned into a comedy, he would instantly withdraw his funds. Karl-Heinz Retter slammed his *Neue Zürcher Zeitung* on top of the man's head, Karl-Heinz Retter threatened to sue, Karl-Heinz Retter climbed up on the lunch table, unzipped his Vons and pissed in the man's Bento box lunch, Karl-Heinz Retter even took Chrissie Luna to the side to browbeat her just in case she had been withholding details about the true extent of her fortune, just in case she might be able to finance an escape pod to allow Karl-Heinz Retter to tell the producer bastards to go back where they came from.

In the end he was forced to admit there was little he could do -- harsh reality, merciless mistress, had dictated her terms. With a $60 million budget there was nothing for it but to go along with (as he called it derisively) "The Clown Who Saved The World." All things considered, Retter would rather have a seven percent producer's fee on a $60 million film, with the option to take his name off the credits if the film turned out to be a disaster, than a seven percent producer's fee on the original $3 million (which Chrissie had offered to finance) and the chance to show everybody he was right after all. The kind of serene decision that only a man who knows he has precisely a decade to live can make.

A man, moreover, who has already picked out the apartment he is going to move in to, the dream apartment at 515 Park, high above the city. Nobody across from him, an entire floor for the no-less-than twenty purebreds his assistants would walk, and an elevator boy on call around the clock to press the floor button nobody would suspect he could not reach. In his new apartment he wouldn't need curtains or shutters, he could finally walk around naked all day long, scratching his balls, shaving his ears and picking his nose to his heart's content. In his new apartment he could begin to draw up the plans for his mausoleum, which would be made with stain-treated platinum. In his new apartment he and Wella Balsam might have a little peace and quiet to explore what a man and a woman can explore when blessed by a true meeting of minds. In the new apartment he would have enough space finally to write one book about dog training, another one about talking to women, a third about rabbit training and a fourth about horticulture. Not only that, but he would even have enough space to orchestrate the Mata Hari scenario with which he would expose Yuichi once and for all. To figure out exactly who the devious monk really was beneath his many fiendish disguises. The dog-walk usurper? Or the viperish and viperous spy?

It was Chrissie Luna, film producer, who insisted that the premiere of *The Man Who Saved the World* be held at the United Nations. And it was fashionably-late Chrissie Luna, arm-in-arm with a still-disbelieving Yuichi, who escorted him past the bristling, cross-eyed UN guards, and into the Promised Land at last. Into the General Assembly room, where no fewer than 798 other excited guests applauded as the lights went down. After the William Tell logo, a small man shooting an arrow through a big apple, after the Izanami production logo, a man and a woman on opposite sides of a boulder, rolling it away from the mouth of a cave, after the film during which the audience laughed all the way through, it was Chrissie Luna who took the stage as the lights went up to introduce Yuichi, "Ladies and

Gentlemen... The star of the show," and Chrissie Luna, her face streaming with tears, who hugged Yuichi long and hard, then lit a candle on the podium and stepped aside.

Overwhelmed, too moved to say a single word, Yuichi stood in front of the audience waiting for the applause to die down. The flame on the candle got very small, then long again, then small as a pin prick, then long one last time. His cheeks glowing with tears too, Yuichi finally gave up, simply bowed and held out the scroll, just as he had held it out to the soldiers on New Year's Day, a year and a half earlier.

Struck by the display of emotion, hushed and awed by the candle, struck by the sudden realization that their children might have a planet to live on when they got older, and their children's children too, the rest of the audience, all those who helped, and all those who hindered, were soon crying as well. Celestina, who had seen this moment long ago, the union of the moon with the sun, Jack Bravo who fell down on his knees and begged her forgiveness, Motowori and Marakchi, who looked at each other and felt stupid, Wella Balsam, who rushed the stage and covered Yuichi with kisses, Max Gilmore, who held Max Jr. and sobbed, Japheth Joseph Abram Brigham Smith, humbled, mortified, released, and Nat and Sarah Gold, who simultaneously asked each other for a divorce. The only two dry eyes in the house belonged to one Karl-Heinz Retter, who at this moment of great triumph, this moment of confirmation, got a sudden intuition that Switzerland was planning to join the United Nations, felt a sharp pain in his chest, and, in spite of knowing the date of his death, became convinced he was dying on the spot.

When they opened the scroll and the cryptographers finally deciphered it, they found that the Book of the Earth told of many marvelous, miraculous, prophetic things. It told of the wanderings of the twelve lost tribes, of Amen, the Egyptian god whose name means "hidden," of the *kahuna*, the Polynesian sorcerers whose name meant keepers of the secret, of the Hebrew word for rabbi, Cahun, whose origin is also clear. It told of how the initial chaos, A-Na, the exact vibration of the cosmic energy, became Ma-Na[3] as it synchronized with the life rhythm of the brain , which became Ka-Na, the rhythm itself coming out as sound, the Word of God. It told of the location of long-buried relics, Noah's Ark for one, just as rumored, of crystal skulls and various jars in which had been sealed the formula for cold fusion, the method for teleportation and many other secrets lost when Eve gave Adam the apple, when Amaterasu went into her cave and Susano-wo the impetuous male took over. It told of holy places in Latin America, Africa and Europe where the missionaries of the first

---

[3] The exact same thing as manna in the Bible

206

civilization had been laid to rest, and the symbols the ancestors had left behind, the pyramids of course, but also Stonehenge, Easter Island and Carnac where the very rocks magnetized 56,000 years ago also held the secret Word of God. The Word of God, which was not a name, nor a magical formula, but the Kototama Principle, the 50 rhythm sounds in Futonolito order, AIEOU, the very foundation of Yuichi's healing power.

It told of the decade to come, of increasing conflict, as Kanagi and Sugaso fought it out to the end. An inside-out, upside-down time when the basest instincts would dominate and unconscious demagogues on both sides, wielding ignorance and fear, would, with the full approval of their subjects, betray what is noblest in the human race. A decade of trial and doubt and destruction from which the life-will would emerge in spite of the fear. Would emerge because the spark had remained lit in those in whom it lived, because Amatu-Hitugi, the activity which gives force to the soul-intelligence, enabling it to redirect the current of civilization is still strong, because the destruction of the planet is not part of the Great Design.

And, although, strictly speaking, this wasn't exactly in the Book of the Earth itself, it told of a humble healer who was finally free to go home.

THE END

ABOUT THE AUTHOR

Jeff Gross is a film maker, traveler and the author of the novel "World of Midgets." Unable to find a remedy for various aches and pains resulting from an excessively athletic upbringing, he was introduced to Oriental medicine and acupuncture, a passion he has pursued ever since. He spends his time between various ports of call in the United States and Paris, France where he dabbles in stand-up comedy and evolutionary activism.

www.ingramcontent.com/pod-product-compliance
Lightning Source LLC
Chambersburg PA
CBHW051420090426
42737CB00014B/2760